Library of
Davidson College

The Philosophy of Immanuel Kant

A collection of eleven of the most important books on Kant's philosophy reprinted in 14 volumes

Selected by
Lewis White Beck
The University of Rochester

Garland Publishing, Inc., New York & London

1976

Library of Congress Cataloging in Publication Data

Macmillan, Robert Alexander Cameron.
  The crowning phase of the critical philosophy.

  (The Philosophy of Immanuel Kant)
  Reprint of the 1912 ed. published by Macmillan, London.
  1. Kant, Immanuel, 1724-1804. Kritik der urtheilskraft. 2. Judgement (Logic) 3. Aesthetics--Early works to 1800. 4. Teleology. I. Title. II. Series.
B2784.M25 1976   160   75-32041
ISBN 0-8240-2328-5

Printed in the United States of America

THE CROWNING PHASE OF THE
CRITICAL PHILOSOPHY

MACMILLAN AND CO., LIMITED
LONDON · BOMBAY · CALCUTTA
MELBOURNE

THE MACMILLAN COMPANY
NEW YORK · BOSTON · CHICAGO
DALLAS · SAN FRANCISCO

THE MACMILLAN CO. OF CANADA, LTD.
TORONTO

THE
CROWNING PHASE
OF THE
CRITICAL PHILOSOPHY

A STUDY IN
KANT'S CRITIQUE OF JUDGMENT

BY

R. A. C. MACMILLAN, M.A., D.PHIL.

MACMILLAN AND CO., LIMITED
ST. MARTIN'S STREET, LONDON
1912

193
K16 cj- xm

COPYRIGHT

76-6825

TO

MY MOTHER

PREFACE

THIS little work is sufficiently described as a study in Kant's *Critique of Judgment*. But I have made extensive use of Kant's other writings, and perhaps it would be more accurate to say that the *Critique of Judgment* is made the basis in an interpretation of Kant's entire system, with a view to expressing the highest standpoint of his thought. The title of so small a work may seem somewhat pretentious, but it is chosen to indicate the author's opinion that Kant's Theory of Knowledge is not completely understood until it is followed as it passes into the last phase of his system. An essential problem in this study is naturally the relation of Aesthetic to Teleology. This problem is the distinctive feature of the *Critique of Judgment*, and must be taken as a serious contribution to philosophy. Our best authority for this point of view is Kant's own mental history, as it is given in his correspondence and academic lectures. To judge from the trend of recent speculation, the *Critique of Judgment* is about to come into its kingdom for the second time, and this very conjunction of Aesthetic and Teleology, which has been for so long neglected as a literary enigma, will become the natural formula for the philosophy of the twentieth century. It should be remarked here that, coincident with the motive of the present work, the treatment of Aesthetic has only been undertaken incidentally as the typical illustration of Kant's metaphysical position, and no pretension whatsoever is made to a knowledge of art-criticism. It was also inevitable in a study which seeks to commend Kant to the modern mind, that some attempt should have been made to bring him into line with recent philosophers. In particular, the influence of M. Bergson may be noticed. But it would be unfair to suppose that I have attributed to Kant ideas which are foreign to his own; and, indeed, I may be allowed to say that I arrived at my interpretation of Kant before I had read M. Bergson's works. Mr. Creed Meredith's recent book on Kant's *Critique of Aesthetic Judgment* did not come into my hands until after my manuscript was sent to the publishers.

It is with a feeling of deep gratitude that I acknowledge my indebtedness to Sir Henry Jones. With characteristic kindness he has read the whole of the proofs, and I have availed myself extensively of his invaluable help. The works to which my chief obligations are due are those of Caird, Adamson, Basch, Cohen and Stadler. I wish to take this opportunity of thanking Professor Boutroux of Paris for his kind courtesy in directing me to the French literature on the subject. The second chapter originally appeared as an article in *Mind*, and is here reprinted with some additions by the editor's permission. The generous appreciation which Professor Stout incidentally expressed for this article, was a strong encouragement to proceed in an undertaking for which I have increasingly felt myself to be incompetent. I have also to thank my brother, Rev. E. Macmillan, B.D., of Pretoria, for reading the whole of the manuscript in type and for suggesting many improvements in the text.

Since going to press, this book has been accepted as thesis for the degree of Doctor of Philosophy by the University of Glasgow.

It only remains for me to add, that the book was written in its final form under circumstances of peculiar difficulty. It was a serious interruption to my work when I was called to the care of a new Parish in a new country, and I had to take up the broken threads under very unfavourable conditions. I have also, in consequence, been deprived of the assistance which I should have sought from my University Professors and other experts in this particular subject of study, just at the moment when their help was most needed. I shall not therefore be surprised if the book should prove an easy prey to criticism. But if the critic knew the sincere modesty and hesitation with which this volume is launched into the world of letters, he would lay aside his gory spear and enter the field with a sword of lath. I have at least the satisfaction which every author feels who writes to any purpose, that I have seen more than I have been able to express, and may console myself with the lines of Propertius :

Quod si deficiant vires, audacia certe
Laus erit : in magnis et voluisse sat est.

R. A. C. MACMILLAN.

JOHANNESBURG, *Mar.* 22*nd*, 1912.

ANALYSIS OF CONTENTS

CHAPTER I

THE SEARCH FOR A NEW PRINCIPLE

Difficulty of the *Critique of Judgment* chiefly connected with peculiar nature of its problem : double use of Teleology as the conception of subjective harmony and as a concept of Nature—Summary statement of Kant's doctrine with a view to the discovery of a new principle—Two main powers constitute the human mind, Understanding (discursive) and Reason (intuitive)—These two powers seek to supplement each other and thus constitute a new power, the Theoretic Reason, which is indifferently an extension of Understanding in its effort to become intuitive and an extension of Reason in its effort to become discursive—Theoretic Reason or Inductive Hypothesis is therefore more concrete than either of its constituent factors—But Theoretic Reason has only pragmatic validity, and if taken as an ultimate interpretation of Reality leads to illusion : hence the despair of Metaphysics and the need for a new principle—This unsatisfactory result due to a limitation in the constitution of the human mind—In the analysis of knowledge we find that we are limited by something which is *given* ; this is Sensation—Sensation inseparable from the notion of Space—Kant sets out with the erroneous view that sensations are independent of Space—In the *Aesthetic* Space is said to be *a priori* as the *object* of perception : Kant means to say that it is only *a priori* as a *power* of perception—In the Subjective Deduction this erroneous view, which arose from Kant's anxiety to distinguish between Sense and Thought as separate faculties, fades into the background ; now it is shown that every element of sensation, including the perception of space, is due to the synthetic activity of the subject—The Objective Deduction corrects the subjective idealism of this position, by showing that synthesis presupposes analysis or previous synthesis—What gives objectivity to the relations in Knowledge is the Transcendental Object—This Transcendental Object not to be confused with the Supersensible Thing : the former represents only the actual relations which constitute Knowledge, or, just that objective order in sensation which is necessary for the consciousness of our own identity; the latter stands for sensations as they exist in themselves, or, as they may be supposed to exist in the Divine Mind—Comparison with Plato's *Philebus*—Thus the doctrine of the Supersensible Thing is a return to Kant's original doctrine of Sensation as independent datum—But this does not mean that the Supersensible Thing is inherently incapable of appearing: Kant prefers to think that it is our minds, theoretical and practical, which are not adapted for pure perception—Even our so-called intuitive Reason is abstract, being based on the distinction between 'ought' and 'is'—Hence the discrepancy in the factors, the possible and the actual, which make up both Theory and Practice: moral intuition is possible but may not be actually realised; sensation is actual but may not be capable of rational explanation—But since our apprehension of Reality, with its acknowledged defects, is itself due to the influence of the Supersensible, it is only natural that we should look to the Supersensible for greater completeness in our apprehension—The question, then, put forward in the *Critique of Judgment* is, Has the Supersensible any favours for us beyond what is necessary for simple perception or the consciousness of our own identity?—Kant finds three such favours in artistic phenomena, organic life and moral man; and the higher type of perception corresponding to these objects is Reflexion—Hence a new problem—The factors in both science and morality are unequally yoked, the unity (corresponding to the notion of possible) being *conceived* by thought, the parts (corresponding to the notion of actual) being *perceived* by sense or imagination—If now it were possible to discover a greater degree of facility in the way these factors come together, it would argue spontaneity in their relation: our thoughts would not be empty possibilities which only come to realisation in sensational shocks, but would be inherently actual; sensations would not be regarded as foreign elements, but recognised as if they were the products of our spontaneous perception—The new principle, which is required for this further determination of the Supersensible, is based on the analogy of Technical Judgment or the practical application of principles—The advantage in this mode of determination is that, while we are *making* a thing, our thoughts are not unduly in advance of presentations: possibility and actuality are both present to consciousness in an equal degree although vaguely and incompletely—Reflexion, therefore, as based on this analogy, will be that power of mind for which the factors of experience exist in an equal degree of reality *but also in their completeness.*   Pp. 1–38

ANALYSIS OF CONTENTS   xiii

CHAPTER II
REFLECTIVE JUDGMENT

Literary history of the new problem in Kant's mental development—
The distinctive feature of Reflexion that, unlike the Hypothetical
Reason of the *Dialectic*, it claims to be a science of the ultimate
without falling into antinomy—Preliminary justification of this new
science—(1) It is first shown that Judgment and Feeling must
have identity of nature on account of their respective positions as
corresponding elements in cognate systems of faculties—These
systems are : the wider system of Mental Powers (*Gemüthskräfte*)
with its three faculties, Cognition, Feeling, Conation ; and the
subordinate system of the Cognitive Faculties (*Erkenntnissvermögen*)
including Concept, Judgment, Reasoning—Kant had already
derived the categories of Knowledge from the concepts of Understanding, and also the maxims of conduct from the principles of
Reasoning ; what more natural than to expect that Judgment will
also prove to be the prototype of Feeling ?—The striking identity
of their respective positions in the corresponding systems—
Feeling mediates between Cognition and Conation : in modern
terms, Feeling is the consequent of Cognition (modification in the
sensory-continuum) and the precedent to Conation or Desire
(modification in the motor-continuum) ; if experience be regarded
as a kinaesthetic-continuum, Feeling will be *the self-consciousness of
experience*—Again, Judgment mediates between the Concept and
the Syllogism—A concept is a microscopic judgment from which
the appearance of synthesis has vanished : a syllogism is an extensive judgment in which the synthesis is further developed ; but
Judgment is the original mental function in which the synthesis
of whole and part is first seen in the making—Therefore Judgment
is *the self-consciousness of Cognition*—The further important consequence follows that the self-consciousness of both Judgment and
Feeling is of the same character, viz. indeterminate : the formal
or contingent relation of subject and predicate in logical judgment
is the prototype of the indeterminate content of Feeling—Hence
Urteilskraft (*The Power of Judgment in general*) is the original and
wider type of Judgment from which scientific or determinant
judgment is derived, just as the *Gemüthskräfte* are a wider and
more original system of faculties than the *Erkenntnissvermögen*, in
which Feeling and Judgment are elements respectively—(2)
Judgment and Feeling show a further mark of identity in their
subjective character—The subjectivity of Judgment not at first
apparent—Confusion of meaning in terms 'subjective' and
'objective'—Objectivity with Kant refers to *province* rather than
to content of Judgment, namely, province of sense-objects—Hence
his 'subjective' need not suggest the ordinary contrast with

xiv ANALYSIS OF CONTENTS

'objective'—On the contrary, Kant's 'subjective,' like the Cartesian use of the term, is what *underlies* the sense-object, the subjective unity of self-consciousness being indistinguishable for Kant from the unity of the 'transcendental object'—The Judgment is subjective in the sense of *personal* as distinguished from divine or absolute mind—Subjectivity of Judgment further illustrated by the contrast between Productive and Reproductive Imagination—The conclusion of this chapter, that while Kant appears to reduce Feeling to a form of cognition, he really shows that cognition is a product of the spontaneous function of mind—Hence Reflexion has an original province of its own of which it will never be completely despoiled by Science (—Suggested here, and further maintained in concluding chapter, that Teleology rather than Aesthetic is the connecting link between Nature and Freedom). Pp. 39–59

CHAPTER III

AESTHETIC AND THE FIRST CANON

The *Critique of Judgment* to be regarded as constructive rather than critical, in spite of its polemical appearance—Kant mistaken in his criticism of his predecessors—The true meaning of the doctrine of Confused Knowledge (*cognitio sensitiva*) as taught by Baumgarten: it is the content apprehended rather than the act of apprehension that is intellectual—Baumgarten's position well defined in Erdmann's paradoxical statement, that *cognitio sensitiva* is a perception that is (*though clear*) confused—The strength of Baumgarten's position, that the content of all perfection is intellectual and that therefore it is the same content that is differently expressed in Science, Ethics and Aesthetics—Its weakness, that the content is properly and only *intellectual*, so that Aesthetic is the beauty of knowledge (*pulchritudo cognitionis*)—But this is just Kant's own error, viz. that significant content is impossible without intellectual form—On the other hand he saw the contradiction in Baumgarten's view, that intellectual relations can be apprehended by a non-intellectual mode of apprehension—But his escape from this contradiction is no advance on Baumgarten: for he severs form from content and does not provide Aesthetic with a peculiar content of its own—The First Canon, that the Judgment of Taste is disinterested—Contrast of the Beautiful with the Pleasant and the Good unsatisfactory—'Disinterestedness' should only mean that we have no interest in the *existence* of objects, or that our interest is confined to their *form*—The implied contrast here not the same as that of 'form' with 'matter' in Kant's doctrine of phenomenalism: for space, the form of

ANALYSIS OF CONTENTS

phenomena, is excluded by Kant from Aesthetic—Put otherwise, Aesthetic is an independent, original interpretation, an apperceptive function, and therefore of the nature of Judgment—On the one hand the basis of aesthetical judgment must be sensation (αἴσθησις, *Empfindung*), on the other hand it is that peculiar form of sensation which can never be the concept of an object, viz. the feeling of pleasure and pain, that is, the *apperception* of all sensation—Must now show difference between aesthetical and logical judgment, the latter being also essentially apperceptive—While the apperceptive function in logical judgment is definitely restricted by the systematic end of knowledge, the aesthetical judgment is conditioned by no end other than the harmony of its processes: in Kant's words, the aesthetical judgment is the free-play of Imagination and Understanding—Thus Aesthetic may be defined as Ideal Judgment—Though this means for Kant *abstract* judgment, his theory is capable of a higher interpretation: —Degrees in subjectivity—Art a creative or ideal imitation—A test-problem in Kant's theory:—If the space-form be excluded from Aesthetic, what is to be said of geometrical figures which are nothing but representations in space?—Kant gives no satisfactory reply—But even here his *principle* holds, viz. that Aesthetic takes no cognisance of the *existence* of objects but only of their *form*, that is, the way in which the subject is affected: not the perception but the *apperception* of a representation in space—The implied antithesis of geometrical (Greek) and characteristic (Romantic) Art—Kant's false statement of the antithesis as between Beauty (meaningless representation) and Art (intentional representation)—Other views:—Lessing, Tolstoi, Croce—The problem limited by the alternatives whether expression must be subordinate to Beauty or Beauty subordinate to expression—Admitted that pure representations in space, *apart from all acquired significance*, may be beautiful—We are not committed, however, by this admission to a mimetic theory of Art, for the representation is not beautiful because Nature gives it but because it is *chosen*—Aristotle's view of historical incidents as adapted for poetical treatment—Tentative solution of the problem: formal representations without content may be beautiful, because in their destitution of significance they simulate the ideal conditions of artistic truth—Thus Imitation, in sense of literal reproduction, has no place in Aesthetic—How far Photography may be considered a form of Art—The superiority of Art that it does not rival Nature as *actual*, but for that reason Art, in its ideal, independent world, is able to outrival even Nature—Criticism of Signor Croce's view that the distinction between perception and artistic expression is only quantitative. Pp. 60–94

CHAPTER IV

AESTHETIC AND CAUSALITY—THE SECOND CANON

The subjectivity of Aesthetic as disinterested is corrected by the Second Canon :—that Aesthetic must have universality—Comparison of the Beautiful with the Pleasant—While the aesthetical judgment is at once singular and universal, the judgment on the Pleasant can only be singular without universality—Kant's confusion of transcendental with logical universality—The real ground of the comparison is Kant's distinction between judgments of perception and judgments of experience—The contradiction in his view of the Pleasant : the basis of the judgment on the Pleasant is not sensation but apperception of sensation (feeling of pleasure-pain) and the judgment is therefore something more than an ordinary judgment of experience, *i.e.* it is *reflective* ; on the other hand, in order to give the advantage to the Beautiful, Kant identifies this basis with empirical sensation and this means for Kant that the judgment on the Pleasant is not even an ordinary judgment of experience but a purely subjective modification—On the contrary, the Pleasant is a form of universal experience but *with a minimum of content* ; that is, a parasitic form of consciousness —Significance of Kant's contrast of the Beautiful with the Pleasant expressed in the doctrine of the aesthetic senses—The universality of Aesthetic essentially the same problem as in *Critique of Pure Reason* :—How are synthetic judgments *a priori* possible ? —The Beautiful must be a *real* connection of elements and at the same time a connection which is not simply *given* in Nature—The technical deduction of aesthetic universality quite straightforward : —that the aesthetic disposition must be universal because, as indeterminate, psychological process, it is the original implicate in all experience—What calls for criticism is the original deduction in *Critique of Pure Reason*—On the ground of Kant's theory of knowledge, the aesthetic disposition will be just that phase of mentality which can never be universal because there is no reproduction in Imagination—His doctrine of Schematism properly means that the Schema is a transcendental element and therefore original to the nature of thought—But to satisfy his rationalistic prejudice, the Schema becomes a psychological device :—all schemata have time-implication and thus he can provide concepts of experience distinct from what he calls pure categories— Criticism of Kant's doctrine of Schematism :—(1) There are no pure categories which are not already schemata—Kant finds his first instance of a pure category in geometry *e.g.* pure conception of a circle, a conception which is homogeneous with empirical perception of a circle and therefore already schematic—But he thinks that a pure category has nothing in common with concrete

ANALYSIS OF CONTENTS   xvii

experience (which is *in time* as geometrical representations are not), presumably because the pure category has no time-implication—Now, he seems to ask, how does a geometrical conception apply immediately to geometrical representations? By a mental act which implies a process in time: *e.g.* the schema of Number—Therefore we can think concrete experience if instead of pure categories we apply corresponding schemata which have time-implication—(2) But schemata have no peculiar implication of time; the Schema is not a process in consciousness but the consciousness of a process—Hence Kant's distinction between Reproductive Imagination (in time) and Productive (not in time)—Only in the latter, here identified with Inner Sense, can we speak of *Spiel der Kräfte*—But the contents of Inner Sense, not being subordinate to the rule of Understanding, viz. reproduction in Imagination, can only be a contingent conceptual play—Hence Aesthetic, so far from having *a priori* universality, would seem to lack even that amount of coherence which is necessary to the consciousness of our own identity—On the other hand, we recognise Kant's concrete view of Imagination as a single faculty with a double function, productive and reproductive—Why then does he appear to confine the time-implication to the reproductive function ?—Because succession in time was the only criterion by which he could identify the causal sequence of experience—Kant's unpretentious theory of Causality justified—But his official theory in the Second Analogy goes beyond this reasonable position—His conclusion may be regarded as instance of 'illicit process':—he seems to identify the proposition that the consciousness of necessity in time is a factor in Causality, with the proposition that the consciousness of necessity in time contains Causality 'eminently'—But why does Kant throw the whole weight of his proof for Causality on Time, and not rather avail himself of intuition in space which clearly lies in the background of his argument ?—Probably because he felt it necessary to account for the difference between the two kinds of mental states, inner and outer, *independently of intuition in space* :—without appealing to intuition in space, he must explain why some mental states should realise themselves in space-relations and others not—Since all mental states are ultimately elements of Inner Sense, the reason for this difference between the kinds of mental states must be found *within Inner Sense*—Hence the consciousness of determined succession in time is consecrated to causal sequence—Thus the peculiar contents of Inner Sense or the contents of Productive Imagination purchase their freedom in Aesthetic only by forfeiting all implication of succession in time and therefore all coherence—Kant however has a double view of Time :—besides the empirical representation of Time as succession, there is Absolute Time which can never be perceived but is felt as duration—It is possible to think that Kant had this deeper view of Time in mind when he seemed to

b 2

isolate Productive Imagination as a timeless faculty—Not only so, the aesthetic Imagination as it appears in the *Critique of Judgment* is certainly not timeless; nor is the aesthetic Understanding devoid of schemata—But this schematic interpretation of Aesthetic demands a modification of Kant's theory of knowledge and particularly his doctrine of Inner Sense. Pp. 95-140

CHAPTER V

ANCIENT AND MODERN—THE THIRD CANON

Like the last moment in the Hegelian triad, the Third Canon is a restatement of the First with a deeper significance :—While in the Second Canon Aesthetic gains universality at the risk of being identified with cognitive process, the Third reverts to the first conception of Aesthetic as disinterested under the deeper conception of *indeterminate coherence* (purposiveness without a purpose)— In this canon Kant's positive and negative views of Freedom struggle for the mastery—Conflicting tendencies of Eighteenth Century :—The *Aufklärung* and its negative conception of Freedom : Positive tendency of the *Sturm und Drang*—Kant's want of sympathy with the latter, and his false antithesis of Ancient and Modern—Schiller's true interpretation of the antithesis in his *Naïve and Sentimental Poetry* :—distinction between formal and characteristic Beauty only logical—Kant adopted the negative conception of Freedom of the *Aufklärung*—His distinction between Free and Dependent Beauty (*pulchritudo vaga* and *pulchritudo adhaerens*)—False antithesis of meaning and expression in Art :—no successful expression without artistic *motive*—Schiller's criticism of the *Aufklärung* ; shows how its contingent conception of Freedom did not realise the Infinite but an infinite *finite*, an inexhaustible *material*, the indeterminate of sense-affection— Kant's rigorism saves his theory from this disastrous consequence : —his exclusion of Charm and Emotion from Aesthetic—Charm excluded on the ground that it is empirical : Kant's doctrine of Sensation (*Empfindung*) as the specifically empirical element in Perception (*Wahrnehmung*)—Thus Aesthetic is form exclusive of matter—But this is not the aesthetical conception of form, which transcends elementary distinction of form and matter, but mathematical form—Kant's mistaken conception of aesthetic purity illustrated in his theory of the arts :—it is the drawing that is essential in Painting, the rhythm in Music—Criticism of his theory of Music :—tones are not any kind of analogical symbolism but direct expression—Kant's highest conception of Music a wealth of *extensive*, not *intensive*, symbolism—Schopenhauer's theory, that the true parallel is not between musical expression and linguistic signs but between musical expression and Nature—Music an independent articulation of the Supersensible, co-ordinate with the language of Creation—Significance of Kant's exclusion of Charm brought out by Schiller in his *Anmuth und Würde* :—Charm, like the Belt of Venus, may be an objective characteristic without being an essential constituent of the Beautiful—Kant's uncompromising attitude to Emotion (*Rührung*) as a possible factor in aesthetic experience—His narrow view of Emotion as exclusively volitional—Moral Emotion as the feeling for Nature not aesthetical for Kant or Schiller : the former regards it as intellectual interest in the Beautiful, the latter as moral sentiment—Both Kant and Schiller failed to assimilate the Sublime to Aesthetic—Their error consists in a false conception of Immediacy—In contrast with Science Aesthetic is immediate, but there are degrees of immediacy in Aesthetic :—the feeling for Nature not an external interest beyond " the mere act of judging," but the consciousness of depth in aesthetic content—Kant's singular admission of mediation in Aesthetic as expressed in the principle that *the pleasure must follow the judgment*—He does not mean that the pleasure must be consequent on *a prior intellectual act* but on a prior act of Reflexion (*Beurtheilung*, which is psychological rather than logical), *i.e.* there is mediation peculiar to Aesthetic itself—Thus the whole of Nature, as mediated through Reflexion, may be regarded as the content of Aesthetic—Original problem of *Critique of Judgment* was the union of the abstract factors in this poetic idea of Nature, viz. Sense and Reason or Mechanism and Freedom—Since he cannot find the union of these factors in the abstract conception of Beauty, Kant professes to find it in the Moral Ideal (Beauty of Character)—But the Moral Ideal is only the *Idea* of Humanity, the abstract Man of Freedom in which Nature and Freedom are never completely reconciled—Only in Aesthetic do we find the *Ideal*, or the realisation of the Idea in individual form ; *i.e.* the reconciliation of Mechanism and Freedom must be found in Characteristic Beauty and not in the Beauty of Character—This conclusion confirmed by Kant's theory of Genius :—the supersensible substrate in Aesthetic is not abstract Freedom but Human Nature in its catholicity : hence the aesthetic powers must be extended beyond the *Erkenntnissvermögen* to the *Gemüthskräfte*—Significance of the Feeling of pleasure-pain (*Gefühl*) as denoting the elemental harmony of consciousness :—the term 'empathy' (*Einfühlung*) here suggested as an adequate description of this state—Conclusion of discussion up to this point, that Nature and Freedom are completely reconciled in Aesthetic but only as *symbol*—Kant unable to carry out the consequences of his theory of Genius :—he could not assimilate the moral consciousness to the conception of natural liberty, as is evident in his doctrine of the Sublime.

Pp. 141-186

CHAPTER VI

THE SUBLIME

Kant distinguishes Sublime from Beautiful as moral emotion (*Rührung*) from pleasurable feeling (*Gefühl*) : the former being volitional, the latter ideational—Thus the feeling of the Sublime is indirect and negative, being mediated through reaction of will—Psychological theory of Burke—Kant's explanation of the Sublime metaphysical : a new order of Imagination peculiar to the moral consciousness—Imagination inadequate for the estimation of greatness—The scientific consciousness evades the difficulty by using Imagination in the form of numerical schemata, which are capable of infinite multiples and have therefore no maximum, no *standard* of greatness—It is only in the conjunction of Imagination with the *moral consciousness* that estimation of greatness is possible, sublimity consisting precisely in the failure of Imagination to keep up with the moral consciousness, or, as Kant says, in the play of Imagination and Moral Reason as harmonious through their contrast—But Kant did not recognise that the first appearance of Sublimity must be an *aesthetical* moment : for no contrast is possible without ground of comparison, *i.e.* unless the object of Imagination is expanded as *aesthetic symbol* of Reason's object, viz. the Supersensible—In this indefinite expansion the Imagination breaks down and the feeling of pain gives way to a feeling of pleasure—Criticism of Kant's theory :—in the unqualified sacrifice of Imagination, the Sublime becomes essentially non-sensuous and is therefore not aesthetical—This negative view of Sublime adopted by Schiller and Hegel—Difference between moral and aesthetical sublimity :—the former implies opposition to, the latter implies *reconciliation* with, Nature—The Kantian theory suffers from a narrow conception of Emotion as *volitional* reaction ; on the contrary it may be *ideational* or sympathetic reaction, whence it follows that there need be no permanent opposition to Nature—Schopenhauer's advance on Kant :—by recognising degrees of sublimity he shows the continuity of Sublime with Beautiful—The difference is that in the Beautiful there is a minimum of discrepancy between meaning and expression, and we are therefore able to grasp its ideal significance without effort : while in the Sublime the expression is out of sympathy with the ideal form to which therefore we can only penetrate by a forcible breaking away from the hostile appearance—Synthesis of Sublime and Beautiful only possible on the aesthetic principle of graduated indifference to harmonious expression—Kant approaches towards aesthetical conception of Sublime, (*a*) in the idea of Nature as symbol of Supersensible, (*b*) in the idea of Subreption (both noticed in earlier part of this chapter) and (*c*) in the sense of Security—None of these constitutes a real advance, the latter being a restatement of his formalism—Our final conclusion that Kant's interpretation of the Sublime is *not* aesthetical —The Sublime as the test in aesthetic theory :—its important bearing on the relation between Beauty and Expression— Doctrinal significance of the Sublime :—Reflection has for its general principle the conception of Nature as adapted to our intelligence—So far this principle is only subjective, an hypothesis—But the Beautiful, as a 'disinterested' harmony of perception in which the mind is at rest, is a *visible demonstration* of this hypothesis : it will therefore be in the interest of this subjective principle if we extend the conception of Beauty so as to include the intransigent phenomena of the Sublime, which contradict the purposive disposition of Nature ; and this can only be done by defining Beauty in terms of expression—Kant, however, does not avail himself of this advantage, though he acknowledges the teleological value of the Beautiful—By sacrificing the ideational Imagination (Nature as sensuous representation), he professes to find in the sublime a new order of *intensive* Imagination as "the instrument of Reason"—This comes very near to our view that Nature as sensuous representation must be *re-instated* in the Sublime by *sympathetic symbolism*—But a closer examination shows that Kant is not prepared for this conclusion —Kant makes radical separation between intellective and moral consciousness :—Beauty is form without spirit; Sublime is spirit without form—Thus there is no connecting medium between the *extensive*, ideational Imagination of the Beautiful and the *intensive*, mystical Imagination of the Sublime : stated abstractly, no connection between Nature and Freedom—On the other hand Kant transcends these limitations in his theory of Genius, which demonstrates the elemental community of man as Nature and man as Freedom in the concept of *natural liberty*—Thus Aesthetic is not subjective in sense of abstract : on the contrary, it is the primordial harmony of mental life raised to a higher immediacy —Aesthetic as *refined* sensation is not therefore a less but a *more intensive* consciousness. Pp. 187–228

CHAPTER VII

TELEOLOGY OF NATURE

The view here taken that there was an implicit intention in Kant's Teleology of Nature, which he did not carry out in his exposition, viz. to emphasise and develop the *psychological* aspect of Natural Teleology which it has in common with Aesthetic, rather than its logical aspect as an ancillary instrument of Science—A manifest difference between Aesthetic and Teleology of Nature, that while aesthetic representations have no existence outside our subjective interpretation, our interest in organisms takes its character from the thought that the organism has *independent existence*—But the psychological aspect of Natural Teleology not affected by this difference, which refers to the *province* rather than to the process of judgment—Kant's restriction of Teleology as subjective or regulative, for the behoof of our reflective faculty—Metaphysic as Science of Nature impossible—Maxims of Teleology not scientific principles but economic devices of Reason :—Homogeneity, Specification, Continuity—Thus the predicate of teleological judgment not a constitutive concept but an affective idea, which illustrates the way in which we are affected by our consciousness of objects—Kant seems to have lost sight of this aspect of Teleology, and practically does no more than repeat the argument of the *Dialectic*—On the other hand a new element is introduced in *Critique of Judgment*, viz. the organic conception—Formal Teleology only a *logical* disposition of Nature, which completes the mechanical interpretation of Nature; but Organic Teleology presupposes a purpose in organic products themselves which is independent of our subjective or logical interest in Nature—No doubt an organism may be regarded as a system of mechanism, and therefore generically identical with the totality of Nature conceived as a logical system :—thus Organic Teleology would be nothing more than a particular application of Formal Teleology—But the point is, How far is the conception of Formal Teleology valid as applied to Nature?—Criticism of Kant's theory of knowledge: objectivity in knowledge requires necessity in Nature but not that this necessity should be merely mechanical :—*i.e.* mechanism may be only a factor in a Nature that is not itself mechanical—Hence Formal Teleology, as external reflection on a given mechanical Nature, loses its significance—Kant's mistaken conception of Teleology as indefinite extension of mechanical (relative) whole—Superficial identity of mechanical and teleological wholes in respect of timelessness—But teleological whole not timeless like abstract logical unity, for even as perfect realisation it is *conative*—Explanation of Kant's attitude :—that the connection of Objectivity with Reflexion is a contradiction, *i.e.* judgment must be purely subjective (hence the false subjectivity of his Aesthetic) or purely objective (hence the false objectivity and consequent priority of Mechanism in his theory of knowledge)—Therefore Organic Teleology is for Kant neither scientific nor 'reflective,' having nothing to do with a feeling of pleasure (*though he calls it 'reflective'*), but a hybrid hypothetical judgment which determines nothing *either in the object or the subject*—Kant reduces Organic Teleology to the abstract principle of Uniformity :—analysis of organisms as *effects*, not as causes—Intensive predicates (life, human purpose, creative mind) cannot give a more intensive insight into Nature, if Uniformity is restricted to a single kind of coherence—So far Kant's interpretation of Teleology is negative—Special examination of Kant's theory with a view to ascertaining how far it is capable of a *positive* interpretation—Main result of Kant's complicated scheme is to establish a broad distinction between external (conditional, contributive) and internal (organic) Teleology—But organic purpose an enigma for philosophy :—the organism only purposive in respect of internal organisation, not necessarily as *natural product, i.e.* no necessary relation to environment—Crucial problem, how far necessity in relation of organism to environment can be demonstrated, *i.e.* how far organic conception can be applied to whole of Nature—Views of Ernst and Pfannkuche :—does Kant mean an External Teleology?—Kant actually did entertain this view in an earlier period, and its traces remain in *Critique of Judgment*—Discussion of Occasionalism and Preformation in *Der einzig mögliche Beweisgrund*—Kant's criticism of Preformation, that it only differs from Occasionalism in the time of divine interference—He adopts Epigenesis or genuine Evolution as opposed to Preformation, which is Involution (*Einschachtelung*)—Kant's conception of Evolution as distinguished from Darwin's :—the production of species is natural, but not their *origin*—What is transmitted by natural causes are *generic* preformations originally created by God—Kant's explanation of 'contingent variations' as variations which are not necessarily hereditary, and which, as such, are accounted for by the original tendencies (*Keime*)—Thus Kant's theory of Evolution a *Minimum* Occasionalism :—organic life introduced into dead matter by original creative act—This unquestionably an External Teleology of Nature—Advance on this position in *Critique of Judgment* :—matter is brought into existence by same creative act as endows it with life—How far Mechanism and Teleology may be regarded as united in a single principle :—distinction of Mechanism from Causality—Supersensible substrate of Nature substituted for theistic God of his earlier theory of Evolution :—Life the spontaneous product of unknown, inner ground of Matter—This not Mechanism but 'Creative Evolution'—Criticism of M. Bergson's interpretation of Kant—The inner ground of Matter (*Grundkraft*) for Kant is of the same nature as that of the subjective mind, viz. purposive reality without a purpose—The *Grundkraft* ought therefore to be accessible to knowledge : but for Kant it remains unknowable because he regards knowledge as prevailingly discursive—Discursive nature of thought means that, given a presentation, we must first think it in the most general terms, then advance from this unspecified thought to a more conditioned until we arrive at an adequate conception—This is the apperceptive nature of thought and unquestioned—The point is that undefined does not mean analytic, unconditioned, as Kant thinks

xxiv ANALYSIS OF CONTENTS

—In his view thought becomes intuitive for first time when it arrives at an *adequate* conception, *i.e.* becomes *schematic*—On the contrary, schemata are not confined to adequate conceptions : it is the schema that lies at the back of all our thinking and institutes the discursive process, which must therefore be intuitive also—Aristotle's view similar to Kant's :—discursive inconsistent with intuitive thought—Criticism of the theory. Pp. 229–292

CHAPTER VIII

AESTHETIC AND TELEOLOGY

The predicate in Teleology of Nature at once a purposive feeling and a concept of purpose :—*i.e.* the subjective or aesthetical teleology in the judgment takes its character from the thought of independent purpose in a being which enjoys its own existence— This independence in the organism, which is something more than the ideal independence of artistic objects, a stumbling-block for Kant—His restriction of *a priori* to extensive magnitudes : we have certain knowledge only of what we can ourselves *construct*— His view of intensive magnitude not an exception but a corollary to preceding principle—On the contrary, we understand an organism better than anything else *just because we cannot make it*— Mathematical knowledge the most certain only because it is the most abstract—Real knowledge only possible of that which can *react on and so confirm* our knowledge, *i.e.* a self-subsisting centre of Reality—Kant makes one exception :—there is one type of experience which is *not* mathematical and yet is a *fact*, the consciousness of Freedom—Personality thus the only valid category outside mathematics : what falls below Personality (biological unity) has no independent substrate of reality but only an external entelechy—Similarity of M'Taggart's view that biological categories are invalid, being due to a defect in our thought —Clear from the above that in Kant's view Natural Teleology obtains its sanction from the *moral consciousness* (self-conscious purpose)—Discussion as to whether this interpretation is valid— Stadler's position, that Theoretic Reason is alone sufficient to account for Organic Teleology—True, in so far as organisms are only regarded as *effects*, but *not* in so far as they are regarded as *causes*—Already asserted in preceding chapter that hitherto Kant's New Principle (the psychological idea of Nature as conceived on analogy of our practical causality) has stood for nothing new, being only an alternative statement of the *logical* disposition of Nature :—this the substance of Stadler's contention—Evidence now adduced to show that Kant did take his new principle in earnest :—it is from our moral consciousness that our conception of the organic takes its rise (contrast with his prevailing view that the organic conception is solely due to discursive nature of thought)—But moral consciousness must be reinforced by the conception of organic purpose in Nature, or, the realisation of moral ends in a *natural* way—Kant goes further:—the moral consciousness really abstract, being an accident of our Practical Faculty, corresponding to discursive nature of Understanding—Criticism of Ethical Nihilism implied:—conception of Obligation not eliminated even for divine mind—But there is this much truth in the criticism of the moral consciousness, that there is something deeper in us than the *mere consciousness of Freedom* and that is the consciousness of ourselves as Nature—Particular examination of the relation of Aesthetic to Teleology:—they stand in the relation of content to form—Aesthetic the felt knowledge (content) of a principle (form), viz. teleology in general, or, the harmony of our consciousness of Nature with the consciousness of ourselves—Thus Teleology, or a judgment of purpose, makes its first appearance as a *purposive judgment, i.e.* the *felt* knowledge of a principle before it is *noticed*—Inevitable that Teleology should lose much of its intuitive power—Maintained that Teleology rather than Aesthetic is the middle term in the Critical Philosophy—The fundamental consciousness of ourselves as Nature a first entelechy which, through the process of morality, is destined to issue in a higher immediacy, the regeneration of Man—This latter Aesthetic alone can express as the Ideal, the complete realisation of the Idea in individual form—But the aesthetic Ideal only a symbol—It is in a teleological interpretation of Nature, whose highest predicate is ethical, that we must look for the *actual* reconciliation of Nature and Freedom.

Pp. 293–329

CHAPTER IX

CONCLUSION

Ethical Teleology the highest level of experience—Its claim to Science defended—Difference of method in Ethical and Natural Teleology—Ethical Teleology as empathic consciousness—Argument in favour of Indeterminate Coherence on the basis of Kant's theory of moral Imagination.

Pp. 330–347

CHAPTER I.

THE SEARCH FOR A NEW PRINCIPLE.

IT is remarkable that the work in which an author crowns his speculative effort, and which stands for his final, if not in some respects for his greatest achievement, should have received comparatively little attention. The criticism of Feeling, which is the chief subject of our study, has only a small share in the colossal literature which has grown around the Critical Philosophy and which has been so largely devoted to the criticism of Theory and Practice. While in France and even in Germany the literature is mean, there is not yet in English a single book which deals exclusively with the *Critique of Judgment* in its entire range.

Two reasons may be found for this apparent want of interest. There is not the slightest doubt that Kant's greatest and most fruitful work is the *Critique of Pure Reason*. The natural failing to extol our chosen subject of study as the author's greatest work, can have no place here. There is no other writing of the great philosophers, except the dialogues of Plato, which warms the brain with the same intellectual glow. The forbidding style, the uncouth language, the interminable periods and continual contradictions, yield the same pleasure to the strenuous thinker as the perilous ascent to the mountain-climber. And they who have gained a summit in Kant's laborious thought shall never forget the clarity of vision, merged in the opal haze of the infinite void. The *Critique of Pure Reason* is Kant's most original work, and it is not surprising if it has absorbed the minds of philosophers. It is the mould in which his spirit was cast for all time, and no study of Kant will be effective which does not make continual reference to its contents.

The second reason is connected with the nature of the problem in the *Critique of Judgment*. Evidently Kant is less easily master of the situation. His aesthetic theory, which makes up the greater part of the book, is not nearly so original as it appears to be. He gathered his ideas from many different sources. From Hume he learned the subjective character of Aesthetic; the influence of Shaftesbury and Hutcheson, who taught a community of nature in the Beautiful and the Good, is very marked in his "Observations on the Beautiful and the Sublime," and appears later in his moral Ideal; the conception of the Ideal he learnt from Winckelmann's researches into Greek Plastic, while Baumgarten and Gerard supplied him with the theory of Genius.

It is not suggested that in the third *Critique* originality is displaced by an eclectic tendency. Never was there a thinker more severely independent than Kant. And though he gladly availed himself of foreign ideas, they must first pass through the alembic of his own mind. As he told Herz in October, 1790, he felt less inclined every day to accept from others the speculative setting of their ideas, and must follow the track which his own thought had cut out for itself during many years.[1] But there is an evident want of fitness in the speculative

[1] *Briefwechsel*: Kirchmann, p. 439.

form he has given to the material he collected and developed. In the programme of his lectures for the winter-session of 1765-66, he proposes to give some notice to the criticism of Taste in connection with the study of Logic;[1] and from that time onwards he elaborated, from various sources, in his lectures on Logic and Anthropology which are now being published in the standard edition of the Prussian Academy, practically all that he has to say on Aesthetic in the *Critique of Judgment*. These discussions were undertaken apparently without any definite systematic intention. But when he came to write the third *Critique*, the mould of his mind had already been fixed in the *Critique of Pure Reason*, and he felt bound, in the interest of unity, to impose this speculative form on his aesthetical ideas. The result could only be disappointing. In the *Critique of Pure Reason*, notwithstanding its artificial structure, there is a certain natural affinity of form and content, and a great part of the originality consists in the marvellous symmetry of method with which its ideas are developed. But in the *Critique of Judgment* the ideas are forced into an alien structure, and both form and content suffer in consequence.

And there is a further complication. Under the influence of Baumgarten and Gerard, Kant came to see that the aesthetic consciousness, as it is most perfectly expressed in Genius, is a harmony of mental activities and might therefore be called a kind of Teleology. By the year 1787, as he indicates in his letter to Reinhold, his intention was to write a book exclusively on Taste which he identified with this subjective Teleology, not as a logical judgment but as a psycho-

[1] Hartenstein, ii. pp. 318-9.

logical process. Meanwhile, in his anthropological studies, he had become interested in the origin of species, and in the following year, 1788, published a short essay on the use of the teleological principle. This, of course, is a very different kind of Teleology from the former. It is a logical judgment, and while it may also be partly a harmony of our mental states, its distinctive character as Teleology consists in having a predicate of purpose. In the one case it is our mental states that are purposive; in the other their content or meaning is purposive, and is the predicate in our judgment upon things which have teleology in themselves, namely, organisms.

Now Kant had no clear idea of bringing these two forms of Teleology under a common principle at the time he wrote to Reinhold.[1] He does this for the first time in the two introductions, the original form of which must have been cast not later than 1789. What helped Kant to make up his mind was the unsolved problem in the *Critique of Pure Reason*. There he had developed the principle of the specification of Nature into classes and kinds. This principle naturally takes cognisance of organisms, for the first specification of Nature is into organic and inorganic. But, at the same time, it does not pretend to discover the real purpose or final unity in things, and is only introduced for our own sakes in order to complete the unity of our knowledge. It is therefore a Subjective Teleology which fulfils a purpose of our own in maintaining the harmony of our mental states. Here, then, is a principle which can ostensibly unite, under the comprehensive name of Reflective

---

[1] Erdmann is decided on this point. *Kant's Kritik der Urteilskraft*, Einleitung, p. xx.

Judgment, the two distinct kinds of Teleology. In a somewhat surreptitious manner, the scientific judgment of objective purpose is affiliated with the aesthetical judgment of subjective purpose. At first sight it is almost incredible that a serious writer should have dreamt of forcing a marriage between such unwilling parties. It practically means uniting such divergent forms of experience as Art and Science under a common principle. Probably this extraordinary connection of ideas is the chief reason for the comparative neglect which the *Critique of Judgment* has suffered. And Kant himself seems to have lost all consciousness of the connection. But the intellectual charm of the book consists precisely in its paradox. Our curiosity is stimulated and maintained in seeking to understand as a natural relation what is apparently a *tour de force*. And I hope to show, before we have finished, that what Kant blindly approved in a fit of literary desperation is justified on Cromwell's principle that a man never mounts so high as when he does not know where he is going.

Besides, the *Critique of Judgment* has unquestioned importance in the history of literary criticism. It gave formal expression to the spirit of the Romantic movement, and placed Aesthetic, for the first time, on a genuine philosophical basis. It is true that Kant was incapable of appreciating the literary movement of his age. He lived in the middle of the *Sturm und Drang*, but was only sensible of what he regarded as reprehensible features, an untempered lust for novelty and extravagance in fanciful expression. He thought deeply about Genius and was a genius himself, but he failed to recognise it in Goethe. His attitude to Schiller was naturally different. He acknowledged in him a kindred spirit and made light of the differences between them, so long as Schiller remained his disciple.[1] But when Schiller rose to Goethe's expectations, he fell out of the sphere of Kant's sympathies. And still it is true, to use Windelband's expression, that the great philosopher constructed the poetical idea of Goethe, notwithstanding his remoteness from the spirit of his time.

The *Critique of Judgment* is also of capital importance for the influence it exercised on the subsequent development of philosophy and theology. Schelling made it the basis of his system, and gave to aesthetic intuition, as the reconciling medium of Nature and Spirit, that substantive existence which Kant had denied to it ; and from Schelling it passed to Hegel, who has much less to say in criticism of the third *Critique* than of the other two. Contemporary with the Romantic and Pantheistic tendency in philosophy at the beginning of last century, the foundation of modern theology was laid by Schleiermacher. Kant's Reflective Judgment, as independent, subjective, individual experience, but at the same time as self-approving, communicable and capable of universal validity, is the natural parent of the great theologian's religious intuition—the feeling of simple dependence on the supersensible ground, a feeling which is neither theoretical nor practical, but akin to and inclusive of aesthetic experience. Later the *Werturteil* of Ritschl is a specification of the *Urteilskraft* ; and even Pragmatism, if its feelings were less arrogant and more sensitive to the discipline of Religion and Art, could put in a small claim to the rich inheritance.

---

[1] Note to *Religion within the limits of Reason alone* : Abbott, *Kant's Theory of Ethics*, p. 330.

THE CRITICAL PHILOSOPHY 7

But apart from its historical connections, the *Critique of Judgment* is the high-water mark of the Critical Philosophy itself, and may indeed be called its crowning phase. We lose its significance if we consider it only as an episodical treatment of what lay outside Kant's proper study. It contains a further development of principles without which it is hardly possible to interpret, with some measure of fairness and appreciation, his theory of knowledge. While the second edition of the first *Critique*, notwithstanding its polemical aim, is a reply to Kant himself rather than to his critics, the *Critique of Judgment*, which is also polemical with a different intention, as Schlapp has shown, contains Kant's further criticism of his own position, and might be called the third edition. Although the peculiar form which the problem eventually assumed is very obscure, the problem itself lay in the trend of Kant's thinking, and arose quite naturally in the course of his reflections as an extension of our hypothetical knowledge. In its simplest terms Kant's position may be stated as follows.

There are in the human mind two distinct types of apprehension, Understanding and Reason. The faculty of Knowledge, in the common perception of scientist and ordinary consciousness alike, by which we articulate Nature into a world of things, arranged in space and successive in time, is the Understanding. Its characteristic objects are incomplete unities which are dependent for their boundaries on their relations to each other. It is not necessary for our present purpose to specify Sensibility as a third and distinct faculty of mind, for the Understanding as Kant finally conceived it is organised sense-perception. Reason is an intuitive power, which comes to the clearest expression in its typical form as moral consciousness. It is not able to specify its objects in the diversity of their relations, but it does perceive their abstract unity.

These two faculties, the discursive and intuitive, always tend to appropriate each other's merits. The Understanding is vaguely dissatisfied with aggregate unities of objects whose parts are externally related, and continuously but vainly aspires to completeness. Reason, likewise, is not always content to dwell in sanctuary, and seeks to make plain the mystical and indivisible perception of Duty by explanations which Understanding alone can approve. These two tendencies meet in a third mode of apprehension, the Theoretical Reason, which is indifferently an extension of Understanding in its effort to become intuitive, and an extension of Reason in its effort to become discursive. There is the advantage in this manner of statement that it resolves the ambiguity of meaning in Reason as two distinct functions, theoretical and practical, which Kant does not notice or explain. In Kant's conception the Reason is fundamentally moral —the apprehension of truth in the practical decisions of the will. But whenever there is danger of confusion, we shall adhere to Kant's terminology and call it the Practical Reason, in order to distinguish it from the Reason which is theoretical.

Now the Understanding, though itself a discursive apprehension of parts in their discreteness, is based on an intuitive principle. For in order to grasp the parts in relation at all, their unity must at least be thought. We are not indeed able to perceive Nature as a whole, nor therefore any object in the complete conditions of its existence. The relativity of human knowledge means that all our explanations of objects are extraneous to themselves and in consequence unending. There is, therefore, no question here of unity in the object itself. But that they should be connected for us at all, we must furnish that unity to the parts of an object which is necessary to the consciousness of our own identity. The fundamental principle, then, of Understanding is itself an 'analytic proposition,' the immediate consciousness of a unity which is indivisible. But it is precisely the complete sum of conditions which exhausts the existence of an object that Understanding, in its extended form as Theoretical Reason, requires; the intuitive principle must not only be felt as the anticipative idea of unity but must be maintained until it becomes the perception of a whole whose parts are all transparent.

This attitude of mind, which may be called the inductive, is quite distinct from the other two, as its logical prototype shows. Kant indeed, in keeping with his general scheme, would seem to derive the Ideas of Theoretical Reason from the deductive syllogism, while the Understanding is modelled on the logical judgment. But we know very well how wooden these procrustean structures are, and how frequently Kant's meaning is obscured by his method. In fact, the notions of Understanding take their character from the whole procedure of deductive reasoning, as Kant acknowledges when he opposes the discursive to the intuitive nature of Understanding in the *Critique of Judgment*. And it is not the deductive syllogism that prefigures the Ideas of Reason, but the prosyllogism which leads us backwards in a train of reasoning to the unconditioned major premiss. Deduction proceeds through episyllogisms, by taking the conclusion in the preceding syllogism as the major premiss in that which follows, until it has exhausted the entire range of consequences. But it is the totality of conditions and not of consequences that the prosyllogism seeks to determine; and what is in question is the major premiss, the truth of which is assumed in the deductive syllogism. Taking the major premiss, then, as the conclusion, we try to construct a new syllogism in which the major premiss is less conditioned, and so ascend through syllogism to syllogism until we reach, if possible, a premiss that is self-evident and needs no further qualification.[1]

The value of this inductive method is that it combines the discursive process of Understanding with the intuition of Reason. Understanding is the knowledge of related perceptions circumscribed by a certain unity of form which is called the object, whose limits, however, are quite arbitrary and subject to incessant change, as the piece of wax loses its rigidity and becomes a fluid mass in the presence of heat. The political divisions of the same continent on maps which represent different periods of history, are a good illustration of the fluctuating boundaries which define the objects of Understanding. And the Understanding resembles the deductive syllogism in assuming the validity of the provisional system within which its attention is confined, as if all the conditions were present which make up the existence of the object. But only so many conditions are present as are needful for immediate perception, and therefore what is actual for the Understanding cannot be the object itself but only the relations. Reason, again, may be said to have

[1] *Critique of Pure Reason*: Meiklejohn, p. 231.

its type in the final moment of the inductive process (ἐπαγωγή) when the absolute premisses (ἀρχαί) are discovered. In all probability Kant had the Aristotelian conception of induction vaguely in mind. In the absence of methodical rules, we come upon our first truths more or less contingently. With the same appearance of suddenness our moral convictions seem to dawn upon us, and no analysis of motives will ever make explicit the mystical voice of Duty. It is the intuition of an analytic unity in the sense that it can never be completely resolved into its elements, and therefore what is actual for Reason is the unity and not the diversity, for this latter is only ideal. Waiving for the moment the extreme formalism in Kant's Ethics, his fundamental principle is ultimately sound. The motives into which we are able to resolve a moral act make up such an inconsiderable part of the total conditions which are necessary to originate such an act as to be practically negligible in view of a complete explanation.

This double limitation in our Theory and Practice is transcended, it would seem, in Theoretical Reason. It employs the intuition of Reason as practical in aspiring to a perception of totality, but at the same time, unlike Practical Reason and in furtherance of the Understanding, it seeks to enumerate discursively the particular conditions which in their sum make up this total unity. Both Understanding and Practical Reason are abstract forms of apprehension, the former having a relatively coherent content without an object, the latter having a complete object without any content at all. Reason has intuitions of God, the Soul and Immortality, but these are so remote from the conditions of existence that it must assume the rôle of Theoretical Reason to give them articulate expression in the form of Ideas; and in the degree that these Ideas are able to supply the total conditions of existence, the intuitions of Reason will be actual as well as possible, and so become necessary. Thus if we were able to have a complete insight into the nature of man, immortality would follow as a necessary attribute of his being; and, conversely, the intuition of immortality would no longer be an abstract thought without content, but the perception of a real quality of existence in the complexity of its relations as they are known by Understanding. Similarly the Understanding appropriates these intuitions of Reason, and uses them as guiding Ideas in order to present its fragmentary perceptions in their completeness.

Theoretical Reason, then, is more concrete than either Understanding or Reason, and it should mean that the tale of existence is completely told. But this is not the case. The knowledge given by the Understanding as it is extended by Theoretical Reason is only hypothetical, and, if taken in earnest, leads to illusion. In the end as in the beginning, the complete unity which alone deserves the name of object is merely ideal, and the initial feeling of unity, with which the Understanding sets out in constructing experience, appears in its final form as the distended bladder of its own enthusiasm, which at a touch may explode into vacuity.

We must remind ourselves, however, that Kant is talking at a very high level. He does not mean that our efforts to give an exhaustive explanation are illusive, but only that we are in danger of illusion when we forget our limitations. This hypothetical knowledge has for its results such excellent and useful information

THE CRITICAL PHILOSOPHY 13

as the classification of Nature into genera and species, what we should call to-day the contents of the special sciences. But for a transcendental philosopher this knowledge does not touch the root of the matter. In Kant's opinion, no science will ever be able to get beyond appearances. There is a limit to our intensive perception, while its extensive range is boundless. We pass through an interminable maze of facts, and not a single fact is exhaustively explained. And Science often deludes itself in thinking that it is exploring the secret of existence when it is only spreading itself over a vast area. The agnostic tendency, however, in contemporary Science is hardly in danger of this error.

This limitation in knowledge is due to a defect in the constitution of our minds. When we analyse a piece of knowledge we discover that there is something given which we have not contributed. This is sensation. Kant sets out from the assumption that sensations are produced in us by an unknown, supersensible thing, and are passively received; and although he considerably modifies this doctrine in what is known as the Subjective Deduction, he never quits hold of its implications. In the first instance, sensations are described as a manifold of unrelated impressions, which are simply given from without; and what makes them our own as possible elements in knowledge is our form of Sensibility in the pure representation of Space. In the *Aesthetic* Kant speaks of Space as if it were the object of a pure perception and therefore *a priori*, and he puts forward as a chief argument that sensation would lose all its quality as having relation to something outside of us, and would be nothing more than a subjective feeling or idea, without the presupposition of Space. No element of sensuous perception can be imagined which has not a spatial quality, "although we can quite readily think of space as empty of objects";[1] we must therefore have an antecedent perception of empty Space, to account for that quality of 'outness' and of their external relation to each other which we observe in sensations as they enter into consciousness.

Evidently Kant has here anticipated his proof in the *Analytic*, and already finds an ordered physical world in the pure form of Sensibility. If this view of Space were sound, the problem of knowledge would lose its meaning. For it is quite as difficult to think of an empty space without any objects as to think of objects which are not in space. And not only is the argument invalid, it is in conflict with Kant's primary intention. His real proof is based on the established science of Geometry, which shows that we have the power of constructing relations in space according to our own conception of what those relations should be, and that in consequence we may be said to have an *a priori* perception of the nature of space by which the process of construction is controlled.

It is quite misleading, then, to speak of Space as a perception. We ought rather to say that it is a power of perception; and in the opening passage of the *Aesthetic* Kant defines his problem as "the capacity for receiving representations," which we call Sensibility.[2] It must therefore be said, and probably this is Kant's real position, that Space as a perception is inseparable from sensation and arises simultaneously. His view of sensation as an unrelated manifold of impressions, which are arranged for the first time in our pure perception

---

[1] *Transcendental Aesthetic*: Watson's *Selections*, pp. 24-5.
[2] Meiklejohn, p. 21.

of empty space, is contradicted by his own admission further on, that sensations have degrees and therefore dimensional quality. Or if we refuse to introduce the conception of quantity into sensation, and prefer to say with M. Bergson that degree in sensation means a more or less extended area of affection, it is all the more certain that sensations have no meaning for us unless they have the qualification of Space.

The reason for Kant's insistence in the *Aesthetic* on Space as an object of perception, is his anxiety to define Sense and Thought as quite distinct faculties. But in the *Analytic* this motive, which had been taken over from the Dissertation of 1770, naturally fades into the background. All that he had wished to prove was that Space as a form of our perception renders subjective the primary qualities of extension and figure, and that therefore the objects of perception are only phenomena and not things in themselves. But since the *Analytic* shows that nothing can become an element in perception without the activity of thought, the insistence on Space as *a priori* perception in its own right is no longer necessary; for now all the qualities of matter, primary and secondary, extension and figure as well as impenetrability, hardness and colour, are found to be mental. Space itself is a construction due to the synthetic activity of thought, and what is *a priori* in our perception of Space can only be the original apprehension of the relations to be constructed. Accordingly, Kant now says that, without this mental synthesis, which alone is able to hold things together in the identity of one and the same unity, "not even the simplest and most elementary idea of space or time could arise in my consciousness."[1]

[1] Watson's *Selections*, p. 59.

Perhaps some of the confusion, which inevitably attends the discussion of this elusive subject, will be avoided if we say that Kant reversed the order of the problem as it had appealed to Berkeley. The problem for Berkeley was: granted that the secondary qualities of matter, which are due to sensation, are mental, to prove that the primary qualities are likewise mental. Kant, on the other hand, appears to take it thus: granted that our apprehension of Space is independent of experience, as Geometry conclusively shows, and that therefore the primary qualities are mental, to prove that the secondary qualities, which are due to sensation, are likewise mental. This may seem strange, but it is a fair statement of Kant's position; and though he riddles the independent existence of sensation by showing that nothing can enter into consciousness without the synthesis of thought, he reverts to his original view and maintains it to the end, as we shall presently see.

Synthesis, then, is the paramount factor in knowledge. The connection of elements in perception, which is the distinctive feature of knowledge, could not even be imagined unless the relations among things were considered as held together in the unity of a conscious mind. That there should be relations at all, means that a plurality of elements are perceived by an identical mind, which abides one and the same throughout succeeding impressions. But when Kant was rightly advised by his critics that his doctrine would only account for a purely subjective world, confined to the individual mind, he replied in the second edition of the *Critique* by pointing out that synthesis is not self-explaining and involves a circular argument. Kant believed in good faith that this is not a vicious circle;

THE CRITICAL PHILOSOPHY

and though it must be admitted that his reply is as much a criticism of his own position, and particularly of his doctrine of sensation, as an answer to his critics, we should not discredit his method until we have considered the peculiar nature of his problem.

The ordinary mind knows the difference between stable objects and illusions, and distinguishes them as reality and appearance. To this Kant would say: Retain this distinction, but remember that the medium in which it is made is itself phenomenal. He sought, then, to interpose this phenomenal medium—as consisting of mental states and something more—between the realm of subjective illusion, which exists only for the individual mind, and Reality which exists for itself. And his proof is, that while consciousness is the source of relations, consciousness itself presupposes a fixed order of relations. Let it be granted that we know nothing except our mental states: on the other hand we can only be conscious of ourselves in a succession of mental states; and if these did not succeed in a certain fixed order, our consciousness of the preceding states would drop out of memory before we reached the others, and at each moment we should be confined to an isolated perception and lose the consciousness of our own identity. There must therefore be an objective ground in sensations which informs them with that connection which is necessary to the consciousness of ourselves. Of that ground we can say nothing more than that it is there, and mark the spot with an algebraical sign. This is what Kant calls the Transcendental Object.

This transcendental object is on no account to be confused with the thing in itself. As every student of

Kant knows, 'transcendental' has always for him the suggestion of immanence, while the supersensible Thing is completely transcendent. It may be a very subtle distinction and hard to define, but it was quite sufficient for Kant's purpose. He wanted, in fact, to return to his original view of sensation. What gives rise to sensations in us is this supersensible Thing, not indeed as cause, for then it would be a term in our knowledge, but as indeterminate ground. And sensations in themselves are quite independent and have no necessity for our Understanding, or, as he says in the *Critique of Judgment*, the particular is contingent for the universal of our Understanding.

I do not think there can be any doubt of the exact parallel, in this connection, between Kant and Plato. In the *Philebus* the phenomenal world is composed of two factors, the Indeterminate (τὸ ἄπειρον) and the Limit (τὸ πέρας); the first corresponds to the contingent material of sensation, the second to the transcendental object. Then the cause of the Mixture, and not the Limit,[1] is what answers to the Ideas of Plato's earlier doctrine, and the Ideas are Kant's things in themselves. Since the Indeterminate has a nature of its own, the resulting mixture can only have a relative necessity. Phenomena are not indeed representations confined to an individual mind; for consciousness implies a fixed order in representations, and we are therefore limited by the obligation to think in a certain way which is

---

[1] [To equate the πέρας with the Ideas, as *e.g.* Ritchie does (*Plato*, p. 117), would identify the Ideas with a purely quantitative conception. In favour of the view we have adopted, cp. the causal relation of Ideas to particulars in the *Phaedo*: τῷ καλῷ πάντα τὰ καλὰ γίγνεται καλά. 100 D.]

THE CRITICAL PHILOSOPHY 19

universally valid for all minds. But this necessary connection in knowledge does not affect the original factor in sensations themselves. Kant only means that, to be our objects, sensations must have a certain limit imposed upon them in order that we may be conscious of our own identity, and all he wants to prove is that they are only *our* objects or phenomena.

The consequences of this position now easily follow. The primary element in sensation, of which we can only speak as a presentation to consciousness, is not perceived by us as it is in itself. We could only have a real perception if the total conditions which make up a presentation were present to consciousness. But, as it appears to us, a presentation contains no more than the minimum conditions, which are necessary for the perception of ourselves as an abiding unity in a permanent order of relations. It may indeed be true, though Kant's theory would deprive even this assumption of security, that the limited series of conditions which we perceive is a real part of the presentation, as the initial members in an infinite series of numbers may be judged to be continuous with the last term. But we are never able to follow the terms in such a series to infinity, and to do this a completely different order of perception from ours would be required. This is what the Understanding aspires to do in its rôle as Theoretical Reason, but all that it succeeds in procuring is an ideal sum to n terms, which is a very different thing. The qualification that the conditions appear to us in consciousness seems to constitute them into a different series, and the inference then follows that a perception, or a judgment of fact, contains no more than the minimum of categorical truth contributed by the original shock of sensation, as it is expressed in the completely abstract and indeterminate judgment, 'something is.' Kant frequently speaks in the *Aesthetic* of empirical judgments as if they were immediate and self-evident, and in our easier language this means that in simple perception we are in touch with actual fact and that our judgment is true without further condition. But this is denied in the *Analytic*, which shows that all judgments of fact are hypothetical. We are in touch with fact indeed, Kant would say, but only under the form of our perception; as Mill afterwards maintained, the matter of sensation, which occasions our first contact with Reality, is not affected by our consciousness. Presentation is therefore not itself perception, but a suggestion which is constructed by our thoughts into that diluted kind of perception which we call appearance.

We quite mistake Kant's meaning, however, if we allege, as the reason for this conclusion, that the supersensible Thing cannot appear. I wish to insist on this point because it is of the first importance to the *Critique of Judgment*, which has for its problem, from one point of view, whether and to what extent the Supersensible can enter the realm of appearance without impairing its quality. Kant prefers to think that the limitation is due to the entire structure of our minds, not simply as Understanding, but also in their function as Practical Reason. Both in our Theory and Practice the same defect is exhibited. It is not the Supersensible that is inherently incapable of appearing, it is our minds that are not adapted for pure perception. This criticism is made of the Practical Reason in the *Critique of Judgment*, § 76. Like the Understanding, Practical Reason supposes two different orders of existence, the actual and the possible. The recognition of commands implies a distinction between what ought to be and what is. We are so made that we can think relations which are not actual, and enact moral decisions which cannot become effective until they are realised in sensible conditions. For a higher order of mind there would be no such distinction; what is thinkable would be a necessary perception, and a possible determination of will would also be actual just because it is good. The Will, however, is in its very nature more happily equipped than Intellect, and it is not without just reason that Kant gives it the primacy. To a certain extent it is able to overcome this dualism by procuring its own sensible conditions. Volition is the concentration of the mind on an idea which it has united with itself completely and not in part, as happens when we only wish to understand; and this continuous effort of attention can originate presentations in the motor continuum without waiting on corresponding changes in the sensory continuum. We can will to believe that we shall recover from an illness, and in many instances we do recover, because the nerve-centres have been instructed to initiate those sensible conditions which would otherwise require to be passively supplied. But our success only reminds us of our defect, for it is achieved through a laboured process, and is not immediate as it should be in a mind for whom the possible is inherently actual. The Understanding, too, realises the same measure of success when it unites with the Will in that mixed practice which we may call pragmatical activity. But in itself it is particularly helpless, for the creative power which it does evince in synthesis has only application to possible relations and none whatever to actual conditions. And what spoils the Understanding is just this want of sustained attention, of which even the Will is only capable by an extraordinary expenditure of effort.

Whenever a presentation occurs we inevitably wander away from it and begin to think of something else, because we can make nothing of it by itself. What is given is a mere blank point of sensation which we must think discursively by means of 'wandering adjectives.' To make it intelligible at all, we are driven to think it first in the most general terms and we then advance to more conditioned thoughts, striving at each successive step to apperceive its meaning by affiliating it more and more closely with our notions of possible experience. What controls this process throughout are schemata, abstract thoughts which are the dynamic in all our thinking and have a natural tendency to what is actual. But they never do become actual of themselves; not even as sensuous images can we perceive them. In Kant's somewhat artificial language, schemata have only the form of what is actual, and are nothing more than possible representations until they are applied to the matter of sensation. We are able, however, to detect their presence in the process by which we advance from thoughts which are relatively unconditioned to those which are more conditioned, until we finally reach those notions of similar presentations in our past experience which are most nearly akin to the objects of present attention.

But clearly this is thinking the presentation in terms of others. Like the bee which goes from flower to flower, we gather our knowledge discursively and never exhaust a single presentation. Instead of dwelling on what is actual until it tells us its story, we dissipate perception in external relations. To be inherently perceptive the Understanding must be instinctive, but in such a way that it shall lose itself in the presentation without at the same time losing its self-consciousness. Then it would approximate to that ideal Understanding which is able to recognise sensation as its own product rather than as coming from a foreign source. Instinct has all the necessary equipment for intensive insight because it is not self-conscious, but for that very reason it can never discover its secrets. Only self-conscious Understanding can ask the proper questions of a presentation to elicit its meaning, but this very habit of asking questions causes its attention to wander, and for that reason it will never find what it seeks. In M. Bergson's words: *il y a des choses que l'intelligence seule est capable de chercher, mais que, par elle-même, elle ne trouvera jamais. Ces choses, l'instinct seul les trouverait; mais il ne les cherchera jamais.*[1] If Understanding confined itself simply to asking questions, it would not go far astray. For if we can believe what George Meredith says in the fourth chapter of *Harry Richmond*, the quickest way of getting at facts is to leave off answering and limit ourselves to questioning one another ; at least he thinks that this is true of boys and women, and it is surely the same elemental kind of intercourse we must use in addressing a presentation. But the Understanding insists on answers, and, if it gets no reply, it invariably inquires next door.

[1] *L'Évolution Créatrice*, p. 164.

It will be clear from what has been said that Understanding is a superficial faculty, because it has not sufficient sympathy to exercise patience in dealing with presentations. Our heads are too big and our eyes are too small, we can think more than we can see. But this is the failing of what is really a virtue, for we should be reduced to the level of animal instinct and could never extend our knowledge if our thoughts were not in advance of sensation. Whatever criticism may have to say in disparagement of knowledge, we find, on analysis, that it is not our making so much as it is due to the influence of a Power not ourselves, and may therefore be regarded as a secure basis for a deeper apprehension of Reality. It may be that the very same factors as are at work in knowledge may be so adjusted, that we can have a purer perception than an unequal mixture of thought and sense, which will approximate to that ideal Understanding whose thoughts are themselves perceptions. That these factors are heterogeneous is unquestioned, for how else could there be a problem of knowledge? But it is all the more wonderful, just because it makes a problem for us, that an idea in my head should indicate an object outside of me. It is to the Supersensible that we owe our most ordinary knowledge, the immediate perception of an ordered world in space and time. For knowledge means synthesis, synthesis is the work of consciousness, and consciousness supposes connections which are already implicit in the very things which we unite, and this logically prior connection, or transcendental object, has a supersensible ground. We cannot have erred, then, in being under the influence of the supersensible Thing.

And there is a further concession on the part of

Nature. Phenomena are so intimately bound up with the consciousness of ourselves that they may be regarded as dependent on our consciousness. But the material of sensation is contingent and independent of our minds, so far as we know, for we have no means of determining whether the conditions under which sensations enter into consciousness, are also the real conditions under which they exist in themselves, or, what is the same thing, in a perfect Understanding. This means that our objects are never exhaustively defined. Now this is just what Theoretical Reason professes to do, and Nature helps us by yielding the presumption that the material basis of existence is also adapted to our Understanding. But this hypothetical knowledge is not different in kind from Understanding, its objects are not a different kind of perceptions but phenomena to the nth power. And although we spoke of these approaches on the part of the Supersensible as concessions to our Understanding, this is only a manner of speaking and we must not mention them as favours. Rather they are a bare necessity, for, without these adaptations, there would be neither knowledge of phenomena nor thought of the Supersensible for us; just as the adaptation of our eyes for sight is no argument for a special design on the part of Nature, because if we are to see at all, our eyes must be suitably adapted and they must be good eyes too. If the Supersensible would have us know that it is there, it is in its own interest to give us a lead. And all that it has done hitherto, both in the Understanding proper as the limited knowledge of immediate perception, and in its extended form as hypothetical Reason, without which the Understanding would have no security, is only what is strictly necessary for the coherence of our thoughts about Nature or, what is the same thing, the appearance at all of a uniform world.

We are brought thus far by the *Critique of Pure Reason*. Nature is so adapted to our intelligence that our intelligence can find itself in Nature as a logical system. Without this necessary hypothesis, there would be neither a Nature nor a coherent consciousness of ourselves. The question now put forward in the *Critique of Judgment* is whether the Supersensible has any favours for us, and if so, whether we have a higher form of apprehension than the hypothetical Understanding, which will bring us into closer touch with the Supersensible in these gratuitous appearances. Kant finds three such favours in the phenomena of Beauty, organic forms and moral Man. To these orders of Reality the corresponding form of higher apprehension is Reflective Judgment. We are encouraged to look for these concessions, not only because the Supersensible has been the moving principle in our ordinary apprehension, but also because this apprehension is so remote from Reality and is shot through with the marks of imperfection. There is a lack of spontaneity in the way the factors come together, which make up both Theory and Practice. I have been careful in this discussion to include Practical Reason in the criticism which Kant passes on the Understanding as discursive. He only mentions it incidentally in the *Critique of Judgment*. But though the imperfections of the Understanding and of Practical Reason start from opposite sides, they are clearly parts of the same defect, and, without the reference to Practical Reason, Kant's argument would be incomplete. The third *Critique*, especially in its treatment of the moral Ideal, makes an evident effort to improve upon the abstract exercise of Reason in the Categorical Imperative; and Reflective Judgment is a form of apprehension which is intended to supersede both Practice and Theory. The whole structure of our minds is awry so long as they have no immediate connection with feeling. Without this mark of spontaneity, we cannot have a sympathetic insight into Reality, and we are suffering in consequence from a sense of obligation.

To take Knowledge first, it is true that we have an *a priori* apprehension of objects : we know that they must appear in space and time and in causal connection. But this simply refers to the form of apprehension, and only means that in no other way can they appear. That sensations should come to us at all and when they please, is completely beyond our control and we must simply take our cue from them. And even when we anticipate Nature, as we do in experimental science by making her answer our questions, and thus exercise an *a priori* apprehension of her material basis, these questions of ours are ultimately conditioned by Nature herself in the influence she exercises over us. We cannot escape the conclusion that knowledge, determinate or hypothetical, is what we are compelled to believe.

Obligation, again, lies in the very nature of morality, and it is not well to conceive of a transcendent ethic from which it has vanished. But in our naturality, this sense of obligation acts on us in the form of a foreign compulsion which is not good. Conscience, as the bare recognition of good and evil, evokes a spirit of antagonism, and, in appealing to the highest, rouses the worst passions in our nature. To use the language of St. Paul, the consciousness of Law works all manner of concupiscence in us and produces a state akin to death. In the days of his naturality, St. Paul was "alive without Law," a free, breathing animal (ψυχὴ ζῶσα) like Adam in paradise, but when the commandment came, sin revived and he died. (Rom. vii. 9 ; 1 Cor. xv. 45.) The self-realisation of Idealism endangers morality by giving the law completely into our own hands, and it can only deliver the commandment unimpaired on the precarious assumption that our nature is completely good. In confusing the psychical state with the content which it bears, it identifies psychology with metaphysics. In order that morality may be possible at all, its law must be realised in me, but while the way in which it is realised is mine, the content is not mine ; otherwise the whole conception of obligation is destroyed. Much worse is the self-assertion of Pragmatism, which has neither the power nor the wish to discriminate a lower from a higher self, as Idealism undoubtedly and most jealously does.

There is more truth in Kant's ethic, notwithstanding its limitations, than his critics have been willing to recognise. He saw that Law puts such a strain on the rivets of pleasure and pain, to use Plato's expression, that morality as realised capacity is impossible in threescore years and ten. And his theory moreover implies, what neither Idealism nor Pragmatism sufficiently recognises but what is attested by the history of human experience, that unreasoned constraint remains a dominant factor in the best of lives, and that a complete acquiescence in the Law only comes in intermittent flashes of the "faith which worketh by love."

THE CRITICAL PHILOSOPHY 29

The divine command confronts us in majesty, and while it requires our loving obedience, does not explain the reason for its authority. The Law appears to us in its abstract totality, but systematic disposition of its parts in their relations there is none. And since the Law is not explicitly defined in Nature, our discursive method of interpretation must be supplemented by the feeling that Nature is a divine organisation in sympathy with our will; and this is not a feeling that is readily acquired or easily maintained.

From this universal criticism of the human mind a new problem arises. While the factors in experience are out of gear, unequally yoked and grasped in different ways, the unity conceived by thought, the parts perceived by sense or imagination, our apprehension of Reality is one-sided and imperfect. We recognised at the outset two cardinal functions of mind, Understanding and Reason. Then from the combination of these two we deduced a third type of apprehension, which we fondly hoped would repair their inherent defects, by giving articulate expression to the unreasoned intuitions of the Will and a completely coherent unity to the fragmentary perceptions of Understanding. But we have found this principle of Theoretical Reason to be illusive, and incapable of anything more than a hypothetical determination of the Supersensible. For while the elements of perception are apprehended in their discreteness, their unity is not perceived or imaged in the same way but imagined or conceived. To realise the total conditions which would make up the exhaustive unity of these elements, Understanding, in its hypothetical function, must run into an indeterminate series which is impossible without antinomy, for the series may equally be regarded as finite or as infinite and the final sum is not actual but ideal.

If now we could discover a greater degree of facility in the way these factors come together, this would undoubtedly argue a certain spontaneity in their relation, and we should confidently assert what Kant only ventured to surmise, that sense and thought spring from a common root. It would be a real concession on the part of the Supersensible to our Understanding, or in Kant's own words, "a favour which Nature has felt for us."[1] Our thoughts would not be empty possibilities which can only be realised when they are limited by sensational shocks, but would be themselves interpretative perceptions which are able to dwell in the actual as a kindred element. Nor would the Understanding, a sober sentinel, restrain the spontaneity of Sense, calling after it, 'Hold there, you have forgotten the categories,' but freely move with it in play. The whole is not produced in utter nakedness nor are the parts received in shreds, but an Individual of flesh and blood is revealed to our eyes. This disposition of material existence to our apprehension, in which the Supersensible may be said to rise to the surface, is found in Aesthetic and Teleology of Nature, and they have this at least in common that their problem is the Individual. But to compass this end we require a new principle.

As I mentioned in an earlier part of this chapter, the search for a new principle arose naturally out of Kant's reflections on the hypothetical nature of knowledge. Both in the received Introduction to the third *Critique* and in the earlier sketch, now called 'J. S. Beck's *Auszug*,' he distinguishes practical from pragmatical.

[1] Bernard, p. 286.

THE CRITICAL PHILOSOPHY 31

For himself the term 'practical' always signifies the pure activity of will, and of this alone can there be a philosophy. But he finds that people often use the term to denote the application of a particular science, as for example, mensuration the practical philosophy of arithmetic ; or we might speak of a practical geometry and a practical psychology. But this is misleading, for it implies that these applications are a distinct kind of Theory from the science in question, whereas they are only consequences of the same in the nature of a scholium or corollary. Under this false use of the term would fall the practical philosophy of Mr. Squeers. In his educational scheme, theory is exemplified in spelling 'winder,' but if you wish to learn the practical philosophy of the subject, you must go and clean the 'winder.'

These applications are but extensions of Theory and form no part of Practical Philosophy at all. In order, then, to avoid ambiguity, Kant proposes to call them technical, judgments of industrial art and skill—"for they belong to art (technical), which is the procuring of what one wills a thing should be, and which is in each instance a mere consequence of a complete theory."[1] The distinctive character of these technical judgments lies in the presence of human purpose. Although Technic involves the activity of will, it is not the pure exercise of will but of will as united with a "natural concept."[2] In the application of theoretical principles to legislation, politics, industry and agriculture, the will is not actuated by a pure conception of duty, but by our own idea of what a thing should be according to the end we have in

[1] *Über Philosophie überhaupt* : Rosenkranz, *Werke*, i. p. 585.
[2] Bernard, p. 7.

view. Precepts of morality, on the other hand, are "not merely precepts or rules in this or that aspect, but without any preceding reference to purposes and designs, are laws"; [1] and it is their characteristic feature to exclude interest or purpose. The will is only supersensible when it represents an act simply in its intention as prescribed by the moral law, and "without regard to the means whereby the object is to be realised." [2]

It is from this mixture of Theory and Practice in the execution of human purposes, over which the god of Pragmatism presides, that Kant takes his cue in the search for a new principle. Technical judgments follow naturally as corollaries from the whole body of theoretical knowledge, determinate and hypothetical. But they differ from their sources in an important respect. Theoretical knowledge is certain because it is independent of experience, and, even as hypothetical, the regulative principles by which it guides the procedure of inductive science, are "immanent in their exercise and sure." [3] And Duty has no uncertain voice. But in Pragmatic, our will descends from its high eminence into the hands of natural concepts, our smiths, our shoemakers and builders. And we no longer hear the clear direction of a single voice, but a Babel of earth-born tongues which brings confusion. Kant has brought us to the strange conclusion that the realm of purpose is the realm of contingence.

Now Kant proposes to use this term Technic to denote Reflective Judgment. But he makes it quite

---

[1] Bernard, p. 9.
[2] *Über Philosophie überhaupt*: Rosenkranz, *Werke*, i. p. 585.
[3] Bernard, p. 317. Cp. *Appendix to Dialectic*: Meiklejohn, p. 394.

THE CRITICAL PHILOSOPHY 33

clear that it is only on the analogy of these technical judgments that we are to think of Reflexion.[1] For Reflexion is neither theoretical nor pragmatical[2] since it determines nothing either in the constitution or production of objects, but is merely the way in which Nature is conceived on the analogy of technical art.[1] And he further adds, it is not the reflective judgments themselves that we shall call technical but the whole reflective outlook, the *Urteilskraft*, on whose laws they are based; and Nature also we shall call technical as the object of Reflexion.[3] This evidently means that the relation between Reflexion and Technic is a loose analogy.

It is difficult to say what exactly we have learnt from this obscure language, and the reasonable doubt arises whether it contains a new principle at all. These technical judgments are easily confused, in a vague way, with the inductive procedure which Kant calls the hypothetical function of Reason, and he never clearly distinguishes Reflexion from hypothetical Reason. Thus in the Logic edited by Jäsche he defines determinant and reflective Judgment as deduction and induction respectively, the former proceeding from the universal to the particular, the latter from the particular to the universal. Only, Reflexion is here further defined

---

[1] 'Reflexion' is a highly technical term in Kant's writings. I have therefore adopted this form of spelling to distinguish it from its use by other writers, *e.g.* Locke, who spells it 'Reflection.' For Locke it only meant ordinary apperception, while for Kant it meant a higher apperception on the basis of the ordinary process.

[2] The text is : theoretisch noch praktisch (in der zuletzt angeführten Bedeutung) = technical or pragmatical. *Über Philosophie überhaupt* : Rosenkranz, *Werke*, i. p. 585. Cp. Bernard, p. 19.

[3] *Ibid.* ; Erdmann, *Kant's Kritik der Urteilskraft*, p. 347.

c

as the wider process of arriving at certain general conclusions from particular concepts, with its two specific forms, induction and analogy: the former reasoning from many to all things of one kind, the latter reasoning from many features common to things of the same kind to the remaining features.[1] The point of distinction is so fine that it is hardly appreciable; and it raises the whole question, on which expositors are divided, whether Reflexion, apart from its aesthetical function, really goes beyond the *Dialectic*. So eminent an authority as Stadler, for instance, is decided that it does not. But I think the evidence in Kant's own writings is sufficient to make it worth our while contending for a new principle. How could Reflexion be identified with inductive procedure when it is expressly based, as we have seen, on the analogy of what are direct corollaries of all Theory, including the hypothetical principles of induction? Technical judgments are but the application of these inductive principles in experimental science, or, as it is stated in the *Critique of Judgment*, Reflexion is based on the analogy of our causality according to purposes.

Reflexion, then, as derived from this new principle, means that we think of Nature as an artisan. It will be said, however, that this is only another expression for the specification of Nature into genera and species, which is the very principle of hypothetical Reason. Undoubtedly; but while the *Dialectic* only insists on the bare principle itself, we are here putting forward a new way of envisaging this principle, and we think of Nature not simply as an abstract quantity, but with the help of an anthropological conception derived from our

[1] Hartenstein, viii. pp. 128-9.

THE CRITICAL PHILOSOPHY 35

own experience. To put it briefly, the principle in the *Dialectic* is logical, while the new principle of Reflexion is psychological. And this is the significance of the analogy: while the experimental application of principles brings us into the region of uncertainty, there is also the advantage of a more intimate knowledge. We never know exactly how a thing will turn out until it is completed, but also, as Kant says, "we see into a thing completely only so far as we can make it in accordance with our concepts and bring it to completion."[1] And the reason for this insight is that the factors in experience develop simultaneously and are present in an equal degree of reality.

Kant's definition of a purpose in this connection is very instructive. He says it is "the concept of an Object so far as it contains the ground of the actuality of this Object."[2] The concepts of Understanding only represent the possible existence of an object. But when a concept is the ground of its actual existence, we are not simply thinking it but bringing it into being. And there is no longer the discrepancy between possible and actual which we discover in theoretical knowledge, for the possible is restricted in its range and is only paid out in the measure that the parts emerge into existence. We have here no superfluous thoughts in advance of sensation which may only be possible; our thoughts have the perceptive quality of instinct because they are genetic like the parts themselves. And while in Pragmatic, whole and part are apprehended incompletely in the same vague way, Reflexion will be that power of mind for which these factors exist in an equal degree of reality, *but also in their completeness.* In beautiful

[1] Bernard, p. 291. [2] Bernard, p. 18.

and living forms the relation between whole and part is transparent, and we are not conscious of the one without the other. Now "we know in part—but when that which is perfect is come, then that which is in part shall be done away." The parts are not perceived in their stark diversity, but as continuous manifestations of a single reality. And the moment we dissever a part from the whole, it loses its quality and becomes an unintelligible thing. As Aristotle said, a hand cut off from the body is no longer a hand, "except in an equivocal sense as we might speak of a stone hand."[1]

The discrete knowledge of the Understanding is no longer necessary, for Reflexion is itself the articulate expression of what is inarticulate for Understanding. Such was the love of the wild animals for the hermit of the Himalayas, in Kipling's 'Miracle of Purun Bhagat':

"we loved him with the love
That knows but cannot understand."[2]

If we try to explain our actions of whose goodness we are convinced, they lose their ingenuousness and become doubtful; or if we seek to intellectualise our religious convictions, they lose their sanctity and become commonplace. As Goethe says, in one of those frequent perceptions which are so true to fact, "though my experience of the divine mercy has been of infinite importance to myself at the time of its occurrence, the detail would be insipid, and perhaps disbelieved, were I to specify individual cases."[3] In his poem on *Love's Secret*, William Blake gives a touching instance of the

[1] *Politics*, Bk. I., Ch. ii. [2] *The Second Jungle Book.*
[3] *Wilhelm Meister's Apprenticeship*: Bohn, p. 361.

THE CRITICAL PHILOSOPHY

blundering folly of Understanding when it attempts to articulate reflective experience :

> "Never seek to tell thy love,
>   Love that never told can be ;
> For the gentle wind doth move
>   Silently, invisibly.
>
> "I told my love, I told my love,
>   I told her all my heart,
> Trembling, cold, in ghastly fears.
>   Ah! she did depart!
>
> "Soon after she was gone from me,
>   A traveller came by,
> Silently, invisibly :
>   He took her with a sigh."

There is no text-book of Reflective Science. Its perceptions are not scientific judgments which are true for all and therefore for no one in particular, but true for all because they are first true for the individual. Like the μυστήριον of St. Paul, they are secrets which are revealed to the initiate. And though we do not see the face of the Supersensible, from the cleft of the rock we are touched by the glory of its presence while it passeth by, and it is by its hand that the eyes of our Understanding are covered.

In the conception of Technic, then, we are brought visibly, nearer to the Supersensible. Hypothetical knowledge only gives the thought of free, self-determined existence, but in Reflexion we have its presence and appearance. When the divine artisan was polishing the world before he launched it into space, he painted parts of it with the hues of the rainbow, and in other parts he set up magic mirrors in which the divine activity is reflected. The first is the realm of the Beautiful, the second the realm of living forms, who in their purposive activity show forth the perfect freedom of God. These finishing touches Kant calls contingent, not at all in the bad sense of his predecessors, but as we should call an Egyptian mummy contingent because the art of embalming has been lost. Our Understanding has lost or never had the rule of interpreting these data. Such are the unaccountable phenomena of Nature for which there is no certain law discovered, such are the objects of inarticulate emotion and the unsearchable essence of life; such also are the inscrutable ways of God by which He rules the world in righteousness. With the reverence of the Hebrew sage, Kant draws the veil over the appearance of the divine Majesty, and realises with him that "it is the glory of God to conceal."

CHAPTER II.

REFLECTIVE JUDGMENT.

ALTHOUGH the *Critique of Judgment* has its place, historically, as an afterthought in Kant's system, the ideas it contains were present to his mind from an early date. As far back as 1764, there is the short essay entitled *Beobachtungen über das Gefühl des Schönen und Erhabenen*, in which he gives token of an artistic turn of mind with which he is seldom credited. Here Kant suggests that even scientific pursuits have an aesthetical character, so that knowledge may become the subject-matter of Feeling and subordinate to it; thus he speaks of the charm of which a Kepler was capable, who would not have sold one of his discoveries for a kingdom.[1] In an article in the *Kantstudien*,[2] there is an elaborated argument to show that as Kant's Aesthetical Philosophy is open to the charge of intellectualism, his Intellectual Philosophy is also influenced by aesthetical ideas, as when he follows his prejudice in favour of logical symmetry at the expense of truth. One might say that his elaborate trichotomy is the result of the free play of his Imagination with his Understanding.

It may not be readily believed that Kant wrote poetry, but he actually did write five stanzas at least, each of

---

[1] *Briefwechsel*: Kirchmann, p. 4.
[2] Band 2, Anna Cutler.

which is devoted to the memory of one of five colleagues in Königsberg University.¹ And the fact that Herder turned one of his lectures into verse, surely counts for something in favour of Kant's poetic turn of mind. One might also mention a remark of Schiller in his correspondence with Goethe. Writing of his impressions after reading Kant's little treatise on 'Everlasting Peace,' he says : "There is in this old gentleman something so truly youthful that it might almost be termed aesthetic."² It is difficult to say how we are to receive the extraordinary intelligence, which Schiller can hardly credit but which Goethe confirms, that certain artists are putting Kant's Ideas of Reason into allegorical pictures.³ Whether this is to be regarded as indicating the intrinsic poetry of Kant's thought or the madness of human nature, must be left to the judgment of the reader.

Facts like these, though slight, are a sufficient proof in themselves, that this third faculty of the human mind was within the sweep of Kant's reflections before the *Critique of Pure Reason* was definitely planned. To these must be added as conclusive evidence, that he lectured on Aesthetic practically throughout his official career. The *Critique of Judgment*, then, does not answer a newly-born demand, so much as the renewed consciousness on Kant's part of what he had already felt.

These public lectures, however, as we have seen, were originally undertaken as a sidelight on Logic rather than as a distinctive treatment of Aesthetic itself. And in the letter to Herz of 1772, he has already lost sight of the independence of Feeling, for he brings it in

¹ *Briefwechsel*, p. 299.
² *Correspondence of Schiller and Goethe* : Schmitz, vol. i. Letter 367.
³ *Ibid.* vol. i. pp. 144-51.

THE CRITICAL PHILOSOPHY 41

common with Morality under the heading, Practical.[1] But in this letter he is concerned with the central problem of the *Critique of Pure Reason*, how an idea can refer to an object ; and, speaking roughly, one may say that from this time on till 1787, there are only two divisions of mind for Kant, the Theoretical and the Practical. In his anxiety to subordinate sensuous feeling to moral law, moreover, he does not wait to distinguish the finer and higher emotions from those which are lower.

But after the *Critique of Pure Reason* was lifted off his mind, we find the distinction again forcing itself upon him in the *Metaphysic of Ethics*, where he distinguishes "practical pleasure" from "passive satisfaction"; this latter is "not a pleasure in the existence of the object of the idea, but clings to the idea only," and this feeling of pleasure "we call Taste."[2] Moreover he goes on to say that such a thing as Taste can only be treated "episodically" in a Practical Philosophy, "not as a notion properly belonging to that philosophy," thus removing Aesthetic Feeling out of the region of the practical aspect of mind. And when, in the beginning of the year 1787, he sees his *Critique of Practical Reason* so far complete that he hopes to send it to press within a week, he intimates to Christian Gottfried Schütz that he must set about his *Critique of Taste* immediately.[3] It was finally in the same year, in his letter to Reinhold, that Kant made up his mind about the independence of Feeling. There he recognises three parts of Philosophy, Knowledge, Feeling of pleasure and pain, Desire : and

[1] *Briefwechsel*, p. 403.
[2] Introd. : Abbott, p. 267.
[3] *Briefwechsel*: Kirchmann, p. 456.

seeks to find *a priori* principles for the second as for the other two, though he formerly held this to be impossible; he hopes to be ready with this by Easter under the title, Critique of Taste.[1] Here we have the *Critique of Judgment* coming to the birth; it was published three years later in 1790.

But though he now recognises three parts of Philosophy, this does not mean three sets of *doctrine*: there are three Critiques, but only two of them are doctrines. He insists on this in the Introduction to the *Critique of Judgment*.[2] But while he was formerly inclined to give a subordinate place to Feeling, he now excludes it from the dignity of a doctrine in order to raise it to a higher plane. By the time Kant had settled the problems of science and morality, he began to tire of Definitive Judgment, Determination, and felt the need of a judgment which could go as deep as the moral judgment and have all its immediacy, but be as disinterested as science without being science.

Meanwhile, Aesthetics were clamouring for a separate treatment, and the unfinished woof of Teleology trailed across the warp of his system. Out of these coincidences arose the Reflective Judgment, which for Kant means a form of experience which is not doctrine in itself but conditions whatever doctrine there is. It is Reflexion that has been guiding us all along. There is no knowledge but comes to birth with its inspiration in the anticipative feeling of unity with the object to be known; and even morality is at best a form of reflective experience and only so far constitutive: "even Freedom ... is for us a transcendent conception, and is therefore incapable of serving as a constitutive prin-

[1] *Briefwechsel*, p. 461. [2] Bernard, p. 16.

THE CRITICAL PHILOSOPHY 43

ciple for determining an object."[1] We must not say, then, that Reflexion is a loose and therefore useless form of Determination, scientific or moral; it is Determination that is a fossilised or artificially restricted form of Reflective Experience.

It is time that this Fountain of all Experience were "critically" examined. It had already come under Kant's notice as the hypothetical function of Reason, and Kant, in so many words, deliberately speaks of this Hypothetical Reason as the *Urteilskraft*, the term he uses for Reflexion in general.[2] It is one and the same power of Judgment which we have in the *Dialectic* and in the *Critique of Judgment*. In this logical disposition of Nature (*logische Beurteilung*) the *Urteilskraft* exhibits a relation between Nature and the Supersensible: *i.e.* even in knowledge the Supersensible is present. But since the function of *Urteilskraft* is here purely hypothetical and therefore negative, it does not need special justification; it does not pretend to be a Science, it does not teach us nor equip us with knowledge, it is only an *exercise* of Reason (*der Verstand einer Belehrung und Ausrüstung durch Regeln fähig, Urteilskraft aber ein besonderes Talent sei, welches gar nicht belehrt, sondern nur geübt sein will*).[3] It is the specific quality in so-called mother-wit, the want of which no school can supply, or, as he said in the *Critique of Judgment*, the *Urteilskraft* is just "Sound Understanding" (*gesunden Verstandes*).[4] Every one feels the Absolute, the Whole, breaking in upon one's relative knowledge; one knows there is a whole somewhere, and proceeds on this

---
[1] *Critique of Judgment*: Watson, p. 336.   [2] Bernard, p. 4.
[3] Hartenstein, *Kritik d. r. Vernunft*, iii. p. 138.
[4] Bernard, p. 3.

assumption. This is the hypothetical function of Reason.

But the need of a Critique arises when this reflective exercise of Reason actually assumes the form of Science, professing to determine objects of its own *without falling into antinomy*. Regulative Reason, whenever it pretended to be constitutive of objects, fell into insoluble contradictions, and therefore its exercise never rises above a form of inspiration ; the Supersensible, in the shape of the Ideas of Reason, is present in us as the anticipative feeling of totality, indivisible unity, a feeling, however, which is dissipated, and with it the real unity, in the exercise of knowledge. As Kant puts it, "it has no immediate reference to the feeling of pleasure and pain."[1] But in Reflexion, as it appears in the *Critique of Judgment*, there *is* such immediate reference, the feeling of unity is not dissipated, and something, therefore, in the form of an object is determined by the *Urteilskraft*. " This reference is precisely the puzzle in the principle of Judgment, which renders necessary a special section for this faculty in the Kritik." Hence *Urteilskraft* in general, since it is purely hypothetical and negative, needs no special justification ; it is the Judgment in the form of Immediate Feeling that must be established *a priori*.

Deduction, then, of Reflexion is the proof of the validity of this primary immediacy of consciousness, which conditions all other forms of experience and is itself the highest form of experience. Of this Aesthetic provides the aptest illustration, but the problem itself is much wider. Reflexion, for Kant, covers all the different exercises of that free consciousness, 'I think,'

[1] Bernard, p. 4.

which lies at the back of the mind—all experience which is distinctively *personal*, as distinguished from the impersonal experience of science.

Kant's Deduction is characteristically peculiar. It consists in carrying back this primary function of mind, which is covered by such names as Reflexion, Purposive Activity and Feeling, to what he calls the Power of Judgment. Ostensibly he professes to find in the formal judgment of Logic *a priori* principles for this third faculty, just as logical concepts stood sponsor for the categories. If Understanding and Reason have yielded a system of synthetic notions for Knowledge and *a priori* precepts for the Faculty of Desire respectively, "what more natural," he asks, "than to suppose that the latter (Judgment) will likewise contain principles *a priori* for the former (Feeling of Pleasure and Pain)?"[1]

Such statements are not to be taken literally. Kant is dealing with Formal Logic as an analogy or type of the real activity, and this is shown by the fact that the formal concepts in the *Critique of Pure Reason* become added to and change, in the process of deduction, into principles of synthesis. Similarly we are to find the Formal Judgment in this last deduction, changing in process of proof into that original Free Consciousness which conditions all experience, mediate or immediate. Kant significantly names it *Urteilskraft*, the Power of Judging in general, though he sometimes uses *Urteil* as equivalent for *Urteilskraft*.

There are two steps in Kant's curious proof. The one is found in the Introduction to the *Critique of Judgment*, the other in the *Über Philosophie überhaupt*.

[1] *Über Philosophie überhaupt*: Rosenkranz, *Werke*, i. p. 588.

In the first step, Kant points out that Judgment and Feeling must be intimately related, because they bear a similar relation to the two remaining functions of mind in the respective groups to which they belong. He calls it a "new ground"[1] of proof. Feeling mediates in a very real sense between Knowledge and Desire, and also the Judgment similarly mediates between Concepts and Reasoning. The former had already been settled by the Wolffians and may be taken for granted, but the latter, which Kant simply states in the baldest way, does call for explanation. Probably the best way to account for Kant's statement is to say that here Logic is changing in his hands. If Judgment mediates in any real sense between the two, it must have a common nature with both; concepts, judgments and reasonings can no longer be distinct as was formerly assumed. A concept is a judgment from which the appearance of synthesis has vanished: reasoning is a form of judgment in which the original synthesis is further developed or explained. But surely that has the right to the name of Judgment *par excellence* which is the distinctively synthetic activity of mind, in which the relation of whole and part is seen in the making? Understanding is for Kant the faculty of parts without the whole—to determine the whole is to court antinomy: Reason is the faculty of wholes without the parts—there is no differentiation of content in the concept of Freedom, it is a case of all or nothing; Judgment alone is the function of mind in which whole and part are first *recognised* in relation. The Judgment, then, may be said to mediate between the microscopic judgment or the Concept and the extensive

[1] Bernard, p. 14.

judgment or the Syllogism, because it is the *original synthetic activity of mind*. It is no longer the Concept but the Judgment that stands first in the scale of mental activity.

Now when Kant assigns to the Judgment this original power of synthesis, he does not mean a particular or actual synthesis—that is a concept—so much as the activity of synthesis itself in general, without reference to a particular product, in short, the *Power of Judgment*. He thus re-establishes the distinction between Concept and Judgment, but in a way which does justice to them both. They are no longer different in nature, for both are modes of Judgment. But Judgment may be of two kinds; for while it is "the faculty of thinking the particular as contained under the universal,"[1] this subsumption may come about in either of two ways. First, both particular and universal may be to hand when the particular given is only such as can be determined by concepts of Understanding; this is the schematic judgment: "the law is marked out for it *a priori*, and it has therefore no need to seek a law for itself."[2] Particular and universal are adapted to each other by the pre-established harmony of the "transcendental object," and so the universal is applied to an intuition which can only be apprehended in that order which is necessary for determination by the categories. But, secondly, the particular alone may be given for which we have to seek a universal, and here the Judgment is no longer determinant but reflective. Thus, while the logical concept and judgment are both modes of judging, they are different, the one being the prototype of determinate, the other of reflective judgment.

[1] Bernard, p. 16.   [2] *Ibid.* p. 17.

Why Kant calls it reflective is not exactly clear. Probably he just means the activity in which the subject reflects on itself and its processes. The best explanation is given in the *Über Philosophie überhaupt*. "To reflect," he says, "is to compare and hold together given representations either with others or with the faculty of representation itself, in view of a problematical idea."[1] That is to say, Reflexion is just the comparison of a representation with the apperceptive Imagination. Kant goes on to give it a very homely meaning. We may call it, he says, the *Facultas Dijudicandi (Beurteilungsvermögen)*, the term Baumgarten used to denote the critical faculty, the power of discerning agreement in difference, the correspondence of means to ends.[2] Nay, Reflexion even happens with animals, Kant continues, "if only instinctively, *i.e.* not as if an idea were to be obtained thereby, but with a view to the satisfaction of some inclination:"[3] a sense of the term which seems identical with Aristotle's δύναμις κριτική.[4]

In its basal form, then, Reflexion appears to be a sense of want. But this may be of two orders. You may know what you are wanting, and then the Judgment is determinant; a category or "fundamental idea of the object prescribes the rule to the Power of Judgment,"[5] and therefore you no longer need a principle, its place being supplied by a rule. It is only for people who do

[1] Rosenkranz, *Werke*, i. p. 589. Cp. *Anthropologie*: Hartenstein, vii. p. 452.

[2] Erdmann, *Hist. Phil.* ii. p. 240.

[3] *Über Philosophie überhaupt*: Rosenkranz, i. p. 589.

[4] φαίνεται δὲ τοῦτό γε πᾶσιν ὑπάρχον τοῖς ζῴοις· ἔχει γὰρ δύναμιν σύμφυτον κριτικήν, ἣν καλοῦσιν αἴσθησιν· *Anal. Post.* ii. 99 B.

[5] *Über Philosophie überhaupt*: Rosenkranz, i. p. 589.

not know exactly what they are wanting that a principle is necessary. The artist, having a great notion in his head, yet not knowing exactly what it is, casts about him for a principle, and in so doing lets his mind run free. Kant gives an interesting illustration of this distinction; the servant who is required to obey definite orders only needs Understanding, while the officer who only receives a general commission which he must interpret for himself in particular emergencies requires Judgment.[1] This free-play of the faculties takes place when the mind is undergoing experience for which there is no adequate category of knowledge corresponding, whether it be in the apparently passive contemplation of aesthetic perception or in the originative activity of artistic creation. Nor do we need to know what we are wanting, even after it has been realised. In Reflexion, it is the satisfaction, not the definition, of purpose or interest that is essential; the free-play of the faculties is its own end, the mind having no interest outside of its processes.

The great difference, then, which Kant has in view between the Reflective and Determinant Judgment is that the one is free and works under a principle, while the other is not free and works under a rule which is fixed. Reflective Judgment is a "mere faculty for reflecting upon a given representation, for the behoof of a problematical idea";[2] *i.e.* an idea which may be the very thing you want and so an idea which is realised as the definite concept of a given representation, in which case the judgment would become determinant, both part and whole being to hand. Reflective judgment always

[1] *Anthropologie,* § 40; Hartenstein, vii. p. 514.
[2] *Über Philosophie überhaupt,* p. 589.

works with a view to the determinant, or as if a determinant judgment were actually possible.

It must be clear from the above that Reflective Judgment is the wider function of which the Determinant is but a special case. All thinking is the subsuming of a particular under a universal, *i.e.* of a sense-datum under a form of thought. And Reflexion is subsumption in general, Determination is subsumption in particular. In the Determinant Judgment, Imagination, which is the highest faculty of Sense, subordinates itself to the law of Understanding. In apprehending a line, or drawing it even in thought, the imagination must keep reproducing the successive perceptions in order to maintain identity of consciousness and therefore the unity of the object: the object is cognised to order, it is what we are "obliged to think." But in Reflexion it is quite otherwise. Here the Imagination proceeds, not under constraint, but in free play with the Understanding; the object is no longer what we are unconditionally obliged to think, but what we are constrained to think for higher reasons than the laws of Understanding.

Now when Kant says that the Judgment ought to provide this reflective activity with *a priori* principles, he is looking to a certain feature in the class-judgment which may serve as type for the freedom of Reflexion. The judgment in Formal Logic abstracts from all content, and therefore exhibits a quite contingent relation between S and P; and Reflexion is like to it in this, that the subject (Imagination) is not fixed down to any definite predicate (the Understanding), but maintains a free relation to it, whereas the transcendental or determinant judgment has for its predicate a certain unalterable rule, *e.g.* the subject must come under the predicate of causal connection. But in the judgment of Formal Logic, S may come under the class P or P¹ or P². Kant expresses this distinction thus : "the Understanding is the Faculty of rules, the *Urteilskraft* is the Faculty of *subsuming* under rules, *i.e.* of discerning whether something stands under a given rule or not."[1] Kant seems to speak here as if Reflexion were Formal Logic over again, but the latter is nothing more than a loose type of the former. For while the formal judgment abstracts from all content, Reflexion holds itself free rather because its content is so much deeper than that of the determinate judgment; thus, in regard to a living thing, it would be a mistake to bind S down to the predicate of causality, for such a predicate may be quite inadequate to its content.

This seems to throw light on the title of the book, *Kritik der Urteilskraft.* It is a point on which writers on Kant have loftily abstained from giving any satisfactory explanation to the bewildered student, for it is not a little disconcerting to find that Kant, who had already used Judgment in a purely epistemological sense, should without further qualification or comment also use it to denote specifically the Reflective activity of mind. No doubt Judgment was the name he should naturally use to denote the faculty of Approval. And it is interesting to find how exactly this term was defined in eighteenth century usage, both literary and philosophical. Henry Fielding and Baumgarten are practically identical in their analysis of Judgment. In *Tom Jones* Genius is defined as the power, both of penetrating into the essence of things and of distinguishing their essential differences ; and these two powers "are

[1] *Kritik d. r. Vernunft* : Hartenstein, iii. p 138.

no other than invention and judgment." But invention, he continues, "can rarely exist without the concomitancy of judgment, for how we can be said to have discovered the true essence of two things, without discerning their difference, seems to me hard to conceive. Now this last is the undisputed province of judgment" (Bk. IX. Chap. I.). In precisely the same way, Baumgarten analysed the aesthetic faculty into the twofold perception of unity and diversity; of these the first is called invention (*ingenium* or *facultas identitates rerum cognoscendi*) and the second a discriminating power (*acumen sensitivum* or *facultas diversitates rerum cognoscendi*).[1] This shows that Judgment was currently understood to be closely connected with Genius. But it does not explain the whole matter. The *Critique of Pure Reason* might well have been called the Critique of Judgment, for it deals with little else, but Kant has so consecrated the term to denote Reflexion that he speaks of the *Critique of Pure Reason* as dealing with Understanding alone "to the exclusion of Judgment and Reason."[2] The explanation, it seems to me, lies in this, that for Kant the common feature in both Reflective and Determinant Judgment is subordination. But the Reflective is the higher and wider type of subordination; far from being the empty tautology of Formal Logic, it is the subordination of Nature to Freedom, whereas Determinant Judgment is but a subordination within Nature, that of Sense to Understanding. And it is Kant's final view that it is this wider subsumption of Nature under Freedom which makes possible the lower adaptation of sense to

---

[1] See Schasler, *Kritische Geschichte der Aesthetik*, p. 349.
[2] Bernard, p. 1.

thought; determination, whether moral or scientific, is conditioned by Reflexion. Now the Formal Judgment provides the type for this higher form of subsumption in the free relation it exhibits between S and P, and from it Kant would naturally take the name, *Kritik der Urteilskraft.* So we might read the above quotation as follows: the *Critique of Pure Reason* dealt with Judgment (*i.e.* subsumption in particular), to the exclusion of Judgment (*i.e.* subsumption in general without arriving at any particular determination) and Reason. Determination is fixed within definite limits, Reflexion is characterised rather by the absence of determinate bounds; the Determinant judgment is like a land-path definitely marked, the Reflective is like the roadways of the open ocean:

" Thy way is in the sea, and Thy path in the great waters, and Thy footsteps are not known." [1]

What Kant has secured for us, then, out of the Formal Judgment, is really a divine way of thinking, of which the forced subordination within Nature in the judgment of knowledge is but the shadow. Hence the truth of Hegel's dictum, Freedom is the truth of Nature.

The second step in Kant's proof rests on the subjective character of both Judgment and Feeling: " there is here already a certain conformity of the Power of Judgment to the Feeling of Pleasure . . . that whereas Understanding and Reason refer their representations to objects . . . the Power of Judgment refers *solely to the subject,* and by itself alone produces no notions of objects." [2] On the other hand, he points out, the Feeling of pleasure and pain is the only one of

[1] Psalm lxxvii. 19.
[2] *Über Philosophie überhaupt*: Rosenkranz, *Werke,* i. p. 588.

the mental powers which has nothing objective in its representations and is only a susceptibility (*Empfänglichkeit*) of the subject apprehending. In the first step it was shown how Judgment and Feeling respectively mediate in a real way between corresponding functions of mind. Now it is argued that their relative positions in the respective groups is so similar, in respect of their subjective aspect, that they must form part of one and the same mental function: "if the Power of Judgment should at all determine anything for itself alone, it can be nothing else than the feeling of pleasure, and conversely, if this (feeling of pleasure) should have at all a principle *a priori*, it will be found in the Power of Judgment alone."[1] Thus the object of the Judgment—in so far as it has one, seeing that it refers solely to the subject—and the subjective determination which we call Feeling, are one and the same.

But what exactly does Kant mean by the subjectivity of the Judgment? To begin with, as we saw above, Judgment has come to mean for Kant the original synthetic activity of mind; and although the Deduction in the second edition of the *Critique of Pure Reason* consists in the proof that the subjective reference in the Judgment presupposes an objective reference and is only possible through consciousness of objectivity, we must remember that, in spite of this, Kant makes a reservation; he insists that the 'I think,' the subjective element in the Judgment, is itself an *analytic proposition*.[2] He means that there is such a thing as *Cognition in general*, consciousness of the subject without arriving

---
[1] *Über Philosophie überhaupt*: Rosenkranz, *Werke*, i. p. 588.
[2] Watson, *Selections*, p. 69.

at any particular determination; and further, it is this *Consciousness in general* which makes possible the knowledge of the Understanding. But this never means for Kant that a purely subjective function of mind lies at the basis of all knowledge. An enormous confusion arises for us here, because we are thinking of a totally different contrast from that which was before Kant's mind. Objectivity for Kant, it cannot be too strongly urged, means no more than the objectivity of external sense. The sensuous perception of Inner Sense, the sense of time in Imagination, is not for him objective; the proof in the Analogies which appears to base outer on inner sense, the permanence of substance on the permanent in time, should not be regarded as an exception to this but as a fault in Kant's argument. What modern Logic means by 'objective' in the Judgment, is what Kant has in view in the analytical consciousness, 'I think': which differs from the objectivity of the modern judgment only in this, that it is not itself so much a system of consciousness, an objective consciousness, as the basis of all objective consciousness. Kant's position nearly veers round to the Cartesian use of the contrast.[1] They called subjective what is independent of individual mind, what underlies the sense-object; and what is this but Kant's 'transcendental object'? And, as Kant admits, the 'I think' of apperception is really indistinguishable from this independent or objective mind. We should,

[1] I find that Cohen supports this view: "bei Kant bedeutet das Subjective ausschliesslich dasjenige, was dadurch gerade und zwar allein objective ist." *Kants Begründung der Aesthetik*, pp. 103-4. It is of course recognised that, through Wolff and Baumgarten, Kant was the first to fix the modern sense of these terms. See Erdmann, *Hist. Phil.* ii. p. 238.

therefore, hit off Kant's view more accurately, in view of the above confusion of terms, if we said that the 'I think' of the Judgment is not subjective, for this implies a false contrast with objectivity, but personal as distinguished from divine or absolute mind. The 'I think' shares the nature of the 'objective synthesis,' and therefore may be said to lie at the basis of all knowledge. It is subjective in the sense that it is personal and free from the obligation to think the objects of external sense.

The student is more and more impressed with the intimate relation which the third Critique bears to the first.[1] This subjective character of the Judgment may be put in yet another way. It is the same feature Kant is hinting at in the contrast which he makes between Productive and Reproductive Imagination, in the chapter on the Deduction of the Categories. The Reproductive function belongs to Psychology, the Productive alone to Transcendental Philosophy, and "its synthesis is the expression of spontaneous activity."[2] Reproduction is an empirical synthesis of Imagination in accordance with the laws of association, but Imagination in its original function is the "faculty of setting before the mind in perception an object that is *not itself present*":[3] *i.e.* though it may make use of association in its free activity, it is not led by it but leads it, "for unlike sense, imagination is not simply capable of being determined, but is itself determining."[4] There is no such thing as a purely contingent fancy which outrages all the forms of knowledge, and certainly Productive Imagination is no such contingent activity; rather it

[1] Cp. Anna Tumarkin in *Kantstudien*, Band xi.
[2] Watson, *Selections*, p. 77.   [3] *Ibid.*   [4] *Ibid.*

conforms to the categories while it constructs its figurations without reference to any definite object, *i.e.* without compulsion of external sense or fixed direction of association. Hence Kant calls it the "first application" of Understanding to Sense, and so "the condition of all other applications of Understanding to objects that we are capable of perceiving."[1]

There is, then, after all something profound in Kant's deduction of Feeling from the Judgment. He begins with the judgment of Formal Logic, and this changes in his hands into the reality of which it is but the type, the Original Synthetic Activity of Mind. The proof is really reversed and is, that Determination is a subordinate form of Reflexion. The usual criticism is that he has violated the nature of Feeling, particularly aesthetic, by reducing it to a form of intellectual cognition. In point of fact, he does quite the opposite. While in seeming he brings Feeling back to functions of knowledge, in the process of proof he lifts up knowledge into relationship with the personal, free activity of mind. Reflexion is not debased to Understanding but Understanding is elevated by its subordination to Reflexion. Kant, indeed, suggests that the fixed forms of the Understanding were originally spontaneous in their activity. When we go beyond the limits of Understanding as it is now known to us, that is to say, beyond causal connection, and freely classify things as genera and species 'reflectively,' our reflexion is characterised by a feeling of Pleasure, the mark of spontaneity. And though we no longer feel pleasure in contemplating the fixed connections of Understanding, yet it must have been there "at one

[1] *Ibid.* p. 78.

time;" and "it is only because the commonest experience would be impossible without it that it is gradually confounded with mere cognition and no longer arrests particular attention."[1] Determinate judgments are fossilised 'reflexions' upon Nature. These unchangeable forms and connections of Understanding had to be discovered at one time, and their discovery was no doubt attended by the inseparable mark of all spontaneity, Pleasure. What takes place in the history of the sciences is repeated in the growing consciousness. For the child each established law of Nature, when it first secures the attention, is a lucky hit of Reflexion, a fresh discovery.

There is a deeper suggestion here. The bounds of Understanding are not fixed but stretch with the advance of Science. Science progressively feeds the forms of Philosophy with their content. In the light of evolution, we should now add to Understanding part of those forms of teleology which for Kant were wholly contingent and reflective. Scientists largely destroy for themselves the pleasure which the forms of adaptation in Nature afford the unsophisticated mind, and later, through their knowledge, the general consciousness comes to feel

"that there hath passed away a glory from the earth."

But there must be a limit to the encroachment of Understanding. If it be the case, as Kant suggests, that the original function of mind is the spontaneous, if Productive is the condition of Reproductive Imagination, if the free, personal consciousness, 'I think,' be the condition of consciousness of the objectivity of sense-perception and independent of it, then it must

[1] Bernard, p. 28.

lie in the power of this original function to maintain a distinct realm for itself; otherwise the Understanding would devour its parent. There is a limit to the encroaching of the land upon the sea, whose trackless ways best typify the judgment of Reflexion. Therefore Kant is right when he makes Understanding, with its fixity, a distinct compartment of mind from Reflexion. He may have drawn the limits prematurely, but, in the long run, its kingdom has an end. It is not likely that the mind will surrender its spontaneity in the realms of the finer emotions connected with Art, Morality, and Religion. Teleology may linger between the two worlds of determined and free activity, and it cannot wholly surrender to Understanding ; the truth may be that it is the bond of union and transition between these two worlds. Kant seems to take this view in the half-hearted way he connects it with Aesthetic. But the objects of the fine emotions are the private grounds of the sovereign Freedom of Reason which Understanding invades only to court defeat. In this sense M. Basch is right when he says that knowledge and will are sterilised products of feeling : " the individual is more truly himself when he feels " : habit, without doubt, blunts " le timbre sentimental de la sensation." But, he concludes, there is one sphere where Feeling regains its ancient empire, where man is concerned neither to know nor to will, but before all to feel ; where representations become again what they have been from the beginning, the creations of Feeling, and that sphere is the Aesthetic.[1]

[1] *L'Esthétique de Kant,* par Basch, Introd. p. xiv.

CHAPTER III.

AESTHETIC AND THE FIRST CANON.

WE are now in a position to understand how, in the last phase of his system, Kant sought to commend our confidence in a deeper and more immediate interpretation of Reality. We are inclined to think of it as characteristically critical because of the title which the three *Kritiken* bear. But the significance of the term 'critical' is limited to Kant's age; it is the sword which he carried in his left hand to drive away the Horonites of Rationalism, and we must not forget the new temple whose foundations he laid. This positive tendency is particularly prominent in the thoughts of the third *Critique*, notwithstanding its polemical tone, and the function of criticism is little more than a concession to his logical scheme. The subject which forms the distinctive and greater part of the book, Aesthetic, did not need to be critically examined in the same sense as Knowledge and Morality, for its claims had not been exaggerated. The trouble rather was that its claims had hardly been advanced, and Kant's office was not to call it in question so much as to call it into existence. The exercise of his critical faculty, in this instance, seems to have been due to force of habit rather than to reasoned conviction; for if he had examined with more care the views which he opposed, he should have found more cause to excite his admiration than his pity. Neither Burke nor Leibniz, the representatives of the complementary tendencies in European thought which he opposed, is in effect less subjective than Kant himself. Neither says that Beauty resides in objects as a constitutive quality. On the contrary, they commit themselves to a subjective theory. For with Leibniz Beauty is a confused knowledge and therefore rests on subjective conditions, the difference between confused and clear knowledge being a matter of degree. And for Burke it consists in the comparative pleasure we enjoy in contemplating different forms. For, notwithstanding his sensationalism in which the smoothness of objects is a prominent feature, his prevailing conviction is that Taste depends for its existence on our ignorance and the practice of deception in Art: "it is our ignorance of things that causes all our admiration."[1] It follows that Beauty is not a sensible quality in things which is passively received in sensation, so much as a subjective interpretation.

Kant did not understand his authors so liberally. He goes out of his way to correct the Leibnizian theory in which he detected the shadow of a concept, however confused, and the theory of Burke whose physiological language alone was sufficient to favour sensationalism. But there is much more in the continental theory as it was developed by Wolff and Baumgarten than Kant was able to appreciate, and indeed it envisages a point of view to which he vainly sought to aspire. For when we candidly consider what is meant by the definition of Beauty as confused knowledge, we find that Kant's criticism loses much of its point. He makes out that

[1] *Sublime and Beautiful*, Part ii. § 4 ; cp. § 10.

the knowledge of perfection, even while it is confused, remains a form of knowledge with an intellectual content; and if this were strictly true, his criticism would be valid within its own limits. But an impartial examination shows that Baumgarten, at least, did not assimilate the Beautiful to intellectual form. This exception can hardly be made in favour of Leibniz, as we have seen, for his doctrine of continuity provides a complete thoroughfare between sense and thought. But Wolff and Baumgarten had advanced on Leibniz's position. Wolff had not indeed worked out a Logic of sense corresponding to the Logic of thought, but he recognised a distinction between lower and higher forms of knowledge, and in his *Psychology* he gives a table of the obscure forms. It was left to Baumgarten to elaborate into a science, under the comprehensive title 'Aesthetic' which originally means simple perception, those inferior modes of apprehension, including feelings and the obscure sense-impressions which are not accompanied by the reflective activity of thought. Beauty was thus defined as having its place in the region of confused knowledge (*cognitio sensitiva*), and this circumstance takes away our wonder that Kant should have employed the term 'aesthetic,' both to denote the pure perception of objects in space without the activity of thought and artistic intuition. Now Baumgarten set out from this accepted distinction between unthinking perception and conscious apperception of objects. It means that mere sense-perception is possible, in the simple awareness of presentation, without identifying the object in the ordinary associations of apperception which we call knowledge. Probably this is what Kant meant, in what is a rather startling statement for the author of the

Analytic, when he said: "we can represent a thing as given although we have no concept of it."¹ But, as the school of Wolff characteristically taught, the content in every form of mentality is perfection of some kind. Beauty is therefore the perfection of this obscure knowledge (*perfectio cognitionis sensitivae qua talis*).² And manifestly its content is more congenital to intellectual form than to any other, because perfection means the complete agreement of an object with its concept. In no other way is it possible to have a clear understanding of what perfection means. This statement at once reveals the strength and the weakness in Baumgarten's position, as will presently appear.

But let me continue. By defining aesthetic perception as a lower form of knowledge, he appears only to have meant that the content, and not the type of apprehension itself, is of the same kind as in cognition. If his statements are literally understood, as frequently happens, it would mean that the Beautiful is a confusion of intellectual relations, which never comes to clear expression without ceasing to be beautiful, when it passes into knowledge. But this would be to suppose what is nonsensical, that Baumgarten saw the beauty of things in a different way from us, in a confused haze. However theories may alter, the experience of the beautiful remains essentially the same. It is sufficient to recall what Aristotle says, that "a very small animal organism cannot be beautiful, for the view of it is confused."³ It was simply the inarticulate nature of

---

[1] Bernard, p. 315.

[2] *Aesthetica*, Part i. § 14; quoted in Cohen's *Kants Begründung der Aesthetik*, p. 34.

[3] *Poetics*, vii. 4; Butcher, p. 31.

feeling that Baumgarten intended to convey in the definition of the Beautiful as confused representation. The object of Aesthetic would be for the intellect a complex of confused relations, but this does not imply that the aesthetic perception is itself confused; for, as Logic is the perfection of thought, Aesthetic is the perfection of sensible apprehension, and is therefore in its nature intended to have a clear expression peculiar to itself. In Baumgarten's phrase, it is the art of beautiful thinking (*ars pulchre cogitandi*),[1] and this qualification is sufficient to constitute Aesthetic into a distinct type of apprehension from cognition. It is therefore misleading to say, without further explanation, that for Baumgarten Taste is a faculty of knowledge. Every kind of perfection and therefore the perfection which we find in sensible knowledge, is a harmony of differences in unity; but while the content of sensible knowledge is intellectually confused, the aesthetic perception is not itself confused, for the beauty of a representation consists in the degree of clearness with which it is apprehended, or, in Baumgarten's words, it is the perfection of sensible knowledge as such. In the dim twilight of the intellect, aesthetic intuition is able to have a clear perception peculiar to itself. This interpretation is supported by Erdmann's significant statement, that the judgment of Taste "rests upon a perception that is (though clear) confused."[2]

Now it is the very same distinction that Kant sought to establish in his theory of indeterminate knowledge, or, as it is otherwise expressed, the consciousness of an end without any determinate end. This is identical with Baumgarten's confused or indeterminate perception

[1] Erdmann, *Hist. Phil.* ii. p. 239.   [2] *Hist. Phil.* ii. p. 240.

of relations in a unity. But neither in Kant nor in Baumgarten does this mean a confused apprehension, or indeed an intellectual activity of any kind. I therefore think that Basch has misunderstood both his authors, when he criticises Kant on the same grounds as Baumgarten.[1] Indeterminate knowledge does not mean for Kant a hazy conception, it does not mean knowledge of any kind, but the original mental disposition by which all determinate knowledge is conditioned, and which is more akin to feeling and conation than to cognition itself. Basch has certainly a strong case against Leibniz, when he observes that on his theory all confused representations would be indiscriminately beautiful, which in fact they are not, and that therefore he cannot provide an aesthetical criterion. But this criticism hardly applies to Baumgarten with the same force. He could have replied that a confused representation which is not able to hold our admiration for any length of time without thinking about it is not beautiful, and that it is beautiful when we are able to dwell in the mere perception while the activity of thought is suspended. Nor is it necessary to suppose, with Basch,[2] that on this theory the Beautiful would cease to exist with the completion of Science ; for the Beautiful is independent, even for Baumgarten, of the growth of Science, and it will remain for Science a confused representation so long as it is worth our while to think it beautiful.

It is the content, then, that is intellectual for Baumgarten in aesthetic intuition, but the type of apprehension need not itself be intellectual. It is the same content that is differently apprehended in Logic, Ethic and Aesthetic. As the Beautiful and the Good appear

[1] *L'Esthétique de Kant*, p. 186.   [2] *Ibid.* pp. 186-7.

to the Understanding only as Truth, and as the Beautiful and the True are for the Will only the Good, so the True and the Good are for sensuous knowledge only the Beautiful; just as a singing bird exists only as tone for the ear, and as colour and form for the eye.[1] As Schasler says, this conception lifts Baumgarten at one stroke above the confusion of the Beautiful with the Good, which we find in Plato, and later in the English and French Schools.

But we must not be misled by Schasler's generous appreciation. I have only contended so far that, in attributing an intellectual theory of Beauty to Baumgarten, we should be careful to place the accent on the content apprehended rather than on the aesthetic apprehension itself. This latter he conceives, in the only way he could conceive it, in the form of feeling and indeterminate sense-perception. But this implies a contradiction, and it is here the real criticism falls. For it may well be asked if it is possible to apprehend intellectual relations, as such, in a form of apprehension which is not itself intellectual. For Baumgarten the content, not only in Aesthetic, but in every form of mentality, is primarily and essentially intellectual. His theory is based on the rationalistic assumption that the world is perfectly ordered by Reason, and is the best possible. He therefore does not mean, as we should say, that Aesthetic is the expression of the same content which in another form is expressed as Truth, but that it is the sensuous expression of that whose first and proper expression is Truth, and he therefore defines it as the Beauty of Truth (*pulchritudo cognitionis*). He has no idea of Aesthetic as the inevitable expression of

---

[1] See Schasler, *Kritische Geschichte der Aesthetik*, pp. 350-1.

a content which may indeed be described in intellectual terms, but never in a way that is adequate to its meaning ; or, that Aesthetic expresses just that quality in the content of which we can have no clear conception.

The real error in Baumgarten's theory, then, is the contradiction that an intellectual content can coexist with a form of feeling which is not itself an intellectual mode of apprehension, or as Wolff defined feeling, an intuitive mode of knowledge (*cognitio intuitiva*). Kant saw this clearly enough, but, instead of repairing the error by providing Aesthetic with a content peculiar to itself, he deprived it of all content whatsoever. Accordingly, where Baumgarten fell short in the lofty theory of Aesthetic with which he is accredited by Schasler, was in maintaining an assumption which is just the cardinal and intractable error in Kant's own position, that significant content must be intellectual. The only heresy which could call for Kant's serious criticism, and which he really thought to burn in the genial effigies of his predecessors, was not the view that Aesthetic is intellectual, but its rationalistic implication which had been nourished in mediaeval speculation, that Beauty is an evidence of the Divine Reason in a perfectly ordered world. This would make Beauty a part of the economy of Nature and degrade it into something that is good to eat. But such a "fat weed," even for Kant's remote observation, could hardly flourish in the clarified air of the Romantic Revival, which was nigh half a century old when he gave final expression to his opinions.

Altogether we receive the impression that criticism has not the same original force in the third *Critique* as in the first. This is not to say that Kant has made no advance on his predecessors. We shall see presently that he was the first to place Aesthetic on a secure foundation. But the very points in which his criticisms appear to count are those in which he shares the same fault. Thus, while he sought to escape Baumgarten's contradiction by severing form from content, he fell into the same formal conception of Beauty as a symmetry of relations in his theory of *pulchritudo vaga*. It is in the implications of his theory which he neglected to develop that Kant outstrips his predecessors, and therefore our interpretation will be more successful if we consider his work as constructive rather than critical.

I have already tried to explain what the new faculty means, which he calls Reflective Judgment. It will be sufficient to remember that it is not a judgment in the logical sense, although it has a certain affinity with logical judgment which Kant is quite able to justify. Reflexion covers the whole domain of feeling, intuition and unthinking perception, and its objects are just what is inarticulate for knowledge. And the problem is, whether these unthinking intuitions can be entertained with at least the same degree of reasonable conviction, as thoughts whose claim to truth can be demonstrated. Those contingent forms which the material substrate of Nature presents to our Understanding, are quite unlike the causal connection of phenomena. They constitute a purpose in themselves or in our apprehension of them which is not necessary, so far as we can see, to their existence as phenomena. Things do not need to be organic or beautiful in order to appear, but as phenomena they are necessary because completely dependent on our Understanding—*der Verstand ist der Urheber der Natur*. While, therefore, their existence as phenomena is necessary, their existence at all or their purpose is not necessary but contingent, and we can only regard them as emanations of the Supersensible. Of these contingent forms the beauty of Nature, including its ideal imitation in Art, and the adaptation of means to ends in her organic forms, are the two outstanding instances. These are not matters of fact so much as favours of Nature in which the Unknown Matter disports itself before our eyes. But although they are both made intelligible by the same faculty of reasonable Feeling, they are yet very distinct; and Kant has scarcely attempted to show what they can have in common to justify us in bringing them under the same principle. Whether and how far this is possible will form the conclusion to our study. Meanwhile we proceed to consider the first of these, and here Reflexion becomes the Aesthetical Reflective Judgment.

Not so very long before the *Critique of Judgment* appeared, Kant did not think that a philosophy of the Beautiful was possible. He makes this admission in the *Transcendental Aesthetic*, where he seeks to justify his use of the term 'aesthetic' to denote pure perception in space. The Germans, he says, are the only people who have availed themselves of this word to denote Philosophy of Taste, and they have done so in the mistaken hope, which Baumgarten entertained, of finding a rational basis for it and raising its principles to the dignity of a science. - But all this labour is vain, for the principles which govern Taste are in their sources empirical and therefore cannot take the place of *a priori* principles, by which our judgment should be regulated. A judgment of Taste is rather the real touchstone of such *a priori* principles. It is therefore advisable to reserve the term for what is true science, the pure forms of sense; and in this we are much nearer to its original use among the Greeks, with whom αἰσθητὰ καὶ νοητά was a prevalent division in knowledge.[1]

This was written in 1781 when the *Critique of Pure Reason* first appeared. He then thought that the Beautiful could not rise above the low level of psychology, being only capable of empirical principles. Experience gave rise to certain rules, as conventional as the rules of Taste in wine or any other agreeable object; it could not be said that in the very nature of the Beautiful there were principles which conditioned experience, corresponding to the constant and original factors in knowledge such as the principle that all sensible objects must have extensive magnitude. In the second edition, some six years later, he repeats this note with the significant alternative, that Taste may share the name Aesthetic with speculative philosophy and then Aesthetic will be received partly in a transcendental, partly in a psychological sense.[2] But the second edition introduces other modifications which Hartenstein apparently thought were original. Instead of saying that the principles of Taste are empirical in their sources, Kant now says that they are only empirical in their *main* sources (*vornehmsten* Quellen); and it is not *a priori* laws that we cannot discover in Aesthetic but *determinate a priori* laws (*bestimmten* Gesetzen).[3] All these little things count. It means that he does not despair of the

---

[1] Hartenstein, iii. pp. 56-7, note.

[2] See Hartenstein's remarks on above citation.

[3] Kuno Fischer, *Kant und seine Lehre*, ii. pp. 408-9. Cp. Erdmann, *Kant's Kritik der Urteilskraft*, Einleitung, xvii; C. T. Michaëlis, *Zur Entstehung von Kants Kritik der Urteilskraft*, p. 7.

sources. What appears impossible is not to discover *a priori* principles but determinate *a priori* principles corresponding to those in science, and in his most mature conclusions in the *Critique of Judgment* he never aspires to determinate principles.

Then in the well-known letter to Reinhold, already quoted, and written in December of the same year (1787), he advances his new confidence in an undertaking which he formerly held to be impossible, with engaging candour : " I can assure you without being guilty of self-conceit, that the further I advance on my way, the less concerned I am that any contradiction, or (as is not unusual at present) an alliance even, should do considerable damage to my system." The alliance he contemplates is evidently the adoption of Taste into his system of philosophy. He has an inner, growing conviction that even in researches in which he does not know his way, he has only to glance at his table of the Elements of Knowledge to get an opening.[1] He is convinced that no realm of Nature is accidental. We may not have a certain knowledge of the Beautiful, perhaps it is not even desirable, but we can and must have a reasonable appreciation. It is possible to show that the aesthetic sense is an activity of the Human Spirit as primary and essential as knowledge or morality, so that without it we are not complete. Indeed Kant ultimately shows that in Aesthetic we make the nearest approximation to divine Understanding, for its objects are those which our mind would create for itself if it had creative power. It is true that Taste is formed in society and modified by the growth of civilisation, but it is not therefore

[1] *Briefwechsel*: Kirchmann, pp. 460-1.

formed contingently at the wish and will of circumstance; for the Human Spirit has already its idea of what the Beautiful should be. No account of Taste is satisfactory which explains it in terms of other mental functions, and assimilates it to these.[1] It is not a derivative but an original faculty. It is neither a modification of knowledge nor of volition nor of sensation.

He begins his proof by laying down as the First Canon that the Judgment of Taste is disinterested (*ohne alles Interesse*). This is an unfortunate expression and foreshadows all the false formalism in Kant's theory. But particularly with this author, we must take one step at a time and content ourselves meanwhile with his narrowest meaning. All he should intend to say is that Aesthetic has no interest in the existence of its objects. In this respect he compares it favourably with the Pleasant and the Good. It should be said at once that these contrasts are miserable and are never clearly defined. We shall have to notice them later, but this much at least should be said now, that while the contrast with Pleasure is notorious, the contrast with the Good is not so obvious. In the first place, we hardly expect it from Kant for whom the Will has no interest of any kind, not even personal, in its objects. But the change of opinion which we are now remarking, just indicates the modifying influence of his later reflections on his moral theory. He now seems to speak of the Good loosely, as one would speak of good things; he states explicitly, however, that he does not mean the useful only but also " that which is good absolutely and

---

[1] Cp. *Über Philosophie überhaupt*: Rosenkranz, i. p. 586, where he deprecates attempts to reduce Knowledge, Feeling and Volition to a common principle.

in every respect."¹ He appears to have felt the need of explanation, for he adds in a note, that pure moral judgments "may be quite *disinterested*, but yet very *interesting*, i.e. not based upon an interest, but bringing an interest with it."² But in this theory of the Good there is nothing to constitute a contrast, such as he has in view; for it is eminently true of the Beautiful also that an interest follows our judgment. Kant, however, meant it seriously, and it is the burden of his third canon which will be discussed in its proper place.

The Beautiful, then, is occupied only with the form of things. But this proposition is not identical with the ordinary distinction between form and matter, on which Kant's doctrine of phenomenalism rests. For in the Beautiful even the pure representation of space, which is the form of phenomena, is excluded because it is an ingredient in cognition.³ By the form he means rather the way in which the thinking subject is affected. Beauty is not a perceived quality in the object but exists in our minds. It was well said by Hegel regarding this canon that it is the first rational word concerning Beauty, and it is Kant's single triumph over Baumgarten though he did not use it to great advantage. He showed for the first time that the outlook in Aesthetic is peculiar to itself and that the activity in aesthetic perception is of an order distinctly its own. In this sense it may be said with truth that there is no natural beauty, for beauty does not consist in the fact of impression but in the con-

---

[1] *Critique of Judgment*, §4: Bernard, p. 53.
[2] *Ibid.* §2: Bernard, p. 48.
[3] *Ibid.* Introd. §vii.: Bernard, pp. 29-30.

templative state which accompanies the impression. This is proved by the fact that our artistic impressions of the same objects vary, and sometimes do not return to us at all; they are not constant effects like the impressions in sense-perception but depend altogether on the state of the subject. It was to ensure this condition that Kant called aesthetic perception a form of Judgment, for which he has been severely criticised as, for instance, by Victor Basch.

But Kant has certainly something to say for himself. In the first instance Aesthetic is perception, as the word originally means. But if it is to be anything more than a mechanical consequence of sensation, the impression must be mediated through some form of reflective activity akin to the process in logical judgment. A savage cry of pleasure is not aesthetical, because it is an immediate effect of sensation. Now Kant noticed, that while the basis in an aesthetical judgment must be sensation (*Empfindung*), for otherwise it would not be aesthetical, "there is only one single so-called sensation which can never be an idea of an object, and this is the feeling of pleasure and pain";[1] and it is this sensation alone, and not any other, that forms the basis in aesthetic perception. Aesthetic is thus brought at once into line with logical judgment, for the feeling of approval or disapproval is decidedly an apperceptive function, or as Kant would say, the distinctive mark of an aesthetical judgment consists in the comparison of a representation with other representations and with the whole reflective faculty. While therefore Aesthetic is primarily sensuous, there must also be the activity of Understanding.

[1] *Über Philosophie überhaupt*: Rosenkranz, i. p. 598.

At this point Kant has brought himself into difficulty. He saw that there is a spurious kind of judgment which is at once aesthetical because its basis is sensation, and also a reflective activity akin to judgment, because its basis is just that peculiar form of sensation in which all sensation is apperceived. Let it be said here for the sake of clearness, that the immediate sensation of pleasure or pain is not the same as the feeling of pleasure or pain; the former is reflex emotional expression while the latter is a function of conscious apperception. Well, this spurious judgment is no other than that abhorred brood, the Pleasant. In the judgment, 'Wine is pleasant,' the basis is not immediate sensation but sensation as it is mediated through our appreciation, and therefore "an aesthetical judgment of sense (*asthetisches Sinnenurtheil*) is possible."[1] Now Kant is bound over not to admit the aesthetical judgment of sense to the same rank as Aesthetic proper, and he therefore distinguishes the latter as the aesthetical reflective judgment. But the distinction which he makes is nowhere satisfactory. The point of difference for him is that the aesthetical judgment of sense does not involve a process of comparison, and that in consequence it cannot pretend to the universality of the aesthetical reflective judgment.[2] But this admission cancels the peculiar character of pleasure-pain as distinct from mere sensation, and indeed this is what happens, for we find him saying that the basis in an aesthetical judgment of sense is "that sensation which is immediately produced by the empirical perception of the object."[3] The truth is that the Pleasant is not so conventional as Kant imagined.

[1] *Ibid.* p. 597.   [2] *Ibid.* p. 599.   [3] *Ibid.* p. 598.

Let us now return to the more important question which will bring us on to the main track again, how we are to distinguish the aesthetical from the logical judgment, or what is the same thing, Reflexion from Knowledge; for the logical judgment is pre-eminently apperceptive, the synthetic unity of apperception being the supreme principle of Understanding. In the judgment, 'Rust is a form of the process called oxidation,' the presentation first receives adequate meaning in being assimilated to a general process, which is of the same kind in the burning of a candle, an explosion, or the physiological function of respiration. But while in this instance the associations which make the presentation intelligible are necessary connections in experience, and may therefore be said to be reproduced in imagination, the apperceptive function in Reflexion is productive, because the associations are ideally selected from the necessary context in experience and placed in a new relation. The process in aesthetic perception is on a parallel with what takes place in reminiscence. Our memory of the past is always an ideal unity. Dissevered from the pragmatic interest which we felt at the time and which is now diminished in intensity or forgotten altogether, events are reproduced selectively with the impersonal regard of a dispassionate spectator. Even excessively painful occurrences, which are fresh in recollection, are subject to the same principle. For we either seek to banish them from our minds as intolerable, or the acuteness of recollection is so modified that we are able to retain them as detached from our immediate well-being, and then our interest is no longer personal but dramatic, and we contemplate them with the sublime pleasure that we feel in tragedy.

THE CRITICAL PHILOSOPHY

It is the same kind of activity that is at work in Art with this difference, that we detach ourselves from events which are present while in reminiscence the events are past. It is true that knowledge is also selective. The impressions of sense which rain down upon us are not passively received, but organised with a methodical intention into the unities which we call objects. Our selective interest, however, is confined within very narrow limits, being determined by the systematic connection of experience; the associations reproduced are strictly those which contribute to the existence of the object, and our purposive activity is restrained by the end of knowledge as a system of necessary relations. But in Aesthetic our activity is purposive without being controlled by any determinate purpose, for it has no end beyond the harmony of its own processes; it is the thinking part of our mind working unconscious of its accustomed end, or in Kant's words, it is the free play of Imagination and Understanding.

If Kant had developed the principle contained in this canon to its full consequences, he would have practically included all the essential principles in a philosophy of the Beautiful. If Aesthetic is an activity akin to judgment and yet, unlike judgment, takes no cognisance of existential relations, it will be the exercise of an ideal Understanding, and therefore a truer and purer interpretation of Nature than is given in science, without itself being science. But the unconscious Understanding as it appears in Productive Imagination is for Kant a more general and abstract faculty than the Understanding itself, and consequently its objects are not the ideal forms of Nature stripped of their contingencies in the conditions of existence, but a more remote description of Nature which is so general that it has no meaning at all. His principle that every ingredient of cognition must be excluded, should mean no more than Oscar Wilde's aphorism, in his preface to *Dorian Gray*, that "all art is quite useless." As in Aristotle's view the useful Arts, political, economic, industrial, bring to completeness the ends which Nature can only realise imperfectly; so the Art of the Beautiful envisages the ideal intention of Nature, but with this difference which Aristotle appears not to notice, that unlike the useful Arts the end of the Beautiful is exhausted in the harmony of our own subjective processes, and we have no purpose of bettering Nature or anybody else.

It is interesting to find Oscar Wilde anticipated in Kant's Logic Lectures of 1772, where he says: *Das Schöne soll immer ungebräuchlich sein.*[1] But Kant took so seriously what has only truth as an aphorism, that his theory of the Beautiful is useless for the aesthete as well as for the scientist or moralist. He appears to speak of the Beautiful as if it were subjective to the second power and so at two removes from Reality, phenomena being already subjective representations; and the Sublime should consequently be regarded as a third degree of abstraction. But his position that the elements of beauty which we find in objects exist in our minds and not in the objects themselves, must be understood as a peculiar consequence of his theory of knowledge. As Günther Jacoby says, to condemn the subjectivity of Kant's Aesthetic is to raise the whole question of his statement of the problem, whether Aesthetic is capable of *a priori* principles.[2] A harmony

---

[1] Schlapp, *Kants Lehre vom Genie u.s.w.* p. 65.
[2] *Herders und Kants Ästhetik*, p. 255.

of relations like every appearance of purpose in Nature, organic or inorganic, is in Kant's opinion contingent for Understanding, because we cannot see that this character in phenomena is necessary to their existence as objects of knowledge. But on the other hand the Subjective in all its forms, moral, aesthetical and teleological, has for him more worth and reality than the objective region of science; the one misfortune is that its reality cannot be demonstrated. And it is specially important for us to carry his principles to their farthest limits, wherever he gives us encouragement to proceed, because we are not immediately concerned with his aesthetic theory except as it sheds light on the interpretation of his whole system.

The value of his aesthetic principle consists in the discovery of different planes in Subjectivity. The modern commonplace that there are degrees in Reality would be expressed by him as degrees in Subjectivity. And in his theory of Genius he shows, if only incidentally, that he had a true conception of what is meant by the subjective quality of Aesthetic. For Genius does not reproduce Nature according to a rule of Understanding, but works up the material supplied to it according to the law of association "into something different which surpasses Nature."[1] It is not an imitation, but an ideal imitation; for example, when Aristotle says that dancing 'imitates' character, emotion, and action, he is using the term imitation as equivalent to expression.[2] The original elements of Beauty must no doubt be found in Nature, and in this sense Beauty does reside in Nature; yet it is not these elements as they are scattered and dispersed in Nature, or as they

[1] *Critique of Judgment*, § 49; Bernard, p. 198.
[2] *Poetics*, i. 5.

are imperfectly organised into appreciable unities which are hampered and obscured by contingencies, that the artist depicts, but as they are ideally selected to form that aesthetic semblance which their appearance suggests to the artistic mind alone. What he imitates is not the actual but what Nature tried to express and failed. This is the proper and only sense in which a work of Art should be true to life. What the poet represents is not what is but what may be, and even what ought to be if with Schiller we conceive of Beauty as an imperative—"a duty of appearances."[1] All Art seeks to give to the soul of things the expression which is most fitting to its nature. So far it will be a reproduction of what is actual, but, as Aristotle says of portrait-painting, it is a representation "which is true to life and yet more beautiful."[2] For the first time Nature becomes beautiful when she is interpreted by artistic genius. It is not a reproduction but a production, not an imitation but a creation. And what takes place in the mind of the artist is enacted by the ordinary consciousness in a less degree. To have aesthetic perception is to exercise in limited measure the creative activity of Genius.

A clear understanding of the intention in Art is the only standard of criticism. Otherwise we shall oppose the products of Genius as realistic or idealistic in the most bewildering confusion, the former alone being regarded as true. The truth is that realism and idealism in Art are not so different in their interpretations of life as their standpoints are opposite; for while the idealist represents the universal as it may exist in conditions which

[1] *Über Anmuth und Würde: Werke*, xi. p. 402. Cp. letter to Körner of Oct. 20, 1794.

[2] *Poetics*, xv. 8.

THE CRITICAL PHILOSOPHY 81

it chooses for itself, the realist indeed represents what is actual but at the moment when it is most expressive of the Ideal. Or, if the realistic expression should be completely wanting in and even hostile to ideal significance, it will at least be capable, if it is Art, of suggesting by sympathetic reaction the sublime meaning of life. The intention of Art in Dickens is the same in effect as in Balzac and Tolstoi. The characters in Dickens move in an atmosphere of such august universality that they barely touch the ground, but if Mr. Micawber, Mrs. Gamp, the brothers Cheeryble, Mr. Mantalini or even Captain Bunsby, are hardly capable of existing in sensible conditions, it is not because they are unreal but because they are too true to life. And, on the other hand, a realistic writer like Balzac betrays this common intention in Art by overstraining realism as, for instance, in Old Goriot; for it is not necessarily the actual as it exists that he is describing but as it is most representative of what may be. A crucial instance for the unsophisticated mind is George Meredith. Here is an artist who can be indifferently regarded as realist or idealist, the former because he dissects the most delicate and intricate operations of the human heart with so fine a touch that the ordinary mind cannot perceive them, nor even believe that they are actual when the author tells them so; and for this very reason he may be regarded as idealist. The same principle applies to Painting and Statuary. Turner is popularly called an idealist, but in Ruskin's opinion he was the most realistic painter of his age. There remains the subsidiary but important criterion of poetic truth that it must be internally consistent or have ideal necessity; otherwise, even as fiction, it will be alike improbable and impossible.

This conditional necessity is what Kant's Fourth Canon, the modality of the aesthetical Judgment, means when adequately interpreted. It is really a corollary to the Second which treats of the universality in the Judgment, and it would be pedantic to take it separately. We therefore propose to restrict ourselves to three canons.

Kant's principle is capable of a further and final application which brings it to the test, and which raises the whole question of imitation in Art. If the space-form, as an ingredient in cognition, be excluded from Aesthetic, what has he to say of those objects which are nothing but representations in space? I mean geometrical figures. This is discussed in the opening pages of the Teleology, § 62. As might be expected, he wavers and gives no satisfactory reply. He refuses to call aesthetical a simple figure like the circle, because it is capable of many intellectual combinations. He will not even call it intellectual Beauty, because this would destroy the proper meaning of Beauty as free from every notion which contributes to the existence of an object, and he prefers to regard it as a relative Perfection. In short, it is classed with the objective-formal type of Teleology. It is also discussed in § 22, where he gives his unqualified opinion that our interest in geometrical figures is not properly aesthetical but intellectual. His point is that we cannot think of a circle or cube without a concept of mathematical necessity, which puts a constraint upon Imagination; only those drawings can be beautiful which are the work of free fancy, such as arabesques and bizarre decorations of like kind, and which do not serve any intellectual purpose. Here we see the sinister intention in Kant's first Canon; he could not understand how an intellectual interest can be compatible with aesthetic feeling.

But it is really not important what he says. I have only mentioned his opinion in order to introduce a wider problem. There are certain geometrical figures such as the ellipse, Zeising's golden section and Hogarth's undulating line, which are acknowledged to be simply beautiful apart from any mathematical implications. And the question is, if these representations whose significance is exhausted in their linear form have nothing to offer which Art can improve, whether the artistic imagination is not restricted in its activity to imitation in the literal sense of reproduction. Even here Kant's principle still holds in spite of his own opposition. Expressed in its most general terms the question is, as Signor Croce has recently been reminding us, whether all intuitions, as the adequate expression of impressions, are not aesthetical. Here there is implied a distinction between Beauty and Art which may be differently conceived and which must be more or less artificial. Stated abstractly, it is the difference between the Greek conception of Beauty as formal symmetry and the Romantic as characteristic expression. Aesthetic is manifestly more than Beauty in the narrow sense, for it includes the ugly, the sublime and tragic representations which are not immediately pleasing in their form. The dwarfs of Velasquez are not beautiful men, but they do give aesthetic pleasure because they are made perfect of their kind; they are not beautiful in their form, for this is repulsive, but in their typical expression of what a dwarf should be. The difference is seen in the different kinds of pleasure. The perception of formal symmetry is merely contemplative, or, to use another phrase of Kant's, it is what pleases in "the mere act of judging";[1] while the pleasure in sensuous expression as the perfect embodiment of an idea is expansive, soaring, dynamic. Kant himself indeed had observed a distinction between Beauty and Art which has become notorious in criticisms of his theory, but he drew the line at the wrong point. He maintained that while Art has intention, pure Beauty has none, and therefore Art cannot be beautiful. We should rather say that while a representation which has no meaning at all may be considered beautiful, the typically beautiful is only found in Art.

Now the question is not whether certain intuitions as the simple but adequate expression of sense-impressions may be beautiful. This is admitted. The ellipse has undoubtedly acquired content as the orbit of the heavenly bodies and may now be regarded as the aesthetic symbol of infinite spaces, but before this astronomical discovery was made it was beautiful, as a Greek vase is beautiful of which it is the geometrical form. A Greek vase is not beautiful because it is the perfect embodiment of an idea, for there is no good reason why a vase should be elliptical. The same is true of flowers, musical melodies and harmonies which are only made to please. The question rather is whether this narrow conception of Beauty is not the whole of Art as Art for Art's sake, in the "decadent" use of the aphorism. For Signor Croce the distinction only means the difference between simplicity and complexity in expression, while Tolstoi drastically cuts the knot by excluding the Beautiful as meaningless expression from Art, which must always be infectious

[1] Bernard, § 5 and § 45.

expression. Happily we are not called to enter further into this unsettled problem, and may content ourselves by observing that the limits of the discussion are fixed for us in the opposing views of Lessing, who made expression subordinate to Beauty, and Tolstoi, who subordinates Beauty to expression. We may fearlessly admit that simple intuitions can be aesthetical without the least danger of degenerating into a mimetic theory of Art. For if our perception is aesthetical, it is never mere reproduction in imagination. The representation is beautiful, not because we simply perceive it, but because we perceive the very form we should produce ourselves if our imagination were free to create its own objects. The test of its aesthetic quality is that our perception is of the same productive nature as the creative activity of Genius. For the first time the form receives its aesthetic sanction from artistic imagination. Thus a photographic reproduction may have aesthetic quality, for though it is received as Nature gives it, it is not because Nature gives it; it is chosen. As Kant says, the important point is not what Nature is, "but how we take it."[1] And these simple intuitions which Art cannot improve are aesthetical, because our choice rests on grounds which are the same in kind as those on which subjects are chosen from Nature for artistic treatment.

We have already recognised that the elemental source of the Beautiful is Nature herself. Without actual perception of form, colour, sound, emotional expression and character as it is enacted in life, the works of Genius could never arise. In this elementary sense Nature is the beginning of all Art. Kant did not

[1] Bernard, p. 246.

take this into account in his official theory, where he seems to speak of the Beautiful as the mere subjective product of our own minds. But he otherwise does recognise the Supersensible, in the disposition of Nature to our Understanding, as the ultimate source of these favours: were it only what he says in contrasting it with the Sublime, that "we must seek a ground external to ourselves for the Beautiful of Nature."[1] We have now to acknowledge a further concession on the part of the Supersensible. In striving to equip herself to the best advantage, Nature gives token that she is capable of artistic treatment by throwing out, as it were by accident, certain symmetrical collocations, which have this at least in common with the products of Art, that they are wholly undesigned. And just as, in Aristotle's opinion, certain historical facts may be legitimate subjects for Poetry—whose criterion of truth is quite different from that of History—because they are capable of adapting themselves to the ideal conditions of poetic truth; so do those meaningless symmetries commove us to aesthetic admiration, because, in their utter destitution of significance, they simulate the ideal conditions of artistic truth. As by-products of Nature they have only hypothetical necessity, and by this circumstance they are detached from the actual world and claim affinity with Art. Both St. Augustine and Schopenhauer have independently remarked how plants invite our admiration, as if they would compensate for their want of consciousness by becoming known.[2] It is their very poverty of

---

[1] Bernard, p. 104.

[2] Schopenhauer: *The World as Will and Idea*, Haldane and Kemp, i. p. 260. St. Augustine: *The City of God*, xi. 27—"ut, pro eo quod nosse non possunt, quasi innotescere velle videantur."

meaning that gives rise to an aesthetical illusion in which we think them capable of more than they are, and perhaps their barren beauty is best described as due to a kind of aesthetic pity. Certainly to one who has the acquired insight of a botanist or the independent and intuitive insight of Genius, the flower in the mossy dell may be a pure aesthetic symbol as the typical expression of its kind ; and our contemplation is capable of a still deeper poetical emotion. But this is not the place to introduce the fine sentiments of Schiller and Wordsworth, for these are sublime rather than beautiful, and the Sublime forms a separate part of our study. Taking the problem at its lowest, we are asking ourselves just now what happens when a person, who has no scientific apperception and a minimum of poetical feeling, pronounces a flower beautiful in all its simplicity. In Signor Croce's words, it is a perfect expression of impressions, and is it therefore aesthetical? A Greek vase is beautiful because its form is elliptical, but why should that which is nothing but a representation in space, apart from all astronomical implications, be beautiful ? I think the true reason is that, by their appearance of ideal necessity, they decoy into activity the same mental powers as are at work in genuine Art, holding out the hope that something will come of it, which hope is vain. In the smell of a rose and in the simple sight of it, there is an indeterminate foreboding of significance which may only arise from sheer nonentity and which we fondly imagine to contain a fearful depth of inexhaustible reflection ; but we have to turn away from it unsatisfied, or we turn and fall to again, and every time, like Sancho Panza, are robbed of our feast. But once the Powers have begun to move, there is no going back! Our aesthetic appetite once whetted, we in desperation want to eat the rose or shed its glory with our hands. The truth is that we are gently flattered by these empty presentations into an incipient aesthetic emotion, and in virtue of that strange contradiction which pervades human nature, we maintain the double consciousness of truth and error. Our conclusion, then, is that the formal representation of unity in variety, which is destitute of meaning, is not the Beautiful itself so much as its shadow or reflection.

There is thus no place in Aesthetic for mere imitation, whether we speak of Taste or Productive Art. Even when a presentation which claims to be beautiful has nothing to offer which artistic perception can improve, it is apperceived by Productive Imagination, if only incipiently and negatively, and there is no question of mere reproduction. Photography can be aesthetical when it is not a random reproduction, but the choice of what is representative and recurs most frequently in a landscape, and which is so far ideal that it can stand out from its actual context with increased significance; or, again, photography may be able to catch the typical expression in a face. On this ground alone can it aspire to the dignity of Art, and even this is a modest claim, because its selective choice is restricted to the field of vision and does not extend to particular features, except in so far as these can be modified or eliminated in the negative. But as an imitation of Nature, which is faithful to the minutest detail, it is a second-hand copy which falls far short of the original.

This is the truth in Plato's mimetic theory, in which the artist has less to say for himself than the carpenter, and is at three removes from Reality. Art shows its superiority in recognising its inevitable limitations. It knows that the actual can never be reproduced in its wealth and complexity of detail nor with the original thrill of sensation. For while in Nature form and matter are germane to each other, Art must fashion a body for the soul which it imports from another world out of a foreign substance. What have pigments, marble, or words in common with aesthetical ideas? From the point of view of Art, of course, the medium peculiar to each art has everything to do with it. There seems to be a natural affinity between the marble with its "bluish veins of blood asleep" and the conception.[1] But this is only to say that, as the elements of semblance, matter and form are congenital. Out of this unequal mixture of heterogeneous elements one Nature more of the same kind could not be reproduced, but only an aesthetic semblance which cannot compete with the substantial entelechies in Nature. No painting can compare with natural colour, no description can adequately translate the verve of action. Indeed, as R. L. Stevenson observes, literature is not the imitation of life, but of speech; and the nearest approach to a reproduction of life is to be found in the stories of the first men, seated around the savage camp-fire.[2] No Pygmalion can ever again feel the hard marble of his statuary yielding to the pressure of his hand and changing into living flesh and blood. Recognising this limitation, Art contents itself with an independent and ideal imitation, knowing that out of its indifferent material it can never reproduce a second Nature. The artist's one method, to quote Stevenson again, is "to half-shut his eyes against the dazzle and confusion of

[1] See Browning's *Pippa Passes*, ii. [2] *Memories and Portraits*, xvi.

reality"; and in surrendering all pretension to the actual, it not only rises superior to photographic imitation, but within the confines of its independent world outrivals even Nature : perfecting the actual in the higher nexus of imaginative truth, transforming the contingent events of history into the reasonable sequence of ideal necessity, and interpreting the motiveless passions of men as the inevitable consequences of ideal grounds, in a world where character and circumstance are congenital factors in the same causality which makes up human destiny. Othello was "not easily jealous," but in his unsuspecting nature Iago found his opportunity, and the tragedy consists in the fatal adaptation of apparently contingent circumstance to character. "It is impossible but that offences will come, but woe unto him through whom they come." The brute necessity of fact is translated in the world of poetic and religious truth into a moral causality.

But Photography has been hitherto condemned to an inferior place, because it is obliged to attempt what true Art never dreams of doing—to rival Nature. In still life it is more successful as a reproduction because the features of Nature are relatively constant, though even in this instance it is at a disadvantage, for Nature is never really the same. The difficulty of the painter is to catch the representative moment in the ever-changing tints of light which to the ordinary eye are a constant impression, while Photography, because it is instantaneous, can only be successful by a happy accident. But when it attempts to reproduce the mobile, the result is not so satisfactory. Photography is supposed to have proved that no artist has ever been able to catch the exact curve of a horse's legs in motion. But this does not indicate

THE CRITICAL PHILOSOPHY

that Art is inferior as an interpretation of the actual. On the contrary, it is Photography that is unreal because it is subject to the risk of choosing a moment that is not capable of continuity with the flow of living being. Such a beautiful sight as a flock of gulls makes a disappointing photograph because it takes in too much from the point of view of Art, and too little from the point of view of Nature. No gull ever exists in such a moment of isolation; the phases which Photography abstracts are never meant to be stationary, which they must be when the impression is instantaneous. We have all seen the Prime Minister or some other notable person on his way to the House of Commons in the *Daily Mirror*. What a leg the man has! stuck up behind him at an angle of forty-five degrees like a hen in cogitation. Surely he does not exist in that way. The moment of impression must have been very inauspicious. But any instantaneous moment would be equally unreal, for the moments in the mobile do not exist as discrete successions but as continuous transitions, like the flow of water, in the ever-changing stream of life. And it is the genius of Art that it is able to preserve this original continuity of existence in an impression which purports to be a single moment of time, but which has really nothing to do with temporal succession at all. To use a simile of M. Bergson's, Experience is not like the steps of a stair but a gentle declivity (*pente douce*),[1] no section of which exists in isolation, and of which Time with its discontinuous moments of succession is the destroyer. If, therefore, the most fleeting moment in this indiscerptible continuity be represented in the form of temporal succession, it must be shorter

[1] *L'Evolution Créatrice*, p. 3.

than the shortest conceivable moment, and so will escape the most instantaneous photographic impression.[1]

Art does not seek to imitate the continuous duration of the actual, but represents the mobile in a timeless symbol, or to come back to Kant again, every ingredient of existence in the object is excluded. But this is its gain and not its loss. For Time as the endlessly divisible is never actually present, while the moment of Art, in being timeless, is also Present as only the absolutely durationless is present, and as that which is truly now, the revelation of the eternal. In the words of Houston Stewart Chamberlain, "the Present in the sense of durationless is shorter than the shortest conceivable moment, and longer than all conceivable eternity."[2] Like the moment of the Beautiful in *Faust*, it is at once fleeting and imperishable.

We have now pushed Kant's principle as far as it will go and have found it capable of a reasonable interpretation. I wish to close this chapter with a brief notice of a fairly recent criticism of the principle as it has passed

---

[1] Our discussion appears to blench before the extraordinary advances of the cinematograph. The growth of a flower as represented by this instrument, is one of the most divine sights the eye can witness. The unfolding of these god-like creatures in the space of a few seconds, suggests an anticipation of the tardy processes of Nature in a pre-existent state, and produces a feeling in the mind akin to the affection induced by the call of the mothers to the unborn children in Maeterlinck's *Blue Bird*. But as a medium of representation, the cinematograph suffers so much from want of light and from the constant impression of confusion that, in its present state at least, it can hardly be allowed to compare with Nature and Art. This, however, is a question for experts, and what is said in the text must be read within the narrow limits of the intention with which it was written.

[2] *Die Grundlagen des xix Jahrhunderts*, Band ii. p. 953.

THE CRITICAL PHILOSOPHY 93

into aesthetic theories generally. Kant practically says that no intuition can be aesthetic unless we are able to forget that it is an intuition. To this Signor Croce stands opposed, and maintains that all intuitions as the adequate expression of impressions are aesthetic.[1] Intuitions are—this lake, this brook, this rain, this glass of water (p. 36). Aesthetic is thus the science of Perception and unites in one the two kinds of perception which Kant had treated separately under the same name. To be true intuitions they must have successful expression; imperfect expression is no expression at all, it is pure sensation (pp. 13, 129). The distinction which we make between simple apprehension and artistic intuition is for Croce only quantitative, the former being simple, the latter complex. If now we look away from the method he has chosen and try to appreciate the motive of his work, we are held with admiration. Somewhat in the spirit of Tolstoi, he seeks to reclaim the outlying region of common experience which has been banned by aristocratic Art. He refuses to recognise a double order of imagination and thinks it impossible to define the limits between intuitions which are artistic and those which are not. Even the utterance of a syllable, if it is perfectly expressed, is aesthetic. This is a praiseworthy intention, but Signor Croce is quite unable to maintain his position. Indeed his book is to be enjoyed as a piece of literature rather than studied as a philosophical criticism. I only wish to indicate that his opposition to our principle is superficial, and that he really veers round to Kant's standpoint. If he were taken seriously, we should understand him to say that besides intuitions,

---

[1] *Aesthetic as Science of Expression and General Linguistic*: translated from the Italian by Douglas Ainslie, B.A., Oxon.

which are all aesthetic, there is nothing else but pure sensation. Yet he admits that though all impressions can become aesthetic expressions, " none are bound to do so " (p. 30). Must they, then, remain· impressions meanwhile, which cannot be organised into simple perception unless the expression is completely successful ? And in his ' Address to the Third International Congress of Philosophy,' he gives away his whole case. He admits that the perception of a physical object is not a pure intuition but a construct, an impression with an abstract concept, and therefore not aesthetical; and we could only have pure intuitions if objects were things in themselves (p. 398). Thus it turns out that, even for Croce, aesthetic intuitions are not so plentiful. They only become intuitions when we refuse to recognise their "unsuccessful expression" in knowledge and give them form in aesthetic imagination. That objects shall be things in themselves and not abstract conceptions of impressions, is indeed the criterion of aesthetic intuition, and in Kant's theory aesthetic perceptions *are* things in themselves because they are the objects of an independent order of imagination, which transcends the opposition of thought and things. It is a weak evasion when Croce protests against this dualism, the admission of which destroys his theory of Art as pure intuition (p. 398). The dualism is there, whether it be ultimate or not, and is to last out our phenomenal term of life. So long as there is unsuccessful expression, there are phenomenal constructs which are not mere sensation, and these carry in themselves an inevitable distinction between Appearance and Reality.

CHAPTER IV.

AESTHETIC AND CAUSALITY—THE SECOND CANON.

IN the realm of the Beautiful the old things have passed away and are become new. But in the rigorous pursuit of his first canon Kant has slipped his moorings. He has cut us adrift from the familiar roadsteads, and we are floating outwards on the open sea. Every ingredient in knowledge, every character in objects by which they can be recognised as existing parts in a common world, has been sacrificed, and we are landed in a region where there is no knowledge. It would seem that the Beautiful is purely subjective and only exists in imagination. But this is the conclusion which Kant expressly sought to avoid. At some considerable risk to the security of the Beautiful, he maintained its complete independence of cognition in order to vindicate its distinctive position as an original, and not a derivative, type of experience. He must now look around and provide in a new way the universality which he wilfully threw overboard. So the Second Canon ordains that the Beautiful must also be universal.

As Kant himself thinks, this canon follows naturally from the first; because, when our contemplation is disinterested, the pleasure we feel is of such a kind that it can be shared with all, while in the case of the Pleasant our private interests render community of taste impossible.

Although this may be accepted as a convenient contrast, it is not fair to the pleasurable feeling which is more than sensation but is not admitted to the rank of Aesthetic, and altogether it only yields a favourable presumption. Kant, however, states it more precisely in a technical form which is quite misleading, and it is a good illustration of the way in which his theoretical assumptions impaired the expression of his thought. He observes that an aesthetical judgment in its very nature must be singular because it is a judgment of perception; thus, the judgment, 'This rose is beautiful,' is aesthetical, while the judgment, 'All roses are beautiful,' is purely logical. But it is peculiar to the aesthetical reflective judgment that it is at once singular and universal, for it is not based on a feeling alone, but is *at the same time instructed* by the intellectual faculties.[1] The italics are Kant's. It is otherwise with the aesthetical judgment of sense. The judgment, 'This rose is pleasant,' is singular, and because it is singular and nothing more, it is said to be without universality.[2] This is false. Kant is here confusing logical universality with transcendental universality or the *a priori* in knowledge. The logical judgment, 'All roses are beautiful,' does not contain a more constant factor than the singular judgment. Indeed its transcendental quality may be regarded as secondary, for as Kant himself says in this section, it is an aggregate of singular judgments. The universality in the logical judgment is only numerical, and does not affect the *a priori* validity of experience. In the judgment, 'The earth goes round the sun,' there is no

[1] *Über Philosophie überhaupt*: Rosenkranz, i. p. 599; Hartenstein, vi. p. 389.

[2] Bernard, § 8. Cp. pp. 101, 153, 158, 165.

THE CRITICAL PHILOSOPHY

numerical quantity at all, and yet it has transcendental universality. The difference between a universal and a singular judgment, in respect of logical quantity, is that the one is a complex and the other a simple synthesis. Each is a synthesis of elements which is given in experience; but the constant factor in cognition, which enables us to recognise the synthesis as necessary, and therefore not as conditioned by but as conditioning experience, is the same in both.

The real contrast which Kant had in view in this confusion of logical with transcendental universality, is his old distinction of the *Prolegomena* between judgments of perception (*Wahrnehmungsurtheile*) and judgments of experience (*Erfahrungsurtheile*).[1] A judgment of perception is, 'This room is warm,' or, 'This is sweet,' and Kant says that it can never become a judgment of experience because it is confined to individual feeling. This is a distinction which of course cannot be maintained, for it is flatly contradicted by the central argument in the *Analytic*, that not even the perception of a pure representation in space is possible without the original mental synthesis which makes experience possible. Kant, however, clung tenaciously to this artificial distinction, as is evident when we consider that it appears both before and after the decisive proof in the *Analytic*. Before he has come to grips with his main problem he says there, that "objects might certainly be presented to us, even if they were not necessarily related to functions of Understanding, as their *a priori* condition."[2] Then there is the later passage in the *Prolegomena*, and also the still later statement in the *Critique of Judgment*, already

---
[1] Mahaffy and Bernard, p. 55; Hartenstein, iv. § 18.
[2] Watson, *Selections*, p. 54.

quoted, "that we can represent a thing as given although we have no concept of it."[1] But the point of the contrast here is quite proper, because the basis of comparison between the two judgments is their transcendental universality, and there is no question of logical quantity at all.

And still this is not Kant's problem, which is much more subtle. To understand his position we must turn to the *Über Philosophie überhaupt*, which is rich in suggestion on this as on many other points. What he has to prove is a peculiar kind of transcendental universality, whether there is a constant and spontaneous factor in a form of judgment which is neither a judgment of perception nor a judgment of experience, and it is in respect of this reflective universality that the comparison between the Pleasant and the Beautiful must be made. A judgment is aesthetical when it has for its basis not a sensation to which there is an object corresponding but merely an affection of the apprehending subject, the feeling of pleasure and pain. But of this there are two kinds: the aesthetical reflective judgment, as when I say, 'This rose is beautiful,' and the aesthetical judgment of sense (*Sinnenurtheil*), as when I say, 'This wine is pleasant.' In neither is there any reference to the constitution of an object. Now Kant wants to believe that the aesthetical reflective has universality while the aesthetical judgment of sense, or the Pleasant, has none. To put it briefly in our own words, he says that while in the case of the Beautiful the elementary apperceptive function of pleasurable feeling is extended to the intellectual faculty—not in the form of particular representations for then it would be ordinary apperception, but to

[1] Bernard, p. 315.

the faculty itself as the condition of knowledge in general —the Pleasant somehow never gets beyond the bare feeling of pleasure and pain.[1]

So far this distinction is plausible enough and suggestive of very fruitful ideas. It could mean that our experience of the Beautiful has significance while pleasant experience has really none at all. In the former kind of apperception it is our whole personality that is called into activity in the harmonious play of sense, thought and will; but the latter can only be named apperception out of courtesy, for it is a meaningless reiteration of the same feeling which never gets beyond itself. All people who are destitute of ideas are limited to this low kind of aesthetic approval, if aesthetic it may be called. The gourmand smacks his lips and keeps telling himself and others how good it is, lest the counterfeit moment, which has no soul to stay and never is, should take its flight; the unlettered plutocrat and the *crassa minerva* alike betray their anxiety to keep up the show of apperception, in chasing round the fruitless feeling with which we approve a mere sensation. After seeing some grand sight, they want to tell you it was fine, and again, 'That was very fine, *you* know,' and yet again but this time in lowered accents and with some show of caution, for the moment has no stuff to feed on and is going, 'I tell you that *was* fine, and don't tell me.' They try to make up for depth of feeling by a prolonged vigil, while the true artist in a flash of intuition gains the still Beautiful, and is content to know that it can never die. The Beautiful has indeed the preference in point of universal appeal, just because it has a significance which the Pleasant never has. If we wish to

[1] See Rosenkranz, i. pp. 598-9.

maintain that this is true, however, we must not restrict the Beautiful to aristocratic Art, but define it with Tolstoi as the infectious expression of the elemental bond of sympathy among a people, as it is found in their religious feeling. Apart from particular criticisms which will no doubt be challenged by those who are competent to speak, Tolstoi may be said to have wrought out in prose, in his book *What is Art?* the lesson of Browning's poetry that Art is love. When, in his vision of *Easterday*, Browning volunteered to give up the realms of earthly delight, of Art and Mind in succession and made love his final choice, he did not meet with the approval he had expected from the Spirit, who rather reproached him that he should choose at this late hour what he should have found long ago in the pursuits of his soul:

> "—Now take love! Well betide
> Thy tardy conscience! Haste to take
> The show of love for the name's sake."

What gives its worth to the show or the aesthetic semblance is the Name. If it be not the joyous expression of self-effacement, Art is a tinkling cymbal for it is wanting in that which makes it the common possession of all.

But, as was noticed in the previous chapter, Kant made the distinction between the Pleasant and the Beautiful altogether too sharp. The consequence is that the peculiar privilege of an aesthetical judgment, whether of sense or reflexion, that it is based, not on a sensation, but on that form of feeling in which all sensations are apperceived, seems to be destroyed; and then the aesthetical judgment of sense is practically identified with an ordinary judgment of perception.

THE CRITICAL PHILOSOPHY

And so Kant says that the aesthetical judgment of sense is determined by "that sensation which is immediately produced by the empirical perception of the object."[1] As a judgment of perception it is based, of course, on a judgment of experience, and though no longer aesthetical it should at least have some degree of universality. But Kant will not admit that a judgment of perception always implies systematic experience, and he is consequently compelled to regard the aesthetical judgment of sense as a purely subjective modification. As we shall presently see, there is truth in Kant's statement. After all concessions have been made in its favour, the Pleasant remains subjective in a way that is quite peculiar to itself alone. But the Pleasant is not to be put down so easily as Kant thought. It is futile to deny that it implies systematic experience and therefore has universality. When it is said that a certain wine is pleasant, the judgment is not confined to individual feeling; for this pipe of wine cost more than others, and this argues a corresponding consensus of opinion in the public taste. Even a pure sensation is not incommunicable feeling, except in the sense that all our thoughts and feelings are our own and cannot be experienced by anyone else, for it is a sensation which all the world would feel under the same conditions. Since Mr. Bradley[2] exploded the categorical nature of the singular judgment, it has been recognised that the demonstratives in the judgment, 'this' and 'that,' are really kinds of universals; they are particular expressions for all particulars, and so when it is said, 'This is a sensation of coldness,' the use of the

[1] Rosenkranz, i. p. 598.
[2] *Principles of Logic*, Bk. I. ch. ii., § 20, 76, 77.

universal form 'this' which can apply to anything indifferently, intimates that this particular sensation is open to all. If the wild vagary of a dream is totally confined to our experience and cannot be reproduced in another person, it is because the same conditions cannot be realised. Similarly the Pleasant, regarded as a judgment of perception, is universally valid provided that the same conditions, in a given instance, are present to all; and this is a provision which conditions every kind of perception. What constitutes the peculiarity of the Pleasant is the fact, that while it is a universal form of experience it has only *a minimum of significance*, and in this sense it may quite properly be distinguished as a subjective modification.

Kant himself, with all his puritanic rigorism, was no stranger to the all-pervading Pleasant. Wasianski, who would seem to have kept a record of his master's breathing, if we may judge from the painfully minute account he gives of his death-bed, says that Kant's health was so exquisite that his sense of organic pleasure was positively acute.[1] Obviously this was a well-grounded sensation, and Kant could not think of keeping it all to himself. But the question to be considered from the point of view of Aesthetic is, whether there is anything in this sensation worth communicating to others which will infect them with genuine appreciation. When a man begins to discourse on his organic sensations, his audience intimate by their stony looks that they do not wish to understand him. But Kant would naturally take a different view of the matter. Here is a sensation

[1] *The last days of Kant.* De Quincey's translation in *Blackwood's Magazine*, vol. xxi. 1827.

which all should be anxious to experience by taking pains to cultivate the required conditions; and it is on record that when he was packed up for the night by Lampe, "swathed like a mummy" or "self-involved like the silkworm in its cocoon," he would often say to himself aloud, as if for the profit of mankind in general, "Is it possible to conceive a human being with more perfect health than myself?" Moreover he was aware that he had pushed the contrast too far,[1] and he recognised that the Pleasant may have a relative universality. He would probably admit that whoever has cultivated a good taste in wine, communicates his pleasure with a disinterested intention which has some aesthetic quality. In his astonishing statement that the Pleasant is not sociable, it is surely Kant the German who is speaking and not the Kant of Scottish ancestry.[2] Anyone who has attended a students' Kneipe knows that it is not conducive to conviviality; it is a solemn conclave of taciturnity and devout sentimentality, an aggregate of units under martial rule, who stand to sing their songs at the stroke of the hammer, and do everything to order except drink—very different from the hilarious and roaring fun of Tam O'Shanter. The tippler insists on others sharing his pleasures; he regards it as a maxim that private pleasure is a contradiction, and when he is compelled to enjoy himself alone, he addresses himself as an independent personality. Kant would have succeeded much better if he had straightway acknowledged the universality of the Pleasant as communicable. For by

[1] Bernard, § 7.

[2] "Das Angenehme ist nicht gesellschaftlich." Lectures on Anthropology, 1793-4, Schlapp, *Kants Lehre vom Genie*, p. 395.

making unreserved concessions, he could have covered it, heaped coals of universality on its head, until it finally disappeared as an independent type of experience and stood declared for what it truly is, a parasitic consciousness which feeds on the bodies of sensations, an empty form of apperception in which we approve sensations without getting beyond them, a threadbare warp of feeling which, if it be not fed with the woof of mind, becomes indistinguishable from sensations themselves.

But although Kant did not develop his position nor even define it clearly, it is important to understand his meaning; for the distinction he sought to establish between the Pleasant and the Beautiful really turns on what is known as the doctrine of the aesthetic senses. The feeling of the Pleasant is the aesthetic apperception of sensation, but in the Beautiful the elementary apperception in the feeling of pleasure is only the occasion of the aesthetic process, or in Kant's words, it is the sensation which gives rise to the harmonious play in the subject of Imagination and Understanding.[1] The Beautiful has only to do with the form of things, while the Pleasant is more immediately connected with the matter of sensation; therefore the aesthetical judgment of sense may be said to contain material, but the aesthetical reflective judgment formal, teleology.[2] Now this distinction between the form and the matter of sensation, which is characteristic of Kant's whole position and was afterwards developed to great advantage by Schiller, is properly a distinction among

[1] *Über Philosophie überhaupt*: Rosenkranz, i. p. 598; Hartenstein, vi. p. 389.
[2] *Ibid.*

the senses themselves. All the senses are avenues of sensation, but some of them are more easily detached from the sensational stimulus. Particularly in sight and hearing, we are not conscious of the affection of the organ as we are in touch, taste and smell; and therefore these two senses have been distinguished as intellectual, disinterested and sociable, and have become known as the aesthetic senses. Kant himself was aware of this; he isolates sight and hearing as "the only sensations that imply not merely a sensible feeling but also reflection upon the form of these modifications of Sense."[1] We may say with Schopenhauer, that the other senses are identified with the feeling of the whole body and are subservient to will;[2] or with Spencer, that they are immediately connected with the furtherance of the life-serving functions, particularly taste;[3] or in Schiller's rhetorical style: "importunate matter is repelled from the senses by the eye and ear, and the object with which we come in direct contact through the lower senses, is placed at a distance—the object of touch is a force which we suffer, the object of the eye and ear is a form which we create."[4] It should be said, however, that the modern tendency is to extend the number of the aesthetic senses. Schopenhauer recognised that there may be a touch which is neither pleasant nor painful. The feeling of velvet gives in a way peculiar to the sense of touch the same disinterested perception that we have of peachy skin, which is an element inseparable from feminine beauty.

[1] Bernard, § 42, p. 181.
[2] *The World as Will and Idea*: Haldane and Kemp, i. p. 259.
[3] *Principles of Psychology*, ii. chap. ix.
[4] *Aesthetical Letters*: Weiss, p. 156.

And even the sense of smell has been championed.[1] Taste is undoubtedly the Caliban of the senses, for it is immediately connected with the life-promoting functions. From this distinction between the senses as they are immediately or indirectly identified with sensation may be said to arise the comprehensive principle recognised by Spencer and Grant Allen, that Aesthetic is the pleasurable state of feeling in which there is a maximum of stimulation with a minimum discharge of nervous energy.[2] It is a higher rate of apperception.

Having cleared the ground, we may now state the problem. As Kant says, we must not "grope about empirically among the judgments of others" and base our judgments on a collection of their suffrages; our idea of the Beautiful must arise spontaneously within ourselves.[3] The problem, then, is the same as in the *Critique of Pure Reason* on a different plane, how are synthetic judgments *a priori* possible? The point in this time-honoured formula is that we are not to be dependent on experience. It does not require that in order to be *a priori*, our judgment must be free from all mixture with empirical elements, but only that it shall have a more original sanction than the conventional congruity which is produced by repeated associations. Our aesthetic sense must be logically prior to and coincident with experience. The question, then, is whether the feeling of Beauty is an acquired sense or whether there is not some original direction of our mind which gives the lead to experience. Is it only an aimless voice crying in the wilderness which awakens no echo in our soul, or is it not rather the reasonable expression

---

[1] See Tolstoi, *What is Art?* chap. ii.
[2] See Spencer, *op. cit.* p. 644.   [3] Bernard, pp. 153-4.

THE CRITICAL PHILOSOPHY 107

of our own nature which is able to prepare the way ? What occasions a problem is the conjunction of the two factors, synthesis, which is *a posteriori* because it is the putting together of apparently unrelated elements, and analysis, which is *a priori* because it is the breaking up of a whole in which the particular elements are originally connected. The judgments of Geometry and Arithmetic are easily synthetic *a priori* and do not constitute a problem, because the synthesis, though real, is made by ourselves. Geometrical relations are purely logical and have nothing to do with actual succession in time ; the elements being connected in the relation of ground and consequence, the judgments are incontinently true. But it is very different when we have to pronounce upon the succession of events in time, for these are real changes which we do not make and which do not follow one another with the logical certainty of a geometrical consequence from its ground. These changes simply happen as matters of fact, and unless we had an *a priori* conviction that every change must have a cause, the synthesis in experience would have no necessity and our judgment would be purely empirical. To be synthetic *a priori*, there must be a veritable connection of elements which we could not manufacture for ourselves but which must be presented in experience as an independent fact, and yet it must be a result which we can approve with absolute confidence as if it were the product of our own thought.

In the *Critique of Pure Reason* Kant showed that our knowledge of objects is *a priori*, because we realise beforehand that they must be presented as extensive magnitudes and as parts of a necessary system in reciprocal relation ; and when they are so presented, our conviction amounts to the belief that it is we who put them in their places. Now the forms of experience which make up aesthetic feeling are combinations of elements which are brought into quite a new relation, something in advance of what our knowledge gives. They are not representations in space as these are simply perceived but as they are felt; and the question is whether there is a new kind of *a priori* to validate these syntheses. Let us keep in mind the entire extent of the problem. On the one hand, they are real syntheses which are not made by us any more than rocks are. They are not even made by Genius, they are discovered. They are facts of Nature, whether we speak of natural or artistic Beauty, which are not the products of mechanical association nor of contingent fancy, but combinations which have significance as objective and outside of us as if God had made them beautiful by His own hand. They are not obvious analyses, synonymous expressions for what we know already, they are a new language with a real synthetic element which strikes us forcibly : " they go beyond the concept and even beyond the intuition of the Object, and add to that intuition as predicate something that is not a cognition."[1] As free productions of the human spirit, they have yet all the appearance of having been predestined.

This objective character of the Beautiful is seen most of all where we find the greatest freedom in aesthetic experience. Nothing is withdrawn of what has been said of the creative factor in Aesthetic, its complete subjectivity, its disregard of existential relations. The marvel in Aesthetic is that it can combine this freedom

[1] Bernard, § 36.

with a new objectivity, as independent and as factual as any given synthesis in Nature. The work of Genius, while it appears to be the facile play of capricious fancy, conceals a serious purpose of Understanding. The more we dwell upon it, the more it is found to embody a coherent unity of meaning. The numbers flow spontaneously from the lips of the poet, while every verse bears the stamp of perfect workmanship. A musical composition comes warm from the brain of Genius as the free creation of his mind, while its structure is conditioned by mathematical rules. As Kant says in a striking passage, "Taste, like the Judgment in general, is the discipline of Genius; it clips its wings, it makes it cultured and polished, it gives guidance as to where and how far it may extend itself if it is to remain purposive. And while it brings clearness and order into the multitude of the thoughts, it makes the Ideas susceptible of being permanently and, at the same time, universally assented to, and capable of being followed by others, and of an ever-progressive culture."[1] Imagination in its greatest freedom conforms to Understanding, for it is Productive Imagination, and this is just unconscious Understanding.

On the other hand, besides this synthetic element, a genuine *a priori* factor is discovered. The Beautiful appears as if it were the transparent analysis of a whole known to us already, for it conceals its art and looks like Nature : "Art can only be called beautiful if we are conscious of it as Art while yet it looks like Nature."[2] It is familiar without being obvious, new

[1] See Bernard, § 50. I have made a few slight omissions in quoting this passage.

[2] Bernard, § 45.

without being strange. The more we feel its influence, the more does it realise for us the inarticulate, shadowy, forms of our spirit which we have sought to express in vain. It is ourself, for we find ourselves reflected in it. It repeats itself without ceasing to lose its interest for us, because it was not made but always is. As Schiller says in his poem, *An die Freunde*, it is only what has never happened anywhere that never grows old:

> " Alles widerholt sich nur im Leben,
> Ewig jung ist nur die Phantasie;
> Was sich nie und nirgends hat begeben,
> Das allein veraltet nie."

The Beautiful is a real association of elements which yet has never anywhere come to pass in mechanical Nature. Can this *a priori* be justified?

Technically Kant's proof is very simple. What he calls the deduction, a term borrowed from jurisprudence, is little more than an appeal to what was already proved in the *Critique of Pure Reason*; it is the justification of synthetic judgments *a priori* in Aesthetic. In his analysis of Aesthetic, which practically contains all that he has to say in the special proof, he carries it back to the groundwork of cognition. This need not mean, as Basch seems to suppose, that Aesthetic can only acquire universality by becoming intellectual, when it ceases to be feeling altogether. Kant saw that knowledge "is the only kind of representation which is valid for everyone."[1] With a certain latitude of meaning, in the sense of language as articulate expression, this statement may be allowed to stand. But he also perceived that a community in representations implies a common mental disposition (*Gemüthszustand*) which is not itself

[1] Bernard, § 9, p. 64.

intellectual. This original disposition is the purposive activity of the same faculties as are at work in knowledge but without arriving at any particular determination; it is not knowledge but the transcendental, that is, the original and at the same time immanent, conditions which make knowledge possible, not representations but the mental powers themselves by which representations are produced; it is a kind of knowledge in general (*Erkenntniss überhaupt*). In this medium lies the peculiar function of the *Urteilskraft* or indeterminate Judgment. And Kant's argument is that if knowledge be a fact, this indeterminate mental process must be a fact too.

In the *Critique of Pure Reason* Kant showed that Imagination and Understanding, or the faculties of Sense and Thought, must be united in every act of perception. But in this case the faculties are compelled to unite in a fixed relation, for the associated elements which go to make up a perceived object must be reproduced in Imagination in a determinate order; otherwise we should lose consciousness of ourselves, our perceptions would have no necessity and would be the capricious play of mental images. Conceive now the faculties of knowledge delivered from this compulsion and united in a free relation. A mechanical illustration may be taken from the common steam-crane. By means of the contrivance called the clutch, the side cog-wheels can be detached from the main axle. And as these run in free play, still in conformity to mechanical law, it is true, but without arriving at any particular determination, so do the Powers, released from the serious business of Understanding, revolve at a higher rate of apperception. To use a phrase of Plato, our perceptions are no longer " bound by the tie of cause," and yet they do not walk away. This is quite a fair description of Kant's theory on its negative side. He thought that we are only aesthetically free when our minds are off the clutch, and the state of pure aesthetic contemplation, as he conceived it, hardly rises above the disinherited reflections of a person idling in his chair and twirling his thumbs. But meanwhile we are concerned with his general and more positive interpretation of the aesthetic state. This state is a fact because it is a necessary implicate in the most ordinary knowledge; it is "a procedure of the Judgment which it must also exercise on behalf of the commonest experience."[1] All knowledge is conditioned by purposive processes of indeterminate attention, of which we may be aware as a feeling of harmony. No doubt, in the great part of ordinary cognition, this feeling can hardly be said to exist at all. We experience no agreeable excitement in becoming aware that $2 + 2 = 4$. But "this pleasure has certainly been present at one time, and it is only because the commonest experience would be impossible without it, that it is gradually confounded with mere cognition and no longer arrests particular attention."[2] This original factor is most easily discovered when our knowledge is of a more primitive and genetic order. When we are not able to make up our minds about an object, our apprehension is of such a kind that it cannot be said to have a definite content, but what Dr. Stout has called an intent[3] or indeterminate content which specifies itself in tentative judgments. To this order of apprehension the forecasts of induction belong, whereby we seek to organise the contingent relations of material existence into the systematic unity of teleological judgments; and

[1] Bernard, p. 169. [2] Bernard, p. 28. [3] *Personal Idealism*, p. 9.

THE CRITICAL PHILOSOPHY

these are "the ground of a very marked pleasure, often even of an admiration."[1] But whenever a definite object emerges, the attention is shifted from the process to the object of thinking, the anticipative feeling of pleasure dies away, and the infinite possibility of choice is checked by a certain, determinate judgment which we are obliged to accept. The reflective, free spirit, ranging at large, must at length rest in a concept which is strictly limited by presentation. It is the double nature of Judgment that Kant has in view; it is both logical and psychological, a content or meaning and a process of thought. If we devote exclusive attention to the thought, the judgment is logical and our consciousness of the activity is suppressed; if we withdraw ourselves from the thought, the process of thinking comes into prominence, and then the judgment is psychological.

Now in Aesthetic it is not the object as the logical definition of a content that occupies us, but the way in which we are affected, or, more simply, it is not the object as it is perceived or thought but as it is felt. It is true, as we shall see later, that Kant does not succeed in providing a new significance peculiar to Aesthetic itself. And the general criticism that his theory is intellectual, is incontestable in so far as he appears to think that there can be no coherent meaning which is not expressed in logical definition. But it is a different matter, and, I think, quite unfair to say with Basch that Kant is interpreting Aesthetic as a form of knowledge (*c'est-à-dire un connaître*).[2] The subjective conditions of knowledge surely do not need to be themselves any kind of cognition. The significance of Kant's deduction is that if knowledge is an *a priori* function of

[1] Bernard, p. 28. [2] *L'Esthétique de Kant*, p. 181.

mind, this original disposition must also be universally communicable, and may be said to be a *sensus communis*. And in fairness to Kant, it ought to be said that in a decisive passage, such as that in which he discusses the delicate problem whether the pleasure precedes or follows, he is careful to use the specific term *Beurteilung* to denote the aesthetical judgment, a term which is synonymous with Mendelssohn's faculty of approval (*Billigungsvermögen*).[1] What calls for criticism, then, is not so much the aesthetical deduction itself as the original deduction in his theory of knowledge.

Probably there is no part of Kant's system which is so hard to interpret. The *Critique of Judgment* gives no adequate explanation of the aesthetic process, and we are left to conjecture what takes place from what we know of the mental procedure in cognition. The Play of the Powers (*Spiel der Kräfte*) seems the most natural conception in the world, but it is the most elusive and puzzling to anyone who has tried to understand Kant's theory of knowledge. The aesthetic powers of which he speaks in so prodigal a fashion are discovered to be simply the two cognitive faculties, Imagination and Understanding. Sometimes he practically reduces them to a single power, as when he speaks in a more concrete way of the Representative Powers (*Vorstellungsvermögen*), for this expression, which is needlessly suggestive of a plurality, indicates a special order of Imagination which includes the activity of Understanding. Perhaps we should avoid confusion by refusing at this stage to identify the cognitive faculties (*Erkenntnissvermögen*) with the mental powers themselves (*Gemüthskräfte*), of which they are only a specifica-

[1] Hartenstein, v. § 9, p. 222.

tion—as Cohen seems to do. Rightly regarding it as a defect of method on Kant's part that he should restrict the aesthetic powers to Imagination and Understanding, Cohen makes them co-extensive with the entire range of mental powers as the *Bewusstseinskräfte*, which is just another name for the *Gemüthskräfte*.[1] He evidently implies that the behaviour of the powers in Aesthetic is more catholic and objective than the limited and subjective direction which they receive in knowledge, in their specific form as the *Erkenntnissvermögen (vom gleichsam subjectiver Seite zusammengefasst)*.[2] This is indeed the intention in Kant's theory, as we hope to show. But if we straightway identify what are only faculties of knowledge with the mental powers themselves, we shall miss the point of his deduction.

In the *Critique of Pure Reason*, Imagination and Understanding are distinct forms of mental activity, the one being sensuous, the other conceptual. If knowledge is to be possible at all, there must be a mediating factor which is at once sensuous and conceptual. This is the transcendental Schema. In no other way can we understand how an abstract thought should represent an individual object. Kant's definition of the Schema as distinguished from an image is careful and acute. It can never appear as an image, and exists "nowhere but in thought."[3] Again, it is not an image but "the consciousness of a universal process of imagination, by which an image is provided for a conception." The distinctive nature of the Schema is seen most clearly in those representations where an image fails us. If we are to think of a very large

[1]*Kant's Begründung der Aesthetic*, p. 252.   [2]*Ibid.* p. 173.
[3] Watson, *Selections*, p. 86.

number—say, a thousand—we cannot have an image of a thousand points in succession, and our thought is rather of the method of counting. The Schema is this rule of procedure in Imagination. It is not even the most attenuated form of a generic image; it is the bare consciousness of possession.

Now I think it is misleading to say, without qualification, that this is simply psychology and has nothing to do with the problem of knowledge. It has everything to do with it. The criticism is certainly obvious that the process in which we come to apprehend, does not affect the metaphysical relation between our knowledge and an object. But Kant evidently intended the Schema to be a transcendental element, without which no knowledge would be possible. His general account of the Schema, indeed, is the denial of a psychological explanation. His observation that schemata and not images lie at the foundation of our pure sensuous conceptions, evidently announces the doctrine of Implicit Apprehension formulated by Dr. Stout.[1] When we are listening to a speech, we do not apprehend the meaning by the revival of distinct images corresponding to each word, but by a kind of divination which is no other than the transcendental Schema or dynamic faculty of representation. The Schema is of course not required when our apprehension is completely implicit and does not anticipate the tendency of our thought. But when we can be said to understand to any purpose, we are in a creative mood and our apprehension is schematic.

So far, then, Kant rules out psychology from the problem of knowledge; for the Schema, thus

[1] *Analytic Psychology*, vol. i. bk. i. chap. iv. Cp. Bergson, *Matter and Memory*, English Translation, p. 126.

understood, is not itself a process of consciousness but the governing consciousness of a process. But he failed to maintain this level and drifted into what looks very like psychology, because he assigned to the Schema an utterly false rôle as having a peculiar affinity for succession in time, and in consequence practically identified it with what is really a discursive process. It will be noticed that all his schemata are time-implications, as he expressly remarks: thus, the Schema of Quantity is number, "the idea of the successive addition of homogeneous unit to homogeneous unit"; even the Schema of Negation can only be thought as the gradual ascent from the vanishing-point to an increasing degree of continuous reality in time; the Schema of Substance "is the permanence of the real in time"; the Schema of Cause is "the real which is supposed never to exist without being followed by something else."[1] These are the chief, and in all of them temporal succession is said to be a necessary implicate, positive or negative. The simple insistence on time need not in itself excite serious criticism, for it might only mean that the discursive process which is initiated by the Schema, and not the Schema itself, is in time. But Kant meant to contrast schemata with the pure conceptual categories which are themselves inapplicable to experience, just in respect of this very feature of time-implication, and then he falls into confusion and talks of mysteries. The contrast which he really had before his mind was quite different. It was from mathematical conceptions exclusively that he originally drew his definition of a pure category. This definition he extended without warrant to abstract ideas

[1] Watson, *Selections*, pp. 88-9.

such as Substance, which are already genuine schemata but which Kant thought required a sensuous modification. The first transcendental discovery he made was the pure category as the conjunction of Understanding with the pure forms of intuition, particularly space.[1]

Now there is a very rigid distinction between these geometrical conceptions which only determine the formal aspect of experience, and the principles we apply to concrete experience. In Kant's own terms, the former are mathematical, the latter are dynamical, categories. A mathematical category contains the synthesis of its elements analytically, a given antecedent being the ground of its consequent; thus, in an equation of proportions, the fourth term may be inferred if the other three are known. But when we are dealing with actual changes in experience, which are not the timeless relations of geometry but real successions in time, our category is dynamical; because we cannot infer with mathematical precision what the required term will be, and can only state that there is such a term. Experience alone can tell what particular effect will follow a given antecedent. On the basis of this valid distinction, Kant should have recognised different orders of schemata which are distinguished by the nature of the objects to which they apply. But, instead of doing so, he contrasted schemata with pure conceptions, as figurative with purely intellectual forms of synthesis. Thus the pure conception of a plate would be "the pure geometrical conception of a circle," and he says that the empirical conception of a plate, or just its image, is homogeneous with this pure geometrical conception.[2] But in the

[1] See *Analytic*, bk. i. chap. ii. § 24; Meiklejohn, pp. 92-3.
[2] Watson, *Selections*, p. 84.

THE CRITICAL PHILOSOPHY 119

very next sentence he proceeds to say that a pure conception is quite heterogeneous from an empirical conception, and requires a mediating term before it can ever be realised in an individual perception. Evidently he has drifted away from his special discovery in transcendental philosophy, that there are conceptions which are immanent in sensuous experience, into Platonic Idealism. He has quite forgotten that the categories are already limited by the forms of sense and are not notions in general. He speaks as if the Schema for the first time imposed a limit on the pure conception, and favours the suggestion that these pure conceptions " hold true of things *as they really are*, while the schemata present them only *as they appear*."[1]

Let it be observed once more that a mathematical category, such as the pure conception of a circle, is the only pure category which is in question ; and if the image of a plate is already homogeneous with the pure conception, no schema is required. Kant was aware of this and he seems to have reasoned in the following way : I see that mathematical conceptions apply immediately to individual objects. Now the kind of experience to which dynamical categories apply, is quite different from mathematical objects. But if I can show that the mathematical and dynamical categories have something in common, namely, an essential implication of time, I can then assume that there are schemata corresponding to the dynamical categories, and which apply to actual changes in time with the same immediacy as mathematical conceptions apply to the logical relations of ground and consequent. Then events will be determined *a priori* in the relation of cause and

[1] Watson, *Selections*, p. 91.

effect with the same necessity as we find in mathematics.

But this is as false as it is needless. The schema of a geometrical figure has no peculiar connection with time. It certainly takes time to draw the figure on paper or even in thought, but this does not make the *a priori* intuition of the figure a time-relation, any more than the fact that it takes time to pass from the major premiss to the conclusion affects the timeless nature of the syllogism. Thus the category of Quantity has number for its schema, and Kant says that number manifestly implies succession in time. Certainly the process of enumeration is in time, but the schema itself is the feeling of number which is not a succession in time at all. M. Bergson gives a good illustration of the way in which number is felt as a quality rather than perceived as a quantitative succession. The bell of a neighbouring clock is sounding, but he has not noticed it until several strokes have sounded. Evidently he cannot be said to have counted the number of strokes, and yet he is able to infer from his sense of duration the exact number of strokes which he never heard. Suppose that four strokes had sounded before his attention was arrested; if he counts backwards to three strokes, he feels that there must be one more, because the total effect of three strokes is qualitatively different, like a kind of musical phrase, from his actual sense of duration.[1] The Schema precedes and conditions the consciousness of succession. In a communication to Goethe about the psychical origin of a drama, Schiller shows the difference between the schematic conception of a drama and the successive experience in which it is

[1] *Time and Free-Will*, pp. 127-8.

represented. "With me," he says, "the conception has at first no definite or clear object; this comes later. A certain musical state of mind precedes it, and this, in me, is only then followed by the poetic idea."[1] Ned Dennis, the hangman in *Barnaby Rudge*, had a pronounced schema for "working people off." No doubt this schema would be a tendency in consciousness towards varied activity in a specific direction, a procedure in imagination which is eminently suggestive of succession in time. But it was Ned and not his schema who wanted to be in time.

And this device is also unnecessary, because schemata do not need to be derived from pure conceptions. Among psychical elements, there are five possibilities open to our choice. We may have a full-blown image, a generic image, a verbal or other attenuated sign, a schema, or a pure conception. At once the most elemental and virile of these is the Schema, it is the nerve of thought. There remains to decide its relation to a pure conception. A conception may be of two kinds: first, it is completely empirical in origin, being an abstraction from particular images, and as an implicit form of apprehension it may or may not be attended by a generic image; secondly, it is an extinct schema which has lost its light like what are known as dark stars in the sky. I call it an extinct schema when it is a concept whose content is exhaustively specified, such as the concept of a cone; for the sections of a cone are demonstrated to be these and no others. The conception will be schematic to one who approaches the study for the first time, but for the practised mathematician it is a case of completely implicit apprehension or

[1] Schmitz, *Correspondence*, Letter 161.

automatic analysis. Such also would be the category of Causality, if it were true that this category completely specifies all the different causal connections in experience. But it remains a schematic conception because it does no such thing. It only announces the bare principle that every change must have a cause; what the particular cause or effect shall be, is in either case decided by experience alone.

From this it is evident that, in so far as the categories of Understanding are taken to be determinate principles which exhaustively specify the individual instances in experience, the proper place for schemata is not among the principles of Understanding but among the regulative Ideas of Reason. Kant gives a crucial instance of a conceptual category as distinguished from a schema : " substance, for instance, viewed apart from the sensuous determination of permanence, simply means, that which can be thought only as subject, never as the predicate of anything else. But such an idea has no meaning for us."[1] On the contrary, it may have a world of meaning for us. What lies at the root of the philosophy of the Upanishads, the Pure Being of Parmenides and the God of Spinoza, is the mystical schema of a subject which can never be the predicate of anything else. If there are such things as Platonic Ideas, it is because there are schemata, like the concept of the Beautiful, in the *Phaedo*, which generates what beautiful things there are. Platonic Ideas as they were interpreted by Realism are schemata whose original force is spent, without duration or change. But the fate of Platonism is the destiny which awaits the history of the human mind. With every increase of detail in the exact sciences, the possible range of

[1] Watson, *Selections*, p. 91.

presentations is further restricted, the content of our schemata is more and more exhaustively specified, until at last they lose their dynamical character and become fixed concepts. Our pure schemata are going the way of the dark stars, and what remains is little more than their reflex activity. In his Romanes Lecture of November, 1909, Mr. Balfour raised the interesting question why our aesthetic pleasure should diminish in intensity with age. Why should he have read sensational stories in his youth with a more vivid pleasure than the greatest works of Art can minister to-day? It is because our schemata are freezing before the mustering ranks of presentations which despoil them of their spontaneity. The mental life of youth is a presentational continuum with a conceptual background, the mental life of age is a conceptual continuum with a presentational background; in the former our thought is predominantly implicit and therefore schematic, in the latter explicit thought occupies the foreground and is decreasingly schematic. *Hinc illae lacrymae.* Thanks be to Pragmatism for helping us to regain possession of our wasting inheritance!

But Schematism, as Kant conceived it, is a constituent part of his system, and not less essential to his theory of Aesthetic than to his theory of knowledge. The difference between Aesthetic and Cognition is, that in the latter Imagination is reproductive but in the former productive. In its reproductive function the Imagination is subject to a fixed rule of Understanding, without which the associated elements would never constitute an object or necessary synthesis. But while in Aesthetic the Imagination is said to conform to Understanding in some mystical way, it is not subordinate to Understanding, and it would seem that its elements are not associated in any necessary order. There are thus within the same medium of Imagination two distinct orders of consciousness, the one the necessary consciousness of our own identity in systematic experience, the other a mystical kind of consciousness or Inner Sense, in which we are not properly conscious of our states, and can only be said to be aware of them. Perhaps it will seem strange to identify Productive Imagination with the fictitious faculty of Inner Sense, for the one is an active power and the other is expressly understood to be a passive receptivity. But where else are we to put it? Probably the fact is that what Kant at first called an Inner Sense, simply to maintain the parallel in his view of Psychology as co-ordinate with Physics, each having a receptive faculty and material of intuition given, he now introduces in its real character under the name Productive Imagination. And this would be natural enough, for the contents which are peculiar to mental life may at once be described as spontaneous products and as our affective states, as if they were modifications of an internal sensibility.

In the earlier part of his system, Kant would appear to favour the Cartesian position that the immediate data of consciousness are our own affective states, for in order to be objects of consciousness phenomena must be mental syntheses or objects in consciousness. But this is only half his position. His completed view stands opposed to the Cartesian doctrine that the knowledge of objects in space is an inference from the prior consciousness of ourselves. Rather it is the knowledge of our own states that is an abstraction from our consciousness of objects, as he shows in the second edition of the Deduction and in the Paralogisms. And he never succeeded in evading this abstract view of mental life, as the external reflection of consciousness upon a contingently associated manifold. It is surely what Plato calls a bastard kind of thinking that can be aware, without integrating the material of intuition into coherent unities. Probably Kant was never quite satisfied with this position. If we may infer the tendency of his thought from a passage in his Posthumous Work, he seems to have believed that the synthetic process by which objects are determined, does constitute a knowledge of ourselves as object.[1] But this is of merely historical importance. The consequences of Kant's doctrine of Inner sense are inevitable so long as we apply the same method to psychical events as to physical objects. If we are to look for the same kind of objectivity in both, it is obvious that our method will fail just where the criterion of permanence in physical objects is absent, namely, the qualification of space. The conclusion is inevitable, that "in the internal sense no permanent intuition is to be found."[2] But what right have we to suppose that mental states should conform to this criterion? Does not the distinctive circumstance that they are the states

---

[1] "Denn das Subject ist diesen Formen nach ihm selbst Sinnenobject. Das Subject, welches sich die Sinnenvorstellung von Raum und Zeit macht, ist ihm selbst in diesem Act zugleich Object." *Vom Übergange von den metaphysischen Anfangsgründen der Naturwissenschaft zur Physik*: herausg. von Albrecht Krause, p. 29.

[2] *General Remark on the Principles of Understanding*: Meiklejohn, p. 176. Cp. *Transcendental Aesthetic*, p. 30.

of a conscious subject, require a different method and a different kind of coherence? It is an unmeaning question to ask if we can be conscious of them when it is already of their essence that we should be conscious in them. Kant is right indeed when he urges that the source of the categories cannot itself be determined by the categories. But is it needful or even desirable that it should be? And still we are not reverting to the Cartesian position when we immediately identify our mental states with the primary fact of self-consciousness; for Kant's principle remains true that the consciousness *in* our states presupposes our consciousness of objects. To take the problem at its highest level, the world of Poetic Truth is indeed independent but has only a meaning in contrast with the world of Fact, and would not be possible apart from this basic implication.

What then are we to make of this lawless activity of Productive Imagination? Strictly understood, Kant has made no provision even for that primary synthesis of mental states which is necessary to the consciousness of our own identity. He felt that it would be a contradiction to say that the Imagination in its freedom is subject to the fixed procedure of Understanding, and proposes instead the evasive and mystical formula that it conforms to law without a law.[1] And yet even the most contingent vagary of fancy must be governed, within limits, by the determined sequence of fact. For example, I am chased by a bull in a dream and run away, when suddenly the chase stops and I turn round to confront a zinc-pail. But while the chase lasts, a kind of causality must be maintained. Must

[1] Bernard, § 22, pp. 96-7.

I not reproduce my steps in consciousness in order to keep up my own identity? There must be connection and coherence up to a certain point in our thinking even when it is not conditioned by actual presentation, though the kind of connection is certainly different from that which we find in the systematic knowledge of objects.

Now it is impossible to believe that Kant thought of psychical events as undetermined in time. However contingent the play of our affective states may be, they always presuppose the consciousness of an order which is not contingent and therefore the necessary consciousness of ourselves. And in his more sober moments, he would not countenance this unreal distinction in the procedure of Imagination. In the *Critique of Pure Reason* he presents it as a concrete faculty with a lower and a higher form of activity: "imagination can give a perception corresponding to the conceptions of Understanding, only under the subjective condition of time. Imagination therefore pertains to *sensibility*. At the same time its synthesis is the expression of spontaneous activity; for, unlike sense, imagination is not simply capable of being determined, but is itself determining."[1] In another passage he speaks of "the empirical faculty of productive imagination" as synonymous with Reproductive Imagination, and he even defines a schema as the product of pure *a priori* imagination.[2] Above all, we must not forget the supreme function of Productive Imagination in his theory of knowledge. As he says in the first edition, "there is thus in us an active faculty of the synthesis of this manifold, which we

[1] Watson, *Selections*, p. 77.   [2] Watson, *Selections*, p. 87.

call Imagination and whose immediate exercise in perception I call apprehension." And in a note to this passage, Kant practically claims to have been the first psychologist to discover that Imagination is an essential factor in perception. It had escaped the notice of former psychologists, partly because they restricted Imagination to reproductive activity, and partly because they believed that sense in its receptivity alone is able to unify impressions into objects, which is impossible in Kant's opinion without synthesis of Imagination.[1] Why then does he appear to make a qualitative difference in the *Critique of Judgment* between the Productive and Reproductive Imagination?

The answer is not far to seek. It is because determined succession in time was the only criterion by which he could identify the actual knowledge of objects as distinguished from cognition in general (*Erkenntniss überhaupt*). In the case of coexistence in space, which forms the subject of the First Analogy, it is quite clear that the consciousness of our own identity in time proves an objective order in our representations. If there were no such order, our successive perceptions would be discrete units without connection in consciousness. But Kant has undertaken to prove more than the permanence of a world coexistent in space, and it is not by any means clear what this proof has to do with Causality. If we wish to understand what Kant thinks of Causality, which is undoubtedly the *pons asinorum* in the Critical Philosophy, we had better set aside the proof in the Second Analogy. His normal view is contained in incidental passages scattered throughout the *Critique*, and is quite unpretentious.

[1] Hartenstein, iii. *Nachträge aus der ersten Ausgabe*, p. 579.

THE CRITICAL PHILOSOPHY 129

He is prepared to acknowledge with Hume, that by no analysis can we ever resolve a causal connection into the identical relation of Ground and Consequent.[1] It is a relation of fact which Reason cannot justify. But he went beyond Hume in asserting that the category of Causality must be *a priori*, because we could not be aware of qualitative change unless the events were so related that in apprehending them we could maintain the consciousness of our own identity.

This is a modest claim. There is an open appeal to experience. Let it be carefully observed that the fact of change is presupposed as given; and the proof consists in the principle that causal connection, though given independently in experience, is more than empirical, because it has some necessary connection with our consciousness of Time. Two passages may be cited in evidence: in the 'General Remark on the System of Principles,' the representation of motion in space is required as the intuition corresponding to the category of Causality;[2] and in the 'Critique of All Theology' it is said that the category becomes synthetic only in experience, and apart from experience has no significance at all.[3] This principle is not so gratuitous as it looks, and may be justified in the following way. In reply to the elementary question, How is knowledge possible at all? Kant showed that the conception of an ordered World is contained in the analysis of consciousness itself. The crowning feature of self-consciousness is the consciousness of Time, and this

[1] See his 'Attempt to introduce the Conception of Negative Quantities into Philosophy': Wallace's *Kant*, p. 127; Hart, ii. p. 104. Cp. Meiklejohn, p. 465.

[2] Meiklejohn, p. 176. [3] *Ibid.* p. 390.

implies a permanent background in Space. There must, then, be a transcendental ground of connection which conditions the entrance of sensations into consciousness. Obviously this transcendental ground need not imply causal connection. It only indicates the permanence of coexistence. The sole merit in the Second Analogy is the clear distinction drawn between a succession in our perceptions and a succession in the presentation itself. To take Kant's example, I have successive perceptions in perceiving a house, but this does not imply that the parts of the house apprehended are themselves successive. The true direction of Kant's argument in favour of Causality seems to start from this point. Over and above coexistence in Space, there are real sequences in Nature and not simply successions in our perceptions. In the first instance these are simple changes which do not call for a causal explanation, like the motion of a boat down a stream. This example is not an illustration of the special kind of connection to which Causality gives its name, and the same is true of Kant's other example, the successive perceptions of water in its liquid and its frozen state.[1] The position of the boat at any moment is not the cause of its position lower down; it is a simple succession of events. Now when we consider the absolute continuity of Space and therefore also of Time, these simple sequences may be run back as corollaries to the elementary proof for coexistence. However these changes may arise, they need not put us out of our reckoning, for they obviously suppose the permanence of coexistent elements in Space. Further, there are qualitative changes which come under

[1] Meiklejohn, p. 99; Hart, iii. p. 133.

the special relation of cause and effect. This is a particular conjunction of elements, in which the effect emerges as a quite different event from the cause—for example, a chemical transformation. But again we consider the continuity of Space and Time, and think it impossible that these conjunctions of events should stand in singular isolation from the simple sequences and coexistences which are only quantitative. Thus Causality will be run back to the argument from Self-Consciousness which proves the possibility of knowledge at all; and the conclusion will be, not that Change is unreal, being ultimately explained in terms of coexistence, but that every instance of sequence and all coexistence are due to a form of synthesis, which in the long run is similar in kind to that form of connection which we observe in Causality.

But in his official proof as it is contained in the Second Analogy, Kant steps beyond this reasonable position. The special significance of this proof for our discussion is its connection with Inner Sense. His argument now turns wholly upon Time, and Causality is defined as the law of invariable sequence in Time. In itself this may not appear to be different from the principle we have just considered. But observe the point of emphasis. While, in the former proof, Causality is represented as a corollary to the elementary act of cognition in coexistence, and has only hypothetical validity, being as much a regulative Idea of Reason as Organic Teleology, he now seems to discover a purely *a priori* criterion for Causality in the consciousness of Time, and which is quite independent of intuition in Space. He thus confuses two different propositions. We can say that an event can only form part of experience if it comes under the dynamical relation of cause and effect;[1] if it were wholly contingent as that which is preceded by non-existence, it would be something of which we cannot be aware. On the other hand, we might say that the simple consciousness of determined succession in Time is itself an indubitable evidence that our perceptions are events which stand to each other in the relation of cause and effect. Kant's conclusion may be described as an instance of the fallacy, 'illicit process': the consciousness of Time in the one case being only a factor in Causality, while in the other it contains Causality 'eminently.' Given the perception of change, we can then say that the events must stand in necessary relation, for otherwise we should not have been conscious of them. But it is a different proposition if we say that from the bare consciousness of Time we can anticipate the perception of change with *a priori* certitude. And this is Kant's conclusion in the Second Analogy.

Now the reason why the real prop in this argument, an intuition in Space, is only covertly acknowledged in the Analogies although it is explicitly stated in the following 'Remark on the Principles,'[2] is Kant's adherence to his doctrine of Inner Sense. He saw that the real difference between inner and outer objects is the form of space. But, in the Inner Sense itself, it was necessary for him to establish a difference among representations, apart altogether from the qualification of space; otherwise he should have to explain how there can be, in the same medium of Inner Sense or Time, two different kinds of content, the one realising itself in space-relations, the other being a mere play

[1] Meiklejohn, p. 478.   [2] Watson, p. 127; Meiklejohn, p. 176.

THE CRITICAL PHILOSOPHY

of representations in perpetual flux. While the contents of inner and outer Sense are held to be the same, as is maintained in the *Transcendental Aesthetic*,[1] no explanation would be necessary. But Inner Sense has a peculiar content of its own—thoughts, feelings and desires, which have nothing to do with position in Space and may never be realised in space-relations. As they are defined in the *Anthropology*, the contents of Inner Sense are affective states arising from the play of our thoughts (*Gedankenspiel*).[2] The difference can now be explained only by discovering a mark of distinction in the Inner Sense itself, and this mark Kant finds in determined succession. That is why he says with an air of finality, as if he wished to prove a point, that all schemata are "in some way relative to time."[3] We are to understand, then, that schemata, as principles of determined consciousness in Time, have no serious application to the peculiar contents of Inner Sense, and that consequently we have no coherent consciousness of them but only a vague awareness. Perhaps the clearest statement is contained in the section on 'The Application of the Categories to Objects of Sense.' The Inner Sense is always to be regarded as "the passive subject." When there is genuine synthesis, the internal sense is said to be affected by the transcendental act of Imagination "which I have named figurative synthesis," that is, the transcendental Schema. On the other hand, Inner Sense contains merely the form of intuition in the

[1] "In the internal intuition, the representation of the external senses constitutes the material with which the mind is occupied." Meiklejohn, p. 40.

[2] Hartenstein, vii. p. 473.   [3] Watson, *Selections*, p. 90.

empirical representation of Time as a continual flux, "without any synthetical conjunction of the manifold therein, and consequently does not contain any determined intuition."[1] What makes all the difference is the Schema. In the one case the Schema effects a synthesis; in the other, the Schema simply ignores the contents of Inner Sense, which therefore remain an undetermined succession in Time. There is thus no apperception of our affective states.

It might be urged in favour of Kant's impossible theory, that as the pure, analytic unity of apperception is not a fact of consciousness so much as a scientific ideal for knowledge, the incoherent consciousness of Inner Sense may also be regarded as the lower limit of synthetic unity in empirical science rather than as an existing mental state; for however clear to ourselves our affective states may be, they can never be defined with the precision of objects in space. But Inner Sense is too deeply embedded in Kant's philosophy to be dismissed so lightly. Since it was necessary to make the distinction within the Inner Sense, he inclined in the Second Analogy to suppress the appeal to space-intuition, and threw the whole weight of the proof on sequence in Time. It only remained to cover his traces by illegitimately consecrating the consciousness of determined succession in Time to causal connection, while to the other order of succession in Time he denies the authentic recognition of consciousness. Inner Sense is the surd in Kant's Epistemology.

We can now understand the hopeless position in which his theory of knowledge has placed him. It is

[1] Meiklejohn, p. 94.

not by any means clear how Aesthetic may be demonstrated by a simple appeal to the theory of knowledge. The doctrine of Schematism was the discovery of a radical difference in nature between two orders of mind : the Pure Understanding whose principles only contribute to a knowledge in general, and the Applied Understanding whose schemata can procure determinate knowledge of objects. And the cardinal feature of distinction between them is the implication of Time. On this basis he is able to maintain a boundary between the Reproductive and the free or Productive activity of Imagination ; and the inference is inevitable, that the Productive Imagination obtains its freedom in Aesthetic by forfeiting all implication of succession in Time.

This is a strange conclusion, but it is a fair inference from the confused ideas which Kant has thrown out. Whatever we may think of Kant's doctrine of Inner Sense, it is certain that our aesthetic states fall within the region over which this mysterious and sleeping partner of our consciousness presides, a region which corresponds exactly to what Spinoza[1] calls the 'Affects' and to Locke's ideas of Reflection. And while the Inner Sense is for Kant the very and only faculty of Time, it appears that the affective states peculiar to Inner Sense cannot be identified as elements in Time at all. Here we are left entirely to conjecture his meaning. A little light may gather if we carry into the region of Inner Sense, the distinction which he

---

[1] For the parallel with Spinoza, see the reference to the *Anthropology* just cited : " Der innere Sinn ist nicht die reine Apperception, ein Bewusstsein dessen, was der Mensch *thut*, denn dieses gehört zum Denkungsvermögen, sondern was er *leidet*." Hart, vii. p. 473.

applied to coexistence and succession in Space. Perhaps he thought of our affective states as reversible. What our Inner Sense observes as an external succession may only have psychological significance; the elements do not need to appear in that or any other order and may never recur again. In spite of the fact that they are the objects of a sense, they are nothing more than a conceptual play (*Gedankenspiel*). There is a certain amount of truth in this, which no one will deny. The connection of ideas in a dream or meditation is certainly not the same as what we find in objects of Nature; even our artistic impressions are variable, and may never recur to us again in the same order of association. But whatever the difference be, it does not lie where Kant has placed it. He believed that schemata, or, more simply, our principles of thought, only realise significance when they are supplied with sensations, or, what is the same thing, when the contents of inner and outer sense are the same; with the solitary exception of a moral event, he regards nothing in the nature of a fact which does not resonate against the sounding-board of Space. But these floating images are not secondary affections of our Self in its passivity, produced by the friction of apprehended facts; they come to us unbidden with all the force of the actual, and are as objective and outside of us as stones and rocks or the motion of a train. The birth of a poem is as actual as a splash of colour or a fall over a precipice. Indeed they are more aggressive and independent of our control than the objects of sense, for we can escape from these by suspending our perception; we can shut our eyes and think away a world. But if I am possessed of an idea, whither shall I flee?

What is remarkable, however, in the Critical Philosophy is that it provides an antidote, like the bark of the cinchona tree, in the immediate vicinity of its infected areas. Already in the Second Analogy we find the corrective to this false theory of our affective states. Kant has a double view of Time. On the one hand, there is the empirical representation as a succession of continual changes, and this, in Kant's later opinion, is the only perception of Time which we can have. On the other hand, there is an absolute Time which "remains and changes not," a permanent substrate. If we did not postulate this absolute Time as what is not itself affected by succession and change, we should have to think of another Time in which this Time came to be, and still another Time and another unto infinity. Therefore all succession and coexistence are only so many modes or determinations in absolute Time. Here Kant breaks with his early view in the *Transcendental Aesthetic*, that Time is a whole of perception corresponding to the perception of an empty Space; for he repeatedly asserts in the Analogies that "Time in itself cannot be an object of perception." But his position has not really changed. What he renounces in his earlier view is the perception of Time as a quantitative whole of which the successive times are limitations; otherwise he contends, as in the Analogies, for an original consciousness of Time as "unlimited" or absolute, and this Time "does not change."[1] The Time, then, which we perceive always under the form of representation in Space, is only appearance; the real in Time is not thus perceived but felt as the consciousness of absolute duration. This is the distinction

[1] Watson, *Selections*, pp. 30 and 36.

within the Inner Sense which Kant ought to have made, and not the unreal opposition of determined succession and an anomalous succession which is no succession, in which we cannot have authentic consciousness of ourselves. This absolute duration, and not the spurious flux of Inner Sense, which is conceptual rather than sensuous, is the medium of Productive Imagination. In it alone does true Time exist, while determined succession is a phenomenal translation of Time into the language of Space, and never is but always is to be. Kant is right in saying that we do not and cannot perceive real Time in this sense, for, like the musical state of which Schiller tells us, it is felt before it is noticed.

And now, when we turn to the *Critique of Judgment*, we find that the factors which Kant employs in Aesthetic are not a timeless Imagination and a disinherited Understanding, but these faculties as they exist in their most concrete form. What does a faculty of representation in general, as ·distinguished from particular representations, mean if not a schema? The whole point in the conception of a schema is the distinction between discursive processes and the intuitive or dynamic element which cannot itself be representation. It is schemata that are at play in Aesthetic, and these schemata exist in the medium of qualitative Time whose faculty is Feeling. Thus all the forms of human activity, in science or in conduct, may be regarded as the raw fibre of Aesthetic. Their schemata foregather on the common ground of elemental play; like the Gods of Greece, their foreheads are smooth, clear of the furrows of toil and serious care, knowing neither the compulsion of external force nor the constraint of moral laws. There are a few passages which can bear this schematic interpretation of Aesthetic. It is said that the Imagination "schematises without any concept."[1] More explicit is the passage where Kant speaks of aesthetic pleasure as involving causality: "*maintaining* without further design the state of the representation itself and the occupation of the cognitive powers." We are able to "*linger* over the contemplation of the Beautiful, because this contemplation strengthens and reproduces itself."[2] But Kant has no real title to this interpretation unless he revise his doctrine of Inner Sense. He believed that schemata do not seriously affect the contents of Inner Sense because he misconceived the function of schemata, and regarded the ambiguous product as merely ideal. But it would be quite as true, perhaps more true, to say that the determinate perception of objects in space is merely actual. Since he denies objective reality to what he calls the mere contents in time, it follows that there can be no science of Psychology. And this is true, if it be meant that it has no objects corresponding to those in Physical Science. But if there be no science of Psychology, neither can there be a theory of Aesthetic; for the objects of Aesthetic, according to his first canon, have no ingredients of cognition, are not supported by the form of Space as such, and exist exclusively in Imagination. And it is not only Kant who says so. No sound aesthetic theory will deny at least this difference between perception and aesthetic intuition, that in the latter the objects of perception are sympathetically interpreted: our cold scientific interest gives way to personal interest; we confer our emotions and life upon objects, until finally

[1] Bernard, § 35, 1-4.   [2] Bernard, § 12. Cp. p. 197.

we are able to ignore their symbolic character and persuade ourselves into the belief that they are impersonations of ourselves. This is entirely the work of Imagination. The objects presented to us, whether they are in Space or only arise within our own minds, are the materials of this supposed Inner Sense. They are, moreover, objective syntheses as factual as anything in Nature, although they are not Nature. They have for us the significance of objects; they have more meaning for us than objects in Space.

CHAPTER V.

ANCIENT AND MODERN—THE THIRD CANON.

KANT's doctrine of Inner Sense was favourable to the eighteenth-century theory of Freedom, which affected his whole philosophy. On the other hand, he had a genuine, if fugitive, insight into the positive expression of Freedom, although he refused to recognise it in the life and works of his contemporaries. This opposition is most sharply announced in his Third Canon. It says that the Beautiful is the representation of a purpose without a purpose.[1] In itself this canon is little more than a repetition of the first and second; for it excludes an interest, and it might also be taken as synonymous with the formula in the second, that the aesthetic state is conformity to law without a law. But it was convenient and even necessary that Kant should bring it forward, as indicating a further stage in the proof. The universality of Aesthetic was based upon the conditions of knowledge; and it is hard to forget that knowledge in any form, however undetermined, is still a modification of cognitive processes, employs concepts, observes relations among elements, and has a final end in view. He must therefore insist in yet another canon, that Aesthetic has the universality of knowledge without being knowledge, or that it is a

[1] Bernard, §§ 10-17.

purposive (*zweckmässig*) activity without intending any purpose at all. This completes the argument. Obviously this moment in the Beautiful is capable of a double interpretation. It may be understood in the sense of implicit intention or as the absence of intention altogether. It is not difficult to decide which of those views Kant really entertained. His negative conception is in great part theoretical, and, as in the proof for Causality, his true position is obscured by his illustrations. A superficial reading of eighteenth-century literature is sufficient to understand this opposition in Kant's mind.

The eighteenth century is known in European Literature as the Age of the Individual. The quantity of autobiographies, for which Rousseau had set the fashion in his *Confessions*, and the dislike of all corporations and guilds, in which individual freedom is hampered by the collective will, are characteristic of the spirit of the age.[1] The lifeless orthodoxy into which the Reformation had hardened, enslaved both mind and conscience, and it was in emancipating the individual from dogmatic authority that the *Aufklärung* had its first significance. An enlightened Pietism revolted against a form of religion, whose votaries, in some instances, sought to accentuate the supremacy of faith over works by making a parade of loose living.[2] As Paulsen says in his *Life of Kant*, Pietism was Luther rising up against Lutheranism. And it should be remembered that, however defective Rationalism may have been in Germany, it made common cause with Pietism, and was thus distinguished from the materialistic phase of the movement in France by an earnest moral theory, although it did not go very deep. But while it was undoubtedly

[1] Erdmann, *Hist. Phil.* ii. pp. 284-5.   [2] *Ibid.* p. 288.

an age of Humanism, it was old before its time. It was the Humanism of the Renaissance without its youthful vigour. It glorified the individual and made his happiness the chief end of existence, but it was the indifferent individual of abstract thinking, not the historic individual of Rousseau, Lessing and Kant. The Humanism of the eighteenth century only simplified the achievements of a former enlightenment, it did not interpret them with a deeper significance. It was the momentary appearance of the mild light of Mediaevalism which had lived secure on the treasures of past ages, and the same degenerating tendencies which characterised mediaeval times now threatened to corrupt German life. It was not the healthy enthusiasm which attends every re-birth of the human spirit, as it is challenged by the wealth of conquests to be won; it was the much less worthy, though more pleasing, Humanism of the spirit tolerating itself. It was comprehensive and ambitious at the cost of being shallow and pretentious.

We are not surprised, then, to find this movement offending in the very faults which it sought to amend. A false conception of human brotherhood, in the vague latitude of an indiscriminate, cosmopolitan culture, preceded the birth of a national spirit which alone is able to justify the cultivation of cosmopolitan feeling. To become citizens of the world, we must first be true citizens of the city in which we were born. Now Germany did not awake to the consciousness of her national unity until the year 1806, when at the decisive battle of Jena the Prussian forces were routed by Napoleon. She still cherished the idea of the Holy Roman Empire; but while each separate principality was governed by its autocratic prince, supported by his unscrupulous minister and all-powerful favourite, no national conscience could exist. The want of a national spirit is nowhere illustrated so clearly as in the person of Frederick the Great, himself the incarnation of Enlightenment. He hated his own language and would hear of nothing but French literary models, which all ran on the traditional lines; and by withholding his encouragement, he all but stifled the first beginnings of the German Drama. But a very curious phase in this cult of Reason is the exercise of authority which qualified the supposed indulgence of illimitable freedom. It is recorded of Frederick that he threatened to dismiss one of his officials if he should refuse to visit the theatre. And in his famous dictum that the King is the first servant of the State, we may readily believe that the accent was placed on *premier* rather than on *domestique*.[1]

These are characteristic indications that the boasted emancipation of Reason was an ill-concealed dogmatism. The philosophy of Wolff which gave intellectual expression to the spirit of the age, undertook to demonstrate, by the cogency of Reason alone, the existence of everything from God down to municipal regulations; and wherever this facile solvent failed, the law of identity was replaced by the dogmatic assertion that it was the best possible which God could have made, and there was an end of the matter. Like every imperfect phase of development, the age was marked by a double and contradictory character in its strange fascination for logical consistency and inconsequent freedom. The individual of the eighteenth century, unfed on the riches of Nature, at length grew dizzy on an empty stomach with the whirling revolutions of his reasoning

[1] Erdmann, *Hist. Phil.* ii. pp. 301-2.

processes, and, losing his vaunted self-control, showed his true nature in the irresponsible freedom of the French Revolution, which sought its demonstration in blood, not in syllogism. The individual, which it took for its ideal, was little more than the wraith of the lusty individual which came to life at the Renaissance. In spite of national differences the broad principles of Enlightenment are the same, whether we look to the Deistic School in England, to Voltaire and the Encyclopaedists in France or to the Rationalism of Wolff in Germany. The solutions by which it offered to explain all things in heaven and on earth, were far too simple to be true. Life was represented as being much more easy than it is actually, and an unreal optimism lent a false glow to the darkest problems of existence. In his little essay on the question 'What is Enlightenment?' Kant had gauged the situation correctly : if it be asked whether we are now living in an enlightened age, the answer is, "No, but in an age of Enlightenment."[1]

It was against this complacent criticism of life that the Age of Genius, inaugurated by Schiller and Goethe, rebelled. The last quarter of the eighteenth century leaves a confused impression on the mind which it is difficult to analyse with clearness. Probably this counter movement is best described as a revolution within a revolution. Historically judged, and in spite of its reactionary appearance, it was a further development of the Era of Enlightenment. The latter had preached liberty of conscience, political freedom, happiness in time and eternity; but society was not reformed. To this reactionary criticism Kant had made the most permanent contribution in his monumental works. Fichte,

[1] Hartenstein, iv. p. 166.

following on his lines, required that the particular should be reinforced by the universal. But the universalised particular may be as abstract as the particular itself. It was Schiller who first grasped the philosophical significance of the *Aufklärung*, and up to the last his romantic ideas were restrained by a lingering conservatism. In the individual of Rationalism he saw at least the type of true freedom, the ideal of the Greek; and while he acknowledged a qualified allegiance to Kant's moralism, the early influence of Shaftesbury, who echoed the ethical optimism of the *Aufklärung* in the union of virtue and happiness, had made a more favourable impression on his mind. The regeneration of the individual, through the aesthetical harmony of Sense and Reason, is for him the final end of culture.

In the mad pranks enacted by the 'Storm and Stress' party under Goethe's revolutionary influence at Weimar, Schiller took no part. With the sanction of their genial patron, the Duke Karl August, court etiquette and dress were disregarded: blue-coat, yellow waistcoat and high boots were affected; long walks into the country, perilous rides, skating-parties at night and dances in the country with peasant maidens, formed part of their programme.[1] Goethe did not like to look back on these early days of boisterous exuberance, and it soon sobered down into serious devotion to classic form. Now, what grated on Kant's puritanic sense was the literary and romantic affectation which followed in its wake, such as anacreontic odes and the night-singers. In the closing decades of the century, a sentimental cult was in vogue which took the form of excursions into the country, in

---

[1] Scherer's *History of German Literature*: translated by Mrs. F. C. Conybeare, vol. ii. p. 145.

THE CRITICAL PHILOSOPHY

feeble imitation of Saussure's travels in the Alps, an account of which first appeared in 1779 and for which Kant professed the highest admiration.[1] Another, and perhaps the more immediate source of inspiration, was Sterne's *Sentimental Journey*. In what is an evident allusion to this movement Schiller says in so many words, that this sentimental taste is not by any means the same as a love of Nature for her own sake.[2] And, so far, Kant was justified when he reproached his contemporaries with trifling and wantonness: "our age is the century of pretty nothings, bagatelles or sublime chimeras."[3] He found the true standard of Taste among the ancients alone, for they were nearer to Nature.

This was a criticism, moreover, which Schiller candidly acknowledged. While his aesthetical education of Man has the forward view, it has also, from another side, a retrospective aspect. The regeneration of humanity is the becoming again what it was, a return to Nature as she was known to the childhood of the race. In his 'Naïve and Sentimental Poetry,' he contrasts Goethe as naïve with himself as sentimental poet. The difference between the two orders of poets is this. In Goethe's Olympian nature Schiller saw one for whom the Ideal was already actual, and in this naïve character he resembled the Greeks; for the divine Ideal with them was no remote conception but an embodiment in individual form. In a very fine passage, he describes this perfect

[1] Bernard, § 29.

[2] *Über naive und sentimentalische Dichtung.* *Sämmtliche Werke* (1836), xii. p. 200.

[3] *Fragmente aus dem Nachlasse.* Kirchmann, *Vermischte Schriften*, p. 331.

union of Grace or humanity with Dignity or deity in the Greek statues: " with softened splendour the Freedom of Reason rises in the smiling mouth, the gently animated glance, the serene brow, and, sublime in its setting, Natural Necessity subsides in the noble majesty of countenance. On this ideal of human beauty are the antique statues modelled, and one recognises it in the divine form of a Niobe, in the Apollo Belvedere, in the winged genius of the Villa Borghese and in the muse of the Palazzo Barberini."[1] But while the naïve is already natural, the sentimental poet strives to become natural by realising the Ideal. It is the difference, conceived in an abstract manner, between Hellenic and Romantic art. Schiller naturally wavers between these conceptions of the Ideal, in a way which corresponds somewhat to the vacillating movement between aestheticism and moralism, throughout his poetry and prose. In his poem *The Pilgrim*, the only possible conception of the Ideal is the sentimental; for the heavenly goal recedes ever and ever farther from the pilgrim who embarks on the rolling sea of life, in search of the Ideal. In *The Ideal and Life* published in the *Horen* the same year as *Naïve and Sentimental Poetry*, 1795, he recognises the naïve conception; for beside the world of pure spirit there is the Olympic world of Beauty which exists within the sense-world as the mirror of man's perfection.

But Schiller does not mean by this contrast that Nature was known to the Greeks alone. On the contrary, it could be said with equal truth that they never knew Nature at all. In either case Nature has a

[1] *Über Anmuth und Würde. Sämmtliche Werke*, xi. (1836), p. 457. This translation was revised by Prof. Hoernlé.

different sense, and the conclusion of his argument is to co-ordinate the naïve or Hellenic, and sentimental or Romantic, attitudes to Nature as complementary. Thus, arguing from the other side, and this time in defence of the Greek conception, we find him saying in a letter to Goethe, that the distinction between characteristic and formal Beauty is only logical; and he thinks that the absence of characteristic expression in the Greek conception of Beauty has been overstated by critics. In his opinion Aesthetic is at once the serious pursuit and the serene, unthinking possession of the Ideal,[1] or, to adopt the words of the adage, Art is at once *ernst* and *heiter*. What, then, is the difference? Why, he asks, are we so different from the Greeks? They describe Nature as they would a mechanical product or any work of technical art; they have no sentimental feeling for Nature, while we worship Nature. The answer is that the Greeks worshipped the human form, but Nature was in the human form for the Greeks as it is not for us; and they had no eyes for unconscious Nature, only because their connection with her was so close as to admit of no intermediary reflection. It was not Nature in her passivity that they saw, but Nature as animated by the very human form they worshipped, in the shape of Nymphs, Naiads, Satyrs and Fauns. For us, Nature has disappeared from Humanity and we must seek her again in the unconscious world.[2]

But Kant had no proper understanding of this contrast between ancient and modern, as Schiller saw it. While he professed veneration for the ancients as

[1] Schmitz, *Correspondence*, Letter 342, vol. i. p. 378.
[2] *Über naive und sentimentalische Dichtung*. *Sämmtliche Werke*, xii. (1836), p. 222.

having been nearer to Nature, there is no evidence in his writings of appreciation of Homer or of the sublimity of Hebrew Poetry, the two great models of antiquity. In the early struggle of his countrymen towards a national literature, he failed to distinguish the substance from the shadow. It should have been enough for him, one would think, that in the Age of Genius the dissolving criticism of Voltaire had been exchanged for the naturalism of Rousseau, and that, in the love of Nature for her own sake, man might regain the naïve conception of his humanity which he had lost. These, then, were the alternatives presented to Kant's choice. The rationalistic and romantic conceptions of Freedom were both untempered and irresponsible, but in very different ways. The ebullition of the *Sturm und Drang* was a genuine renaissance of the human spirit ; as the first phase of a constructive movement, its extravagant expression had an implicit intention. But the *Aufklärung* was the passing of the human spirit through a destructive moment ; its conception of Freedom was contingent, and by a natural transition pretentious Reason completed its course in the passional abandon of the French Revolution. Yet it was in the latter of these that Kant sought the type of aesthetic freedom.

Consequently, the exposition of his third canon turns on a sharp distinction between Free and Dependent Beauty (*pulchritudo vaga* and *pulchritudo adhaerens*). In the Dependent type of Beauty Kant has in view the confused representation of perfection, which was received in the Wolffian School as the definition of the Beautiful. It is the Beauty of whatever exhibits intention, external or internal. All objects of industrial Art, and Kant

THE CRITICAL PHILOSOPHY 151

would include Beautiful Art, may have this kind of Beauty. In these the intention is external, it is wrought into them, and their Beauty will consist in the relative perfection with which they embody this imported purpose. There are also objects which have an internal purpose, namely, the products of organic Nature; plants, animals and, highest of all, man, realise the idea of their kind, and are judged aesthetically in the degree that they approximate to the generic idea. Thus a flower, although it is Kant's stock example of Free or Independent Beauty, may from another side be taken as Dependent, when it is the object of intellectual satisfaction to a botanist who knows its history and structure and can appreciate how far it fulfils the idea of its kind. The judgment of the botanist is teleological, and whatever Beauty he sees in the flower is mixed with intellectual ideas; it is therefore said to be impure or dependent because it is not inherent but adherent. This relative perfection Kant calls the Normal Idea; it is the generic image such as is obtained by stereoscopic observation or by Galton's process of generalised photography.

But he goes a step further. It seems that in the earlier editions of the *Critique of Judgment*[1] he considered the Normal Idea as the highest type of Dependent Beauty. Now, however, he sees that it is quite inadequate and only provides the necessary conditions for realising the highest perfection. It is so far indispensable that when the expression is extravagant and does violence to the Normal Idea, it becomes caricature. But when individual character is suppressed in favour of generic purity, the product is a lifeless abstraction which contains "nothing specifically characteristic," and is "merely

[1] Bosanquet, *Hist. Aesthetic*, p. 272.

correct."[1] The Ideal must have individual expression, it must be an individual plant, an individual animal, an individual man. Now the individual which most perfectly embodies the idea of its kind is the Ideal. This and not the Normal Idea is the highest type of Dependent Beauty.

Kant restricts the Ideal to the human species because it alone is capable of moral expression. He means that Man is the only being who contains the end of his existence in himself, or to put it in another way, Personality is the only instance of a real individual. This conception of the Ideal is the key to Kant's Teleology of Nature. It implies that all the categories which fall below Self-consciousness, including those of Biology, are only reflective predicates which are due to the dialectical nature of our Understanding; they are descriptions of objects which have no supersensible substrate, and consequently their purposive activity is not the expression of a nature in the objects themselves but only an appearance for us. Thus the Ideal of a flower is inconceivable for Kant, and Myron's Cow is not an Ideal because it has not a moral expression.[2] We have to remember, however, that, as the highest form of the Dependent type, the Ideal loses in aesthetic quality as it gains in significance. It may be said to be at two removes from Pure Beauty, for it is informed by a moral as well as an intellectual purpose. It is now easy to understand what Free Beauty means: it is the representation which is neither normal nor ideal, being completely void of all intention, intellectual, moral, or both together. Such are the meaningless symmetries of decorative art, arabesques and fanciful embroideries

[1] Bernard, § 17, p. 89.   [2] Bernard, pp. 86-9.

which are only made to please, and purposeless formations like flowers and crystals.[1] Even geometrical figures are excluded because they presuppose an intellectual purpose. The Beauty of a representation is only pure when it is unconditionally free. Even the thought of a purpose must not enter into our judgment. As an extreme instance, Kant mentions stone implements which are found in old sepulchral tumuli, with a hole in them as if for a handle. The purpose of these implements is quite unknown to us, but they are not therefore beautiful, for we know very well that they were originally made for a certain use.[2] Similarly in a work of Art, our aesthetical judgment is hampered by the intention of the artist; and Kant thinks that if our judgment is to be pure, we must be able to abstract from the intention altogether and confine our contemplation to the mere appearance.

This principle is plausible and might be accepted as a useful test in settling disputes on Taste: it could be pointed out, in a case of disagreement, that for one person the Beauty consists in the mere act of contemplation, while the other person tries to understand what the artist sought to convey; and it might happen that he could criticise the former's taste on the ground that he was applauding a work of Art, in which, however well executed, the intention was poor or even improbable. But it is precisely this opposition in judgment which is not admitted in a true theory of Aesthetic. The fault in Kant's principle consists in making a dispute possible where there ought to be none. If, as we say, the conception in a work of Art is poor or impossible, nothing in the execution

[1] Bernard, pp. 81, 211. [2] Bernard, p. 90, note.

can make up for this defect. It will remain a body without a soul, and whatever pleasure it may minister to us is only what arises from the resemblance in an imitation; possibly it may have less aesthetic quality than a well-made hoe.

On the other hand, we must not be deceived into thinking that a work of Art is meaningless because the intention is too vague to be grasped. When we speak of the conception we do not mean that the intention ought to be capable of definition, but that the work has an artistic motive and is really the expression of a significant state of mind, though it may be less understood by the artist himself than by the critic. If what is nothing but a study in colour is successful, it is not by any means the empty representation of symmetry in visual sensations, for colour like music is spiritual expression. In so far as I am able to understand Meredith's meaning in his *Hymn to Colour*, it is a metamorphosis of Love which, in this shape, becomes bridegroom to the Soul and opens her eyes to the truth of things. Life and Death are substantial forms only because we see in them, not Love, but our "craving self": in the language of Spinoza, they are born of desire, or as Schopenhauer would say, they are representations due to the pragmatic will. But in the presence of approaching Love, Life and Death, which walk with the Soul on either side, are made to seem as shadows, forms of light which borrow from each other tints and shades of colour:

"Death begs of Life his blush; Life Death persuades
To keep long day with his caresses graced."

And thus these two substantial forms are seen to be nothing more than the abstract factors which make

THE CRITICAL PHILOSOPHY 155

up the variety of existence, as it is expressed in colour. So much may colour mean:

" he leads
Through widening chambers of surprise to where
Throbs rapture near an end that aye recedes,
Because his touch is infinite and lends
  A yonder to all ends." [1]

A successful study in colour alone is the expression of an artistic state which may have its roots as deep as Life and Death where they meet. However unconscious the artist may have been of any such intention, the spiritual meaning will nevertheless glow in his work, and whoever does not see some glimpse of it there is not entitled to pass an aesthetical judgment on the matter.

It is interesting to notice that Kant had a very different opinion in his lectures on Aesthetic. There he says at least three times over, that you cannot tell whether a thing is beautiful until you know what it is for, that the Beautiful cannot be demonstrated *a priori*, and that the idea of the thing as it is found in experience must always be presupposed.[2] In reading these remains, one naturally finds that Kant is comparatively free from methodological caution in delivering

[1] *Poems*, vol. ii. *A Reading of Earth.*

[2] " Wir können eine Sache nicht eher für schön halten, als bis wir wissen, was es für eine Sache sei, und was da schön sein soll. Anthropology 1779. Ohne die mindeste Beziehung auf Nutzen können wir keine Schönheit finden, wenigstens 'darf sie ihm nicht widerstreiten. Anthropology 1784. Ob etwas schön sei, lässt sich nicht vordemonstrieren. Es ist blos durch die Erfahrung zu erkennen. A priori würde er das Schöne als solches nicht gelten lassen. Anthropology 1791." Schlapp's *Kant's Lehre vom Genie u.s.w.* pp. 201, 281, 393.

his opinions; and this seems to be true even of the time after the *Critique of Judgment* was published, as may be seen from the date of the last quotation in the note. It clearly shows that, whenever he sat down to systematic exposition, his mind was overdriven and misdirected by theoretical exactions. And when we consider his moral disposition, we have no difficulty in understanding why he should have chosen the Rationalistic rather than the Romantic type of Freedom. He could hardly rejoice in the legal Freedom of Reason. But human nature must enjoy something, and his aesthetic theory looks as if it were prompted by the revenge of violated Sense on unsympathetic Reason. Since Reason in her freedom was so prudish, it was inevitable that Sense, secured by no weightier influence than a nominal conformity to Law, should become nonsense. Notwithstanding his anxiety to exclude all that savours of Sense, his aesthetic theory becomes in fact the formula for decadence. A theory of Art which professes to have no content, which sacrifices meaning to the cultivation of refined sensations, is, in the long run indistinguishable from vice.

This was in substance Schiller's criticism, perhaps the most penetrating judgment ever passed upon Enlightenment, and it is a criticism which has lost nothing of its force when applied to the downward movements in subsequent literature. He saw that the unsanctioned freedom of the individual did not seek to realise the true infinite of Reason, was not even conscious of its presence, but readily confused it with the specious indeterminate of sense-affection. What the individual pursues is not the infinite but an infinite finite, an unlimited extension of his individuality, an inexhaustible

THE CRITICAL PHILOSOPHY 157

material instead of form, an eternally during mutation instead of the immutable and the absolute security of his temporal being: "while the infinite dawns upon his dazzled imagination, his heart has not yet ceased to live in the partial and to serve the present moment." Incapable of abandoning his individuality to meet the demands of Reason, he lets fall his eyes on something in his sensuous nature which nearly resembles the uncaused causality of Reason, the law of his members which knows no law; and since he cannot lay the questioning intellect to rest by discovering a final motive within himself, he at least brings it to silence through the idea of causelessness.[1]

But Kant has saved his theory from this disastrous consequence by a special application of his first principle, that no ingredients of sensation shall be admitted into Aesthetic. This restriction is now introduced with particular reference to the two forms of sense-affection, Charm and Emotion. So much has been already conceded to this insatiable phantom of negative Freedom, that it is hard to think what remains. The precious toil of science and the ennobling discipline of morality, can contribute nothing of their treasures; and it would seem that even Sense, the aether Beauty breathes, is sacrificed. The reason for his strictures on Charm (*Reiz*) is characteristic. The charm of Sense is empirical and therefore cannot be assimilated to what must be an *a priori* activity of mind. This is a good instance of Kant's weakness for the *a priori*, and is a consequence of his doctrine of Sensation. In the concrete act of perception (*Wahrnehmung*)

[1] *Aesthetical Education of Man*, Letter 24. *Sämmtliche Werke*, xii. (1836), Weiss's translation, pp. 145-7.

there are two factors: the constant forms of intuition (*Anschauung*), Space and Time, and the variable (*Empfindung*). There is thus a constant factor in perception, which Kant ultimately believes to be produced by the synthetic activity of mind; this is how it is stated in the first edition of the Transcendental Deduction: "Now this synthesis of apprehension must be exercised *a priori* also, I mean for the sake of representations which are not empirical. For without this synthesis, we should not be able to have *a priori* representations either of Space or of Time, for these can only arise through the synthesis of the manifold, which is offered by sensibility in its original receptivity."[1] But the variable in perception is empirical, and is not accountable to our minds for its coming and going: at the most we can have 'anticipations' of its behaviour; we know *a priori* that it will have some degree of intensity, but what degree it will have, and that it should enter into perception at all, is outwith the jurisdiction of the mind. It is this specifically empirical element that Kant excludes from Aesthetic under the name of Charm.

His criticism, however, is not indiscriminate. Up to a certain point it is the commonplace observation, that Beauty is not enhanced but spoilt by the excrescences of barbaric taste.[2] An ornamental sword which is not serviceable in the field, is less beautiful than a plain but well-made sword which is perfectly adapted for use. When Aristippus asked Socrates if a dung-basket can be beautiful, he replied: "Yes, by Jupiter, and a golden shield may be an ugly thing, if the one be beautifully formed for its particular uses, and the other ill-formed."[3]

---

[1] Hartenstein, iii. p. 568, *Nachträge aus der ersten Ausgabe.*
[2] Bernard, § 13. [3] *Xen. Mem.* iii. 8. 6, Bohn.

THE CRITICAL PHILOSOPHY 159

But Kant's strictures go much deeper. He reverts to his original distinction between aesthetical judgments of Sense and aesthetical judgments of Reflexion, or, more simply, the distinction between matter and form.[1] Now, Aesthetic can always be adequately defined as what deals with the form of things. But if we are to interpret Kant by his illustrations, he evidently does not mean aesthetical form which is something quite new, transcending the elementary opposition of matter and form in sense-perception, but the formal perfection of objects as unities in variety; and this, of course, is not aesthetical but abstract perception. In a halting manner he does recognise that there are sensations whose matter may be exhausted in the form and are so far aesthetical, such as simple colours and tones. But this concession is only made on the ground that they are pure; for, in themselves, the simple tone of a violin or the green of a grassy plot are mere sensations, and ought to be called pleasant.

The point now to decide is what he means by being pure. In the first place, since he cannot find a distinction of matter and form in these representations, he all but invents one. He should like to think, if he could settle his doubts, that the mind actually perceives the rhythmical vibrations of the aether which constitute sounds and colours; then it would be easy to explain why simple tones and colours are thought beautiful, for they would be the perception of unity in a manifold of sensation. But failing this improbable expedient, he falls back on aesthetic apperception: "We cannot assume that the quality of sensations is the same in all subjects."[2] That is to say, those

[1] Bernard, § 14, p. 73. [2] Bernard, § 14, p. 74.

who apperceive sensations aesthetically will distinguish between the variable sense-affection itself (*Reiz*) and the pure element which alone is capable of universal communication. But this apperception does not constitute aesthetic form. As appears from his later treatment of the subject, his distinction between pure sensations and those which are mixed with the affection of the organ is an elementary recognition of the aesthetic senses ; and by the pure form which is universally communicable, he only understands a moral symbolism : thus the white of lilies suggests innocence, red suggests sublimity, and each of the seven colours has its appropriate moral.[1]

Kant's conception of aesthetic purity either means the abstract factor which is constant in perception, or it lapses into analogical symbolism corresponding to Hegel's symbolic stage in Art, where the sign is in contingent relation to the thing signified like the Bull as the symbol of Deity. This is illustrated in Kant's theory of the arts. In Painting it is the drawing and not the colouring that is essential, in Music it is the rhythm and not the pitch of tones. This statement almost justifies the gratuitous criticism that a colourless painting and a toneless music are nonentities.

We have already said a little to indicate the spiritual nature of colour. In Music there is something which goes beyond the tones, the ineffable which Abt Vogler touched by accident on the keys of his organ and could not recover. The tones are not any kind of analogical symbolism, moral or intellectual, but the pure and direct expression of what is otherwise inarticulate. Kant seems to suggest this idea in his subsequent opinion, that musical composition is a kind of language

[1] Bernard, § 42, p. 181.

THE CRITICAL PHILOSOPHY 161

which expresses the "unspeakable wealth" of aesthetical Ideas.[1] But a cursory inspection shows that this wealth in the aesthetical Ideas is not inarticulate because of its quality or meaning, but because there is an inexhaustible quantity of possible linguistic signs in the musical composition; it is a wealth of extensive, not of intensive, symbolism. This interpretation is confirmed by the fact that he assigns the lowest place to Music among the arts, as being merely a beautiful play of sensations without contributing to the expansion and culture of the mind. He regards the tones as accidental signs, corresponding to the elements of speech, which indicate the affective state of a person speaking, and, by mechanical association, communicate the corresponding idea in his mind. But as Schopenhauer, in his remarkable discussion, has shown, the true parallel is not between musical expression and speech but between musical expression and Nature. All the other arts are imitations, although ideal imitations, of Nature; they are always particular representations of events and things. Painting, Sculpture and Poetry do not indeed represent events and things as they exist in their contingency, but in their ideal forms; and therefore what they copy is the Platonic Ideas. Now Music is distinguished from the other arts in this, that it does not resemble a representation of life and events at all; there is no likeness in musical expression to a world of things, as there is in a painting. What Music copies is not the ideal forms of things but the Supersensible itself; it expresses "the quintessence of life and its events" without resembling any of them. The Platonic Ideas, although they are immediate, and

[1] Bernard, p. 218.

so far complete, organisations of the Supersensible, are after all limitations of the Supersensible; they are a plurality of expressions from different points of view. But Music passes over the appearance of the Supersensible, whether as ideal or as actual, and could be said to exist even if there were no phenomenal world at all. It does not express the Supersensible in terms of Nature, but is as direct and immediate a revelation of the Supersensible as Nature is in her totality, ideal and actual. Music, then, cannot be a language whose elements are conventional signs of the ineffable, but the peculiar language which makes the Supersensible articulate, co-ordinate with the language of Creation. Schopenhauer confirms his theory by observing a certain parallelism between these two expressions of the Supersensible in Nature and Music: the mass of inorganic Nature corresponding to the bass or fundamental note, the vegetable kingdom to the third, the animal kingdom to the fifth, and the kingdom of Man to the octave.[1] The truth is that Kant's opinion of Music was prejudiced by certain intrusive forms of the art with which he was painfully familiar. When an author descends to a foot-note, he generally takes the reader into his confidence. In the text he has been reproaching the noble art with a want of urbanity, because it extends its charms beyond what is desirable in the neighbourhood; and then, in a note, he gives way to his grief against the ranting chorus of his neighbours at family prayers. Bernard recalls his letter to the burgomaster, in which he complains of the annoyance caused by the devotional exercises of the prisoners in

---

[1] *The World as Will and Idea*: Haldane and Kemp, vol. i. bk. iii. § 52; vol. iii. chap. 39.

THE CRITICAL PHILOSOPHY 163

the adjoining jail, and suggests the propriety of closing the windows.[1]

This false conception of aesthetic purity as the abstract schema in perception, is simply a misconception of what *a priori* means. As was remarked above, it is not aesthetic form but mathematical. His exclusion of Charm proceeds on the supposition that the *a priori* is inconsistent with empirical mixture. So, while Aesthetic ought to be regarded as a representation which is *a priori*, he identifies it with the constant factor in an *a priori* representation. If we were to speak of the Beautiful as a fruit, we should say that Kant has given us a dry preserve. But this is not what *a priori* means in the *Critique of Pure Reason*. Knowledge is surely never identified with its abstract conditions. And in another work, Kant was forced to admit that the *a priori* does not exclude what is empirical. He was criticised in the Leipsic *Zeitung* for having made contradictory statements in the *Critique*. He had said that there is no empirical mixture in pure knowledge *a priori* ; then, two pages forward, he used the same example to illustrate pure *a priori* knowledge as he had just used to illustrate a mixed proposition, namely, 'every change has a cause.' To this Kant replied, that by a pure *a priori* he meant what is not dependent on empirical elements (die von nichts Empirischem *abhängig* ist), and not what is absolutely free from empirical mixture.[2] This is an important admission which ought to be printed on the fly-leaf in every edition of the *Critique of Pure Reason*.

[1] Bernard, p. 220.

[2] *Über den Gebrauch teleologischer Principien in der Philosophie* : Hart, iv. pp. 495-6.

Apart, however, from his mistaken conception of *a priori* and his consequent theory of aesthetic purity, the principle which underlies Kant's restriction is sound. If, as Lessing said, Charm is Beauty in motion,[1] those arts which are representations in time, namely, Poetry and Music, can have no expression at all without charm. But otherwise, charm is not essential, and, like the belt of Venus, sits loose to the person of the Beautiful. Schiller took up this idea from the Greek myth, and worked it out in his essay on 'Grace and Dignity.' It is the least satisfactory of his philosophical works, and it is almost impossible to gather its contents under a single, systematic conception. That it was not successful, is sufficiently evident from the fact that it pleased neither Kant nor Goethe. Having studied Kant's aesthetic theory before he wrote this essay, which first appeared in 1793, his main purpose was naturally to correct the prevailing subjectivity in Kant's view by an adaptation of Shaftesbury, and as a consequence to prove also against Kant, that in the beautiful character inclination and duty are reconciled. He observes that without her belt, which gave charms even to the ugly, Venus is still the beautiful Venus, while her beauty she can only give away with her person. Those on whom this favour is conferred, retain it as something external to themselves, and so far the charm of their beauty would seem to be subjective. But the marvel in the myth is, that while they have the belt in their possession, it constitutes an objective characteristic of their person and is not a mere appearance for the spectator. (*Sie . . . kommt dem Gegenstande selbst zu, nicht bloss der Art, wie wir*

---

[1] *Laokoon*, xxi. "Reiz ist Schönheit in Bewegung."

THE CRITICAL PHILOSOPHY 165

ihn aufnehmen.)[1] Now motion is the only change which a subject can suffer without losing his identity, and thus Charm or Grace can be an inherent attribute of the subject without being a constant, objective quality.[2] Schiller advances to his conclusion in what is a chapter of contradictions, which we must pass over. He would emphasise that the motion must be voluntary, and in other places he insists that it must be involuntary. He does not mean to say that Grace is involuntary in the sense of reflex action, but that it is the involuntary element in the actions of a moral disposition; it is what is characteristic in emotional expression, or just that form of expression which follows immediately on a state of feeling before it has passed away.[3] But Schiller has thus restricted characteristic expression to the beauty of character, and we can now understand why Goethe did not like his paper. It marks the middle period in Schiller's aesthetical development, where he tries to co-ordinate aestheticism and moralism. Evidently he has taken the Greek conception for all it is worth; but, instead of applying it to inorganic Nature as Goethe did, he confined it to the Individual of the *Aufklärung*, to whom he looked back with fond regret.

His conclusion is practically the same as Kant's denial of an Ideal to what has not a moral nature. He thinks that the waving hair of a beautiful head has no more grace than waving corn.[4] This statement is one in principle with Kant's criticism of Myron's Cow, that it is merely correct because it has not got

[1] *Über Anmuth und Würde.* *Sämmtliche Werke*, xi. p. 386.
[2] *Ibid.* p. 385.
[3] *Ibid.* pp. 407-13. See especially pp. 408 and 413.
[4] *Ibid.* pp. 386-7.

a moral expression. But Schiller has advanced on Kant in bringing out the significance of his principle when it is properly applied. He has shown how charm can be objective as entering into characteristic expression, although it is not essential to Beauty. To put it epigrammatically, there can be Beauty without charm, but charm must be the expression of a beautiful nature. This somewhat ambiguous place assigned to charm may be clearly understood by a simple illustration. We have seen the features of an ugly musician transformed under the influence of the music he is playing. While he is girdled with the belt of Venus, the expression on his face is a real part of himself. But when the music ceases, this expression dies away and the features resume their forbidding appearance. In one of his stories, Tolstoi tells of a musican who found his way to a ball in a most filthy condition. He volunteered to play, and "at each note that he played, Albert grew taller and taller. At a little distance, he had no appearance of being either crippled or peculiar. ... His face shone with complete, enthusiastic delight; his eyes gleamed with a radiant, steely light; his nostrils quivered, his red lips were parted in rapture." But now the time is approaching when he must give up the belt to the Goddess: "at the end of the next variation, Albert's face grew serene, his eyes flushed, great clear drops of sweat poured down his cheeks. The veins swelled on his forehead; his whole body swayed more and more; his pale lips were parted, and his whole figure expressed an enthusiastic craving for enjoyment. Despairingly swaying with his whole body, and throwing back his hair, he laid down his violin, and with a smile of proud satisfaction and happiness gazed at the bystanders. Then his back assumed its ordinary curve, his head sank, his lips grew set, his eyes lost their fire; and as though he were ashamed of himself, timidly glancing round, and stumbling, he went into the next room."[1]

Now Kant himself recognises, when he comes to treat of the Sublime, that charm is compatible with Beauty because the aesthetic state is a feeling of the furtherance of life, an interplay of the powers in which they promote one another to increased activity.[2] This clearly indicates that he conceived of Aesthetic as an objective, concrete state ; it is the significant play of our mental powers as fulfilling an end of our being. But while he makes this concession to Charm, he will not admit of Emotion (*Rührung*); for this is the feeling of Sublimity, and is not play but earnest activity. Emotion he defines as "a sensation in which pleasantness is produced by means of a momentary checking and a consequent more powerful outflow of the vital force."[3] It is not intellective but volitional, and therefore not aesthetical but a modification of our moral disposition. But with this final limitation we shall have passed the lower limit of polemical criticism and entered on Kant's constructive phase.

This moral emotion, in its most general form, is simply the feeling for Nature which Kant had throughout presupposed in the background of his theory. The insipid simper of Free Beauty, which he thought already sufficiently charming, is only a caricature of the softened splendour in Celestial Being. Referring to the section in the *Critique of Judgment* where this sentiment is

[1] *A Russian Proprietor and other stories—Albert.*
[2] Bernard, p. 102.   [3] *Ibid.* § 14, p. 76.

expressly introduced, Schiller speaks of Kant in the highest terms as the first to reflect on the love of Nature for her own sake, as she stands opposed to Art and puts it to shame: "whoever has learnt to admire the author only as a great thinker, will rejoice to find here a trace of his heart."[1]

Schiller gives some examples. What is it, he asks, that pleases us in a homely flower, a spring of water, a mossy stone, the chirping of birds, the humming of bees? He answers, it is an idea presented through them that we love: the still, creative life, the quiet, self-produced effects, the self-determined existence, the inner necessity, the eternal unity with self. They *are* what we were, they are what we *ought* again to be; hence they transport us into a state of sublime emotion.[2] Kant calls this emotion by the strange name of an intellectual interest in Beauty, ostensibly because it implies some concept of Nature. Schiller more candidly regards it as moral sentiment. Neither of them considers it aesthetical. But Kant did not see that the admission of this feeling for Nature alters his whole conception of abstract Beauty. If we discover that the object of our admiration is an artificial flower, we lose our interest. It is the thought "that Nature has produced it" that creates the immediate interest in our aesthetic reflexion.[3] A mischievous boy can make a perfect imitation of the nightingale, and while the delusion lasts we are charmed; but as soon as the deception is discovered, the charm is gone: "it must be Nature or be regarded as Nature, if we are to take an immediate

[1] *Über naive und sentimentalische Dichtung. Sämmtliche Werke*, xii. p. 198.

[2] *Ibid.* pp. 198-9.   [3] Bernard, § 42, p. 178.

interest in the Beautiful as such."[1] Notice the deliberate use of the term immediate, and then consider that this section is entitled, 'Of the intellectual interest in the Beautiful.' Both Kant and Schiller are thinking of the same thing and both are wrong. Schiller's argument is that the feeling is mediated through an idea, and that it could only be aesthetical if it were the impression received in immediate observation of the form;[2] or as Kant would say, it must be *blosse Betrachtung*.

Here we see Schiller's limitation. Although he developed the conception of Form to great advantage, as aesthetic semblance, he never got away completely from Kant's mechanical distinction of matter and form; and when he comes across psychic phenomena which have a deeper significance than the play of free appearance, he can find no place for them except as affections of our moral disposition. Kant would defend himself by pointing out that we must not confuse this emotional interest with a pure aesthetic judgment, for in the contemplation of a flower as a free beauty, we abstract altogether from the thought that Nature has produced it. But to this we reply that such a flower is as unreal as an artificial flower, and Kant has practically admitted that it is impossible to think away the thought of its connection with Nature; in the case of a counterfeit, our whole interest is based on the supposition that it is natural. Schiller could go a step further. He would admit that the form is deceptive, but it is an honest deception; as the refutation of existence in its naturality, the *ästhetischer Schein* is frankly appearance and is a base

[1] Bernard, p. 182.
[2] *Über naive und sentimentalische Dichtung.* *Werke,* xii. p. 198.

falsehood when it claims to be actual.¹ But this is not an abstract appearance—a new heaven; it is a new heaven and a new earth. It is not an image given off from Nature like the εἴδωλα of Democritus, but Nature herself as appearance in her body and spirit. It is the false appearance that is opposed as form to matter, while the honest appearance transcends and includes this original opposition. This, as will be readily recognised, is practically refuting Schiller by his own words. But owing to his moralistic tendency, he did not see that the naïve feeling for Nature is nothing else than the aesthetic consciousness of Nature's Spirit, which breathes through the poetry of Wordsworth:

"To me the meanest flower that blows can give
Thoughts that do often lie too deep for tears,"

is a purely aesthetic emotion of the sublime order. But neither Schiller nor Kant was able to assimilate the Sublime to Aesthetic.

Let me give one more illustration from Schiller. In a very fine passage he shows, with special reference to children, how the unsightly, the inconsiderable and in itself despicable has a soul of Beauty which does not lie in its form but shines through its formlessness. It is a good instance of the Sublime, which includes the infinitely small as well as the infinitely great. He says it is a mistake to think that the feeling we entertain towards children is due to their appearance of helplessness. This may indeed be the emotion in those who are used to feel towards the weak nothing but a sense of their own superiority. But the feeling for Nature for her own sake is

---
¹ *The Aesthetical Education of Man*: Weiss, p. 158.

"humbling rather than agreeable to self-love; and if there be an advantage on either side, it is not at least on ours. The emotion does not arise within us because we look down upon the child from the height of our power and perfection, but because we, out of the limits of our condition, . . . *look up* to the limitless destination in the child and to its pure innocence."[1] What is this but the sympathetic symbolism of aesthetic intuition, which gives wings to the wind, eyes to the stars, and invests inanimate Nature with the passions of men? Because the child touches the Ideal of our perfection in a single point, we make it impersonate the complete destination of our humanity. In a similar way, the homely flower and mossy stone have what is wanting in our character to make it complete. And although they do not enjoy our divine freedom to change our condition, they suggest the Ideal of our humanity in the simple appearance of self-contained existence; they have necessity, the indifference to change, which we have not, the eternal age of unremembered years is writ upon them. But if both are combined in what can only be an aesthetic intuition, if our uncertain, fitful changes are controlled by and educated into their serene indifference to Time's destroying passage, "there goes the Divine or Ideal."[2]

The whole root of the error of both Kant and Schiller is a false conception of immediacy. The feeling for Nature is the consciousness of depth in aesthetic content. Is our experience less aesthetical because it must sustain an effort of reflexion, is our intuition less serene and contemplative because it

[1] *Über naive und sentimentalische Dichtung. Werke*, xii. p. 200.
[2] *Ibid.* p. 199.

is the penetrating insight of sympathetic feeling? Is not aesthetic emotion the greatest amount of excitation with the least expenditure of energy, and will it not therefore maintain its calm in the consciousness of spontaneous effort? Is our feeling less aesthetical because the soul of Beauty in a thing does not lie in the mere observation of its form, but exists in our sublimity, and must be fetched from the deep by sympathetic symbolism? Kant himself has been telling us that there is a kind of causality in Aesthetic, by which the Powers maintain themselves and promote each other to increased activity. So the question arises whether unqualified immediacy is an adequate description of what is distinctive in Aesthetic. Setting aside for the moment the specific type of emotion which Kant has defined as a violent inhibition of the nerve-centres, we have only to recognise that emotion need not be exclusively volitional. The check may be and is normally ideational, and this is not a rude revulsion of moral feeling but the gentle displacement of one idea or image by another; it is what happens in the almost imperceptible shock of surprise with which we greet recognisable features in a view or work of Art.

Now it will be remembered that Kant stakes everything on this question, and insists that the moment immediacy is surrendered, Aesthetic disappears. But the truth regarding immediacy is the same as we found in the claim to disinterestedness; the two terms are the sides of the same shield. In contrast with Cognition Aesthetic is undoubtedly immediate, for it does not think the object discursively but views it as a whole whose parts are transparent. This perception, however, may be full or empty, deep or shallow,

THE CRITICAL PHILOSOPHY 173

according to the power of aesthetic vision. He may not gain the Beautiful who only glances at her form and is satisfied in "the mere act of judging," he may have to linger long and suffer the displacement of many ideas. And still this mediating process is not the intervention of a concept or a moral reaction; it is neither an intellectual nor a moral interest but the mediation peculiar to Aesthetic itself. This is what both Kant and Schiller have not recognised. It is not a going beyond the appearance into something beneath or above, which would be intellective, it is a modification within the appearance. There are degrees in aesthetic appearance, there are degrees in Subjectivity. When we recognise the qualified sense in which Aesthetic is immediate, we shall not speak of a sympathetic insight into Nature as an intellectual interest or as moral sentiment, we shall call it rather the content in aesthetic judgment.

This completes Kant's critical theory. It was a threefold criticism, directed against the intellectualism of Leibniz, the aesthetico-ethical fusion of Shaftesbury and the sensationalism of Burke. But we have been continually aware that his theory suffers in its several applications. This is partly due to Kant's ignorance of Fine Art, but more I think to the incoherent doctrine of Freedom which he adopted from the *Aufklärung*. The fact is, he had a most profound insight into the original conditions of aesthetic Feeling, such as none of his predecessors had acquired, and the general principles of his theory will never be superseded. As was hinted in an earlier part of this chapter, his limitation chiefly consisted in not being able to develop his own principles. His path was blocked by three obstructions which 'are all hewn out of the same rock, a negative conception of Freedom, an unregenerate Sensibility and a consequent want of schemata in aesthetic Imagination.

I now wish to indicate, in conclusion, the positive and constructive phase of Kant's theory. But before doing so, we ought to notice an apparently unique passage in which he demolishes, at a single stroke, the whole edifice of abstract Beauty. He announced quite early in his analysis, that the key to the criticism of Taste is to be found in the principle that the judgment must precede the pleasure. To an appreciative reader this statement will occasion some surprise. As M. Basch says, a state of feeling is changed into a state of knowledge *sans crier gare*.[1] Although it appears as early as the ninth section I have purposely reserved it until now, because it seemed quite inconsistent with the theory which Kant has developed. We have understood as a cardinal maxim that Aesthetic must not be assimilated to intellectual activity, but explained as being due to an original and independent faculty. Now, however, we are told that we must make up our minds in advance before the feeling of pleasure arises, and this can only be understood as a prior intellectual act. What is more, this principle removes a most important landmark by which Aesthetic is distinguished from other types of mental activity; for it is equally true of a teleological judgment that the recognition of an end precedes the pleasure, and also in the moral judgment the pleasure must decidedly follow the maxim of Practical Reason. Moreover, the statement is not without support. In the original Introduction the same principle is expressed with a more glaring

[1] *L'Esthétique de Kant*, p. 178.

emphasis ; it is said that " the 'subjective teleology is *thought* before it is *felt*." [1]

It might be explained, in the first place, that Kant is here confusing logical with temporal priority. Undoubtedly the conditions which make the pleasure possible as a felt harmony in the mental states must be supposed to exist prior to the pleasure itself, but not for our consciousness. And, in his other statements, Kant makes it quite clear that the pleasure does not follow but accompanies the judgment ; it must be " bound up with the mere act of judging." [2] But this criticism is so obvious that, if it had been proposed to Kant, he would have laughed in scorn. Why then did he say that the pleasure must follow? Because he wished to indicate that there is such a thing as aesthetical Reflexion, quite distinct from the intellectual process, and that if the pleasure is to be aesthetical and not the consequence of sensation, it must first be mediated through this reflexion. And although his language would lead us to believe that he is reducing the aesthetic state to an intellectual process, nothing is further from his mind. Even in the passage quoted from the original Introduction, where the harmony of the faculties is said to be thought before it is felt, he is careful to point out in the next sentence that the ground of this harmony cannot be brought under a determinate concept and can only be apprehended in feeling ; that is to say, it is not thought at all. Evidently Kant is struggling to express ideas which were in advance of his philosophical vocabulary. He has to use the word ' thought '

[1] *Über Philosophie überhaupt*: Rosenkranz, i. p. 599 ; Hart, vi. p. 389.
[2] Bernard, p. 164.

when he should have said 'felt'; and he does so because it is not a mere feeling of pleasure that is in question but indeterminate content, and for Kant significant content was the object of explicit thinking. The unsuspecting candour and the absence of all sense of contradiction with which he introduces this principle in the ninth section, are themselves a clear indication that he had made a discovery of which the mechanical appliances of his age were not able to provide a working model. As to whether he meant an intellectual act when he placed the judgment before the pleasure, this is settled at once by his express use of the term *Beurtheilung*, which does not denote a logical judgment but a psychological process; notice how it is stated: *ob im Geschmacksurtheile das Gefühl der Lust vor der Beurtheilung des Gegenstandes, oder diese vor jener vorhergehe*—the specific judgment of the object, which is said to precede the pleasure, is distinguished from the judgment of Taste itself as falling within it.[1] He does not say that the pleasure follows an intellectual act, but that it must be bound up with and be dependent upon the condition of all intellectual acts and principles, the Power of Judgment in general.

This principle, then, which at first appears so disingenuous, is simply the denial of unqualified immediacy. What must be fundamental, he says, as the basis of the pleasure, is "the universal capability of communication"[2] in the mental state; and this is just another expression for a significant content, a state of feeling that is worth communicating and therefore capable of being understood. The whole point is that the aesthetic powers have it in their own hands, and do

[1] Hartenstein, v. p. 221.   [2] Bernard, § 9, p. 63.

not move at the bidding of Sense without or Reason within. The aesthetic act may be immediate ; but this does not mean that we must be precipitated on to the presentation and be glued to it in a blind panic, and that if it does not happen instantaneously there is a miscarriage. Like Falstaff the Powers refuse to entertain upon compulsion, and whether we shall have any pleasure in the Beautiful is for them to consider. They have instructed the Pleasure not to be tickled by sensation, nor to be cajoled by any intellectual interest or moral sentiment, but to take its cue immediately from them ; when they move, it goes with them, when they begin to play, it announces the fact in cheers. But the Powers may refuse to budge, their motion may be fast or slow, light or heavy, and may vary in intensity. There is therefore such a thing as aesthetical Reflexion, quite peculiar and distinct from thought. There are degrees in immediacy, and each of them as it imperceptibly glides into another is an immediate moment, the *Augenblick der Ewigkeit*. Now when this reflective modification is observed from the outside, it looks like a mediated process; and it is this false external view that led both Kant and Schiller to think that naïve interest in Nature, because it is not immediately connected with the form of presentation, must be an intervention, intellectual, moral or both. It is not an intervention ; it is the mediation peculiar to Aesthetic itself.

Thus Nature as the object, not indeed of Understanding but of Reflexion, is the content in Aesthetic. This poetic idea of Nature, as containing the raw substance to which Aesthetic gives form, is composed of two abstract elements, the systematic knowledge of sense-perception and moral Reason, or Nature as she is interpreted by mind and will. These elements do not enter into Aesthetic by mechanical subsumption as a material which is contingent to and unaffected by the form, and here at least Kant is above criticism. For although this mechanical metaphor is cognate to his mode of thought, he is very careful to insist that it is not concrete representations that are brought into the free relation which constitutes aesthetic form, but the faculties themselves. And this can only mean that, as indeterminate potencies, Knowledge and Morality enter into Aesthetic by inner transformation : foregoing their specific form and subsiding into characterless substance, they are "changed into the same image." Kant unfortunately restricts the faculties to Imagination, or the highest faculty of Sense and Understanding, or the faculty of systematic Thought, and these are only specifications of one direction of mind, the intellective ; but, as will immediately appear, he merits a higher interpretation. He is deserving of all praise for the dogged persistence with which he excludes Knowledge and Morality, as such, from Aesthetic, and his mistaken theory of purity is in great part due to this motive. The artist is capable of perceiving Truth, but he does not think it discursively, and he has also a moral disposition, but its promptings are not commands to be obeyed. Therefore he need not blush to acknowledge the sensuous form nor fear to own its authority, for it is instinct with intelligence, theoretical and practical.

Now the original problem of the *Critique of Judgment*, as it is generally received, was the union of these two elements which are the abstract factors in the poetic idea of Nature; it is the union of Sense and Reason, or of Nature as Mechanism and Nature as Freedom. But it is evident that this union can never be consummated in the artificial type of Beauty which Kant has developed; for, as the very abstraction of Nature and the negation of true Freedom, it is incapable of containing either. Kant is well aware of this and turns to the Ideal, which is not aesthetical but moral, not the Ideal of Beauty but the Ideal of Character. But again this is not the solution of which we are in search. This moral Ideal is the ethical noumenon, the abstract Man of Freedom, which, as Cohen says, separates Nature and the ethical Personality (*Sittlichkeit*);[1] it is an Ideal which is never completely realised and can only be maintained by ceaseless strife. It is therefore not properly the Ideal but the Idea of Humanity. It is in Aesthetic alone that the Ideal can be presented as the complete realisation of the Idea in individual form. There is only one way in which man could contain his own Ideal, and that is by being himself perfectly good.

Kant, however, seems to have found his solution in another and somewhat accidental way, I mean his theory of Genius. It has the appearance of a foreign element which has no systematic connection with the rest of his work. But this is not a true impression. On the contrary, it may be urged with some degree of confidence that it is the primary and original factor in his Aesthetic. For over thirty years he had discussed the nature of Genius in his lectures on Logic and Anthropology, chiefly under the influence of Baumgarten and Gerard. The 'Essay on Genius' by Gerard, a professor at Aberdeen, was known to him as early as the sixties,

[1] *Kants Begründung der Aesthetik*, p. 216.

and he mentions the work as the best of its kind.[1] Meanwhile, in his comparison between Logic and Aesthetic, he was effecting a rapprochement between feeling and logical form, which later emerged in the conception of subjective teleology or Play (*Spiel der Kräfte*). But it is not likely that he arrived at this conception apart from the theory of Genius. We must remember that subjective teleology as aesthetic play does not come into vogue in Kant's writings until so late as 1787. In that year he intimated to Reinhold that Teleology would be the title of his work on Taste. It is surely, then, a correct inference that the conception of Play arises out of the theory of Genius and not the latter from the former, as Anna Tumarkin supposes.[2] But Kant did not seem to be aware of any connection between them, and developed an independent theory of Aesthetic which has nothing in common with the nature of Genius. He did not see that in Genius the distinction between the formal Beauty of Nature and the characteristic Beauty of Art is completely swept away. For the work of Genius is at once Nature and Art; the rule by which he is guided is not consciously applied, it is Nature that gives the rule to Art through him: "it can only be that in the subject which is Nature and cannot be brought under rules or concepts, *i.e.* the supersensible substrate of all his faculties."[3]

> "Nature is made better by no mean,
> But Nature makes that mean; so o'er the Art,
> Which you say adds to Nature, is an Art
> That Nature makes."

[1] Schlapp, *Kants Lehre vom Genie*, u.s.w. p. 244.
[2] *Kantstudien*, Bd. xi. *Zur transcendentalen Methode der Kantischen Ästhetik.*
[3] Bernard, p. 238.

THE CRITICAL PHILOSOPHY 181

It is in this artistic consciousness that we shall find the reconciliation of Nature and Freedom. For the supersensible substrate that utters itself in Genius is not the ethical noumenon but the catholic nature of the individual, not the ethical but the human Personality, not the Man of Freedom but the Man of Humanity. It is therefore the harmony of all the mental powers, and not simply those which are intellectual, Imagination and Understanding : it is the unison in their original simplicity of Intellection, Emotion and Conation ; it is the *Gemüthskräfte* rather than the *Erkenntnissvermögen*.

Kant denotes the consciousness of this state by the feeling of pleasure and pain. Perhaps there is an advantage after all in this nomenclature. In the original Introduction he defined the feeling of pleasure and pain as the only form of sensation which can never indicate a quality in objects.[1] In another passage he goes further and says that it contributes nothing even to a knowledge of our subjective state.[2] Pleasure-pain is not a psychosis but the resonance of a psychosis ; it does not illumine explicit elements in consciousness, it only indicates the practical attitude of consciousness to presentations. And, as the barest form of awareness, it has a close resemblance to that elemental state whose content is indeterminate. But there is a great difference between them. Pleasure-pain is only the qualitative index of consciousness as a succession, while the other feeling-state is the vague sense of duration and only means that we have consciousness. It has a nearer affinity, therefore, with sensation than with that form of sensation whose significance is exhausted in the

[1] *Über Philosophie überhaupt* : Rosenkranz, i. p. 598.
[2] *Rechtslehre* : Hart, vii. pp. 8-9.

bare feeling of pleasure or pain. But it is not sensation. It is the state which exists before the distinction has emerged between consciousness as affective and as affecting. Fichte held a feast on the day his child first said 'I,' because it was the birth of self-consciousness. The child-life is prevailingly objective and impersonal, and even when the first personal pronoun is used, it is more in imitation of the linguistic expression than with a definite sense of the distinction between pure and empirical consciousness. The ego is vaguely identified with the whole mass of sensation, as may be seen from the use of the simple exclamation 'Hungry!' instead of the more subjective expression, 'I am hungry.' Unfortunately, we have no word to express this primordial state of consciousness except the common term Feeling, which is already used to denote pleasure-pain. Perhaps we might use the word 'empathy,' which Dr. Ward has coined to cover *Einfühlung* in its widest sense. It is not a feeling of, but a *feeling in*, an empathy; it is the limit at which consciousness is still possible without a determinate object, the thin, taut rope on which consciousness balances itself without support and looks down into the awful abyss of the thoughts.

This elemental feeling of our identity, in the quiet of our spirit, is a fleeting revelation of a past estate, and is deep enough to justify the thought of pre-existence. In the earliest dawn of human life, mind existed in its original simplicity without specific directions of activity: if there was apprehension it was not intellectual but pragmatical, for it was subservient to Will; if there was Will it was not ethical but instinctive, for it was subservient to the feeling of well-being as it is promoted or hindered; if there was Emotion it was not ideational,

THE CRITICAL PHILOSOPHY 183

for it was inseparable from its physical expression. This is not an estate we should wish to recover, and if we speak of a return to Nature, we mean an ideal regress which is really a progress. But it was a harmony of mental life which we must regain if Nature and Freedom are to be reconciled. Meanwhile we cultivate the tendencies of consciousness in isolation, in order that the original unity may be enlarged and enriched; but we are to come back again. As the human foetus has evolved through the several stages of the animal world, the elemental harmony of human life has broken up into co-ordinate directions of activity and waits in hope of its redemption, when that which is in part shall be done away. Our Intellect is cultivated to excess, and as it becomes more and more conceptual, it loses the intuitive power to realise its ideas in practice :

"Video meliora proboque, deteriora sequor."

There is the correlative defect in our culture that our Will is not intellectual; it is exercised apart in enforced obedience to a Law which our mind cannot approve, a helpless monitor which bids us act or refrain from acting but does not inspire us to obey. Pragmatism is telling us that this is an antiquated theory, and that we must mince the absolute Rule into interesting morsels. But Pragmatism cannot change human nature. Humanism is periodic in the race, but the permanent features of human nature remain unchanged. The youthful exuberance and healthy-minded vigour of the present generation is closely akin to the effete and dangerous *Schwärmerei* of the eighteenth century, and is the passing of the human spirit through a destructive moment. Mankind will ever seek to strive with the Highest and will not tolerate the squandering of its behests in the suffrages of human passion; it will rather battle with uncompromising Righteousness, a hateful Law which intimidates by coercion, than see its mandates weakened. But therein it is not blest. Its morality is warped, a gasping Freedom reft from dishonoured Nature at whose dear price it wins a doubtful victory. To be an offering worthy of God and man, morality must pass through Nature, forgo its rigid form and sink to plastic substance, thence to emerge, empowered by Nature's ministries of love and noble feeling, to serve the Highest. It is not by Law but by "the faith which passes into action through love" that man is made righteous.

Pending this regeneration of the Race, Aesthetic is the "symbol of Morality." The phrase is Kant's and thus we take it in its highest meaning. The moral Ideal was for him nothing less than the consummation of History. Now, the elemental harmony in man, which we may suppose to have preceded the development of distinctive tendencies in consciousness, is already preserved in the aesthetic state as a higher immediacy. But Aesthetic is not Life. As the deliberate refutation of the actual, it is only an incident in Life. Life, on the other hand, is a process of realisation which is never complete. But if man, in the fulfilment of his destiny, attains to perfect goodness, he will then become the Ideal of his humanity which Aesthetic now contains as symbol. His nature will be aesthetical, not in despite of the actual but for its sake. He will carry the ideal world into the actual, instead of sublimating it into an ideal world which ignores its existence. He will not be able to take pleasure in a work of Art which ignores or conflicts with moral instinct, as the artistic consciousness can do and is justified in doing. I do not wish to raise the controversy here whether there ever did exist a sinless man. But, to illustrate what has been said, we may at least observe that the nature of Jesus was an aesthetical harmony just because it was perfectly good. It would be a poor description of the life in God, as he conceived it, to say that it was moral, and in fact that is not the way in which he presented the Ideal of Character. It was as the life without a motive that he commended it, the life of the lily, the end of whose existence is completely immanent in itself. He did not tell men to be perfect *because* their Father in Heaven is perfect, but *even as* He is perfect, or as children say, *just because*. Morality in itself is not spontaneous but artificial, calculating, careful of its reputation; it is occupied with many little things instead of the one thing needful; it is the restless effort to acquire depth of character through breadth of enterprise, to gain intensity of feeling through extensive activity. Jesus told these weary souls to cease from their labour and enter into rest, the Peace of Genius. He showed them that the present moment is rich enough to make a perfect life if it is lived well, and that they need take no thought for the morrow. If we have the strength and the patience of mind to dwell in the actual until it is shorn of its contingency, it will be found to harbour the unlimited content which our minds are informed to receive, and we shall possess that intensive insight at home which the moral consciousness, in its impatient prodigality of effort, seeks to find in a far country. The perfectly good is an aesthetical harmony.

But Kant was never able to carry out the consequences of his theory of Genius. For him Genius is more of an intellectual harmony than a harmony of all the mental powers. Even Cohen, the most liberal and sympathetic of Kant's expositors to-day, does not think that the moral consciousness is assimilated to the aesthetic in Kant's theory.[1] Although it is the supersensible substrate that speaks through Genius, the faculties of Genius are the Imagination and Understanding; they do not include the Will. Kant was afraid of the mental chemistry which could transform the moral consciousness by making it pass through Nature, and this appears in large letters in his doctrine of the Sublime.

[1] "Die Aufhebung des sittlichen Inhalts in die Form des Gefühls der Anlage des Problems nach zwar vorgesehen, aber den Ausführungen nicht als Disposition zu Grunde gelegt worden ist." *Kants Begründung der Aesthetik*, pp. 232-3.

CHAPTER VI.

THE SUBLIME.

IF Kant had been asked to distinguish the Sublime in a single word, he would have said that while the Beautiful is pleasurable Feeling (*Gefühl*), the Sublime is a moral Emotion (*Rührung*); the one is the consciousness of mere observation, the other is the consciousness which follows innervation, the reaction of our will to the challenge of Nature. The Sublime "brings with it as its characteristic feature *a movement* of the mind," while the Beautiful "maintains the mind in restful contemplation."[1] Both are forms of mental movement, but in the Beautiful it is ideational, the play of representations. The Sublime is altogether earnest, and it is not Imagination and Understanding that are in play but Imagination and Moral Reason.

It follows that the satisfaction in the Beautiful is immediate and positive, but indirect in the Sublime, being mediated through the reaction of our will.[2] The very conception of Experience implies the adaptation of Nature to our minds, and the most elementary relation of subject to object is a harmony of our cognitive powers. This is not a state of positive pleasure, it is only absence of pain. The Feeling of the Beautiful is an intensive adjustment of this mental relation.

[1] Bernard, § 24.   [2] *Ibid.* p. 136.

We have positive pleasure in a further adaptation of Nature to our minds, for we perceive objects, not only as we ought to perceive them, but as we should like to perceive them. The Feeling of the Sublime is different. Unlike the Beautiful, which excites the Imagination and Understanding in harmonious activity to a positive degree of pleasure, it rudely destroys the existing harmony. Terrible Nature menaces and thwarts the habitual course of our ideas, and creates a feeling of disquieting fear. In the presence of mountain masses piled in arrogant confusion, forbidding crags with jagged edges impending our path: before the fury of the tempest and the raging of the swollen sea: beneath reverberating thunder-clouds emitting bolts of destruction, we suffer a sense a shock; the even tenor of our life is arrested by invading force. But if our emotion will be sublime, we must win past this first moment of surprise and regain our calm, we must rise above the threatening presentation and our feeling of dismay. It is the difference between sublimity and superstition, and Kant has been careful to remark this distinction: " he who fears can form no judgment about the Sublime in nature; just as he who is seduced by inclination and appetite can form no judgment about the Beautiful." [1]

The satisfaction in the Sublime may therefore be called negative; it is the peculiar pleasure which arises from pain and fear. Kant calls it admiration or respect, Burke calls it delight. The initial shock is followed by an overflow of vital force, the tension of inhibition relaxes in a feeling of expansion, and we are caught up beyond the present danger to an elevation from which we can look down in serene security. The

[1] Bernard, p. 124.

THE CRITICAL PHILOSOPHY 189

explanation of this change in us is that the greatness and vastness of Nature, baffling the effort of Imagination to grasp it, challenges our Reason, the divine power of our mind, to think of something greater still, the infinite power and majesty of God. The greatness of Nature suffers in comparison with the Omnipotent. This feeling is subtly expressed in a well-known Psalm. In the words, "I will lift up mine eyes unto the hills, from whence cometh my help," the dependent clause is strictly interrogative and ought so to be read. The structure of the Psalm is antiphonal, set to be sung in the form of responses by reciprocating choirs, thus:

"I will lift up mine eyes unto the hills—
From whence cometh my help?
From God my help cometh, maker of heaven and earth."

But Burke's explanation is much inferior. It is simply the psychological fact that we do find pleasure in what is painful. He does not only mean dramatic sympathy, the pleasure we take in an imitation of painful facts, but pleasure in the painful facts themselves. He asks us to choose the most affecting tragedy, and to appoint the most favourite actors to act it on a certain day; and just at the moment when the audience is at the pitch of expectation, let it be announced that a criminal of high rank is to be executed in the adjoining square: "in a moment the emptiness of the theatre would demonstrate the comparative weakness of the imitative arts, and proclaim the triumph of the real sympathy."[1] He thinks that terror is the ruling principle in all cases of sublime

[1] *Sublime and Beautiful*, Part i. § 15.

emotion; what makes the sublime a "delightful horror" and one of the most affecting ideas, is its power of appeal to our self-preserving instinct.[1] By defining the Sublime in terms of its phenomena, without discovering any principle which should make them sublime, Burke has practically identified this emotion with the wretched sentiment which draws people against their will to the shambles, or the morgue, or any horrifying spectacle.

Kant's explanation is very different. It is metaphysical and concerns the destination of our humanity. In agreement with his principle that the Sublime is incompatible with charm, the sensational character of the presentation ceases to affect us at the moment when sublime emotion arises. It is not to the stimulus of the presentation that we respond, but to the solicitude of our Reason which it provokes to activity, and therefore horror or charm of any kind is not admitted into the Sublime. The raging sea is not sublime, it is horrible. Kant goes so far as to say that no form of sense can contain the Sublime; we can only say that it is capable of suggesting a sublimity which is found in our minds.[2] These are statements which we cannot accept, but meanwhile they help us to see the inwardness of his position. Before we advance further, we should say that Kant makes a distinction between the mathematical and dynamical Sublime, which we do not intend to consider. There are the two classes of sublime phenomena, those of quantity and those of force. But mathematical extension is unable to affect us unless we conceive it somehow as intensive power. So Burke thought: "I know of nothing sublime which is not some modification of

[1] *Sublime and Beautiful*, Part ii. §§ 2, 5, 22. [2] Bernard, p. 103.

power."¹ Whenever we speak, then, of greatness in Sublimity, it should always be dynamic and not simply quantitative.

Kant has given a very confused account of his ideas, and it may not be possible to obtain a net result. Probably his analysis is consummated in the discovery of a higher kind of intuition. In the magnitudes of Understanding there is no occasion for sublimity because there is no conflict between perception and thought. The mathematical estimation of greatness proceeds by numerical schemata, and it is by this mathematical procedure that our bread-and-butter faculty of knowledge, the Understanding, appreciates greatness. We do not attempt to realise the greatness, we are satisfied if we can measure it or count it; and since the schema of a mile is as easy for the Imagination as a foot, an exceeding great mountain occasions no more surprise than a molehill. Certainly, as Kant reminds us, we must begin with a sensible measure in this logical estimate; the numerical schema presupposes a definite intuition in space, and therefore "all estimation of the magnitude of the objects of nature is in the end aesthetical."² The term aesthetical, as it is here used, has its original meaning of sense-perception and has nothing to do with artistic intuition. But in logical estimation the Imagination does not keep by the original, sensible measure, for its purpose is not to realise greatness but to give it a figure. It shuts its eyes to the solicitude of the presentation and listens to the Understanding. And since the numerical schemata of the Understanding are capable of infinite multiples, the Imagination can have "no

---

[1] *Sublime and Beautiful*, Part ii. § 5.
[2] Bernard, p. 111, § 26.

maximum " and therefore no impression of greatness. The whole which the Imagination seeks to envisage is not real, it is not the intuition of the parts in their completeness but the multiple of an arbitrary unit of measurement; and however far the Understanding may lead, the Imagination is always able to follow by changing its gear. If the Understanding puts up the figure very high, Imagination takes its seven-leagued boots and gallops after.

But Reason will have none of this short work. It requires the Imagination to realise what it is doing at every step. As the faculty of Totality, our sense of the divine and ultimate, it demands a whole of real parts and not an ideal sum; and it asks the Imagination if it is able to keep up intuiting the real parts until the whole is envisaged. Here the unit is no longer relative but a fixed perception, or the aesthetical unit of magnitude as Kant calls it: "it must be the *aesthetical* estimation of magnitude in which the effort towards comprehension surpasses the power of the Imagination."[1] To this effort Imagination is unequal. It can apprehend part after part to any extent, but it cannot comprehend them in a single intuition. Looking up a mountain-side, we run over its features from the base to the top, but we cannot take it in. The total effect in the Powers of Nature is more than we are able to envisage in perception. This is the negative moment of disquiet while we are still under the influence of the presentation, but it is just in this contrast between Imagination and Reason that sublimity arises. The transcendent solicitude of Reason is for the Imagination "like an abyss in which it fears to lose itself."[2]

[1] Bernard, p. 116.   [2] *Ibid.* p. 120.

The painful sense of shock occasioned by the presentation reaches its limit in the completely unthinkable object of Reason, which makes its first appearance in our consciousness as an indefinite extension of the presentation. Were the object nothing more than a piece of finite Nature, we should not be alarmed nor distress ourselves about it. Its sublimity would be simply a want of conformity to our thoughts about Nature and would fall outside the range of our reflections. It is because the presentation is suggestive of so much more than its immediate unform, a Nature-in-itself for which we have no imaginative faculty, a Nature which with its slightest motion would derange our poor subjective principle of adaptation, that we are seriously perturbed. The presentation expands into infinity as the peal of thunder rolls into its interminable echo. In the words of Cohen, it is only as we view Nature aesthetically that there is anything hateful in her; malformations are not yet objects of dislike but of teleological judgment, and only affect us as *furchtbar* and *zweckwidrig*.[1] It is because we interpret Nature into the aesthetic symbol of a Nature-in-itself which to us is all unform, unlike the supersensible harmony of which Beauty is the aesthetical appearance, that it can give us so much pain. There is thus already an aesthetical moment in the Sublime for which Kant has made no provision. In the passage already quoted, he tells us that all estimation of magnitude is aesthetical, because there must be an aesthetical unit. But if he thinks that this proves the Sublime to be aesthetical, he is surreptitiously confusing the two senses of the term. It is quite evident that in this passage aesthetical only means

[1] *Kants Begründung der Aesthetik*, p. 300.

sense-perception as contrasted with logical calculation. But an aesthetical moment, in our sense, is implied in his statement that the feeling of pain arises from a want of accordance between Imagination and Reason.[1] In no other way could we realise the contrast between Imagination and Reason than by the expansion of a presentation into Reason's object by aesthetic symbolism. It is at this moment Imagination calls off. The feeling of discomfort reaches its limit and passes into satisfaction. We are relieved of the irritating effort to assimilate the intractable forms of Nature which now are overshadowed by the Absolute. There is victory in this defeat, for although it is hopeless to contend with the Absolute we have a right to do so and are ennobled in the consciousness of effort. It is a law for us, says Kant, to strive after the Ideas of Reason, and it belongs to our destination to estimate as small in comparison with these Ideas everything which Nature, regarded as an object of sense, contains.[2] Thus in the moment of self-abasement we are exalted and feel with Faust in presence of the *erhabener Geist*:

"Ich fühlte mich so klein, so gross."

It is this self-negating effort of Imagination, the greatest faculty of Sense, which falls so far short of Reason, the highest faculty of Thought, the more it strives, that gives rise to sublimity. It is the peculiar pleasure we take in a unity which is realised by emphasising the differences rather than by making them transparent as in the Beautiful; it is the subjective play of Imagination and Reason "as harmonious through their very contrast."[3] The thwarting feeling that we cannot see is

[1] Bernard, p. 119.   [2] *Ibid.* p. 120.   [3] *Ibid.* p. 121.

THE CRITICAL PHILOSOPHY 195

itself a certain intimation that there is light round about us, for this privation assails us with a challenge : like the dumb conviction which remains with us of the truth we have failed to vindicate in argument. The darkness of Reason is brighter than the whitest light of Sense :

> "in such strength
> Of usurpation, when the light of sense
> Goes out, but with a flash that has revealed
> The invisible world, doth greatness make abode,
> There harbours."[1]

The feeling of the Sublime is thus for Kant a higher power of intuition. The pull which Reason makes on our Imagination to procure a real Idea, a whole in perception and not simply in thought, "excites in us the feeling of a supersensible faculty."[2] Here at last Reason has found an answer to its pathetic cry, and is freed from the reproach of barrenness in the gift of a divine perception which sees the things unseen. There is also a covert rebuke to the arrogance of Understanding, which professed to have the only kind of certain knowledge. Kant is here recovering part of the ground he had so readily conceded in his battle with the Rationalists. He freely exposed the emptiness of Reason, and gave his whole strength to rescue Philosophy from the contempt into which it had fallen by vindicating its existence as a genuine, scientific knowledge of Nature. But meanwhile the Understanding has gained undue ascendancy in Kant's system, and the time has come to define its limits. The scientific conception of Nature is exhausted in a single adaptation to our minds, namely, the world as matter in

[1] Wordsworth, *Prelude*, Bk. VI.   [2] Bernard, pp. 109-10.

motion determined by causality, and it makes no provision for further favours of Nature. But we have already found in the phenomena of the Beautiful an adaptation of Nature which goes beyond the Understanding, and now the phenomena of the Sublime, though they do not promote our thoughts about Nature, are conducive to our knowledge of a Nature-in-itself, the Supersensible. We say knowledge of the Supersensible and not simply thoughts about it, for the supersensible faculty is a power of intuition which transcends the opposition of perception and thought. The Understanding, the controlling faculty of Sense in which Imagination is a subordinate piece like the lens in the telescope, is the knowledge of separation and diversity; it only knows the parts of existence with a suspicion of their complete unity and therefore not as they exist concretely in the whole. Reason can never obtain a real total from these abstract particulars and must be satisfied with an Idea, an attenuated thought about them. For the demand of Reason, that it shall realise existence as a completed whole, can only be satisfied if the parts of existence themselves are known in their completeness as originally connected with the whole and with each other. As we shall see later, Nature favours us yet once more with an illustration of this more intimate relation of whole to part, in the phenomena of organic life. There is thus a conflict of faculties. Understanding and Reason, the governing faculty of Sense and the governing faculty of thought, are not able to supplement each other and supply a real intuition. For the parts of existence as they are known to Understanding are perceived, if imperfectly and even falsely, while the real kinds are not imaged by Reason, but *imagined* or conceived.

THE CRITICAL PHILOSOPHY 197

The particulars and their specific characters exist for our minds in divergent ways.

This is the result at which the *Critique of Pure Reason* arrives: there is a pull between Imagination and Reason, as it is expressed in the *Critique of Judgment*. In the Sublime this silent opposition breaks out for the first time in an open declaration of war. Our power of perception is taken at a disadvantage. What can the Understanding make of arid wastes of solitude, " mountain-masses grandly dumb," or the tragedy of human life? To know their scientific history is not to explain the reason of their existence. Certainly the Beautiful is also outwith the jurisdiction of the Understanding, but of these phenomena it does not need to ask the reason because they confirm its interpretation of Nature as adapted to our intelligence. But these intransigent phenomena of the Sublime help us in no way; they rather bring discredit on the effort of our intellect to keep its hold on Nature. For once the Imagination, which is an unbounded faculty of presentation, is put to confusion. Reason had already been degraded as an empty power; now it is the turn of Imagination, with its controlling genius Understanding, to fall into disgrace, and in their common ruin the supersensible faculty takes its rise:

" in such strength
Of usurpation—doth greatness make abode."

The superiority of this supersensible power consists in its transcendence of the *Streit der Facultäten*. Its object is a "real idea,"[1] the absolute totality which Reason sought but failed to find. It is real because the parts exist in the same way as the whole, there being no outside faculty of Imagination now to raise a conflict. It is the type of real existence.

[1] Bernard, p. 109.

But however valuable this interpretation of the Sublime may be as a moral or religious acquisition, it has little in common with Aesthetic and Kant deliberately calls it a mere appendix to the Beautiful.[1] Imagination having once lost its footing is never allowed to regain it, and "the light of sense goes out." It is true he says that Nature is sublime "in those of its phenomena, whose intuition brings with it the idea of its infinity."[2] But it is by a negative suggestion and not by aesthetic expansion of the presentation that the thought of the Infinite is conveyed to us. The presentation itself suffers in comparison with the Infinite of whose expression it is deemed incapable and even unworthy. "Who would call sublime," he asks, "shapeless mountain masses piled in wild disorder upon each other with their pyramids of ice, or the gloomy raging sea?"[3] Certainly we should. But to Kant these are simply horrible, and although he is superior to Burke in discriminating between the Horrible and the Sublime, Burke was nearer to the truth when he discovered Sublimity in the *frisson* of sensation.[4] What is it that comes to our help when we are confronted with some imminent peril and regains for us our self-control; or what enables us to contemplate the most harrowing suffering at once with sympathy and admiration? It is sublime emotion. It may not happen often. As Kant truly says, sublimity requires moral culture. But if we are not moved to disgust nor turn away in loathing, we

---

[1] Bernard, p. 104.   [2] *Ibid.* p. 116.   [3] *Ibid.* pp. 117-8.

[4] "Der Engländer Burg (*i.e.* Burke) sagt das Erhabene sei schreckhaft, das ist falsch. Anthropologie 1791-92." Schlapp, *Kants Lehre vom Genie*, p. 393.

THE CRITICAL PHILOSOPHY 199

stand our ground in presence of the presentation and are sufficiently reconciled to contemplate it with a curious but ennobling satisfaction. The awful loses its erstwhile hostile form, becomes familiar and even friendly while yet it maintains its distant majesty.

There is a lingering trace, however, of aesthetic symbolism in Kant's view. Instead of confirming our interpretation of Nature as an intelligible order and enlarging our thoughts about it, sublime phenomena call in question the whole principle of natural teleology as unimportant, and shift our attention to the supersensible world of which visible Nature is only a more or less contingent representation : " we are reminded that we only have to do with nature as phenomenon, and that it must be regarded as the mere presentation of a nature in itself."[1] It will thus be employed *gleichsam zum Schema des Uebersinnlichen.* But this is only the analogon of a schema and not an expressive symbol. Perhaps a more decisive suggestion may be found in his idea of subreption : " the feeling of the Sublime in nature is respect for our own destination, which by a certain subreption we attribute to an object of nature."[2] In its highest sense this language would mean the artistic passion which lives itself into the object and makes it personate our feeling. And he uses moderate language when he says that we judge sublime, not so much the object as our own state of mind.[3] I have mentioned these passages that we may not think unfairly of Kant's view. But these modifying statements do not affect his characteristic position. Sublimity is withdrawn from Nature altogether and exists entirely in our minds.

[1] Bernard, p. 135.   [2] *Ibid.* p. 119.   [3] *Ibid.* p. 117.

This theory has influenced later thinkers and may be said to have held the field until we come to Schopenhauer. "Your object is the sublimest, of course, in space," said Schiller to the astronomer, "but friend, in space the Sublime dwells not."[1] Hegel, too, has lent the weight of his great name to the same view. For him there is only one object of sublimity and that is God. But his appeal to Old Testament poetry is a little unfortunate, for it is not true that the transcendence of God exhausts Hebrew poetry. On the contrary, it was not till after the exile, when the fortunes of the nation were broken, that the Hebrew people learnt in their unfulfilled hopes to measure the distance between God and the creature. The theophanies of the earlier records testify to a fellowship with God as intimate, if naïve, as New Testament faith. And God is not only present to His people, He is immanent in His works. The forces of Nature are not analogous symbols but the expression of His presence and power:

> "Yea, He did fly upon the wings of the wind. He made darkness his secret place; his pavilion round about Him were dark waters and thick clouds of the skies.
> "The Lord also thundered in the heavens, and the Highest gave His voice; hail stones and coals of fire."[2]

If the God of the Hebrews is sublime, it is as He is clothed with Nature's majesty and power. And if Nature suffers in any part of her before the glance of the Creator, it is in man. But the vanity and nothingness of human life, so characteristic of Ecclesiastes and many of the Psalms, is a product of scepticism,

---
[1] Kuno Fischer, *Schiller als Philosoph*, p. 60.
[2] Psalm xviii. 10, 11, 13.

which first appears in the prophet Habakkuk and which is not original to Old Testament faith but a consequence of its historical development. The destruction of Nature herself is abhorrent to the Hebrew mind, and is the subject of apocalypse which belongs to the New Testament rather than to the Old.

Apart from this reference, however, it should be remembered in explanation of Hegel, that the rejection of Nature in his theory of the Sublime rests on the general principle of his Aesthetic. For him as for Aristotle, Art is Nature purified and set free from her contingencies; and it has therefore more reality than Nature, as Poetry is higher than History.[1] He scarcely recognises natural Beauty. And since the forms of Nature are more or less contingent because inadequate embodiments of the true forms which are born of spirit alone, it should follow that all Art is in its origin sublime. It is in his impatience with natural Beauty, that is, with ordinary perception, that the artist desires to create an individual form which will perfectly express the specific character of a rock or tree or any other object of Nature. He wants to see the thing in its history and in the variety of its existence; he wants to see a distinct, individual rock or tree and not as it exists for ordinary perception —a generic composition of quartz and felspar or a generic collocation of leaves. Now the state of mind in which he approaches his study is sublime, because it involves some mental strain and a moment of disappointment, followed by the feeling of uplifting, in the effort of imagination to penetrate to the Ideal of Nature in the particular form.

[1] *Poetics*, ix. 3.

But if we are to acquiesce in the rejection of Nature in her sublime appearances, we shall have to face the question whether Aesthetic has any part in sublimity at all. We must not be misled by the peace of exalted emotion into thinking that it must therefore be aesthetical. The sublime peace of a Wordsworth is aesthetical, but not many are able to have the same feeling of peace. Moral determination is self-approving and yields a harmony of feeling, and peace of soul is the grace of religious faith. But neither of these need be aesthetical for they may be very abstract. Morality and Religion can exist on two terms—God and I; and it is even essential to their existence that they should maintain a negative if not hostile attitude to the world. The difference is that Aesthetic must be reconciled to Nature now, while Morality and Religion can afford to wait. It is the genius of Faith that it lives on a promise and does not walk by sight. For this reason we should consider Faith as of a higher order than aesthetic intuition, for the latter is a premature realisation of what Faith will be one day when the old things are passed away. The common interpretation of Faith as a faculty which will pass into sight whenever the eternal things are revealed, is completely false. Faith is not hope; it is a power which will continue to be exercised even by him who is seeing the eternal things. It is in this sense that Kant is justified when he calls the Beautiful the symbol of Morality. Yet Faith may be aesthetical, but it is only in rare, exalted natures that it is able to forget the opposition, suppress the strife and be reconciled to the world. "Father, forgive them, for they know not what they do," is a true instance of aesthetical sublimity.

It was, of course, impossible that Hegel should not

have also recognised an immanent phase in the Sublime, and I only allude to what he holds in common with Kant. If the Sublime were confined to those extreme phenomena which provoke antipathy rather than engage our sympathy, we should not be greatly concerned to win a place for it in Aesthetic. It could be defined as the exalted emotion of moral and religious experience. But this would be unjust to many phenomena which can only be admitted into Aesthetic by the recognition of their sublime character. Now in his analysis, Kant offers no principle which is able to include those phenomena. They will thus be regarded as neither sublime nor beautiful. We have to ask, then, whether this terrible shock of which we have heard so much is essential to sublimity, and is a representative characteristic of all its forms. Certainly not in the sense of violent reaction to a hostile, menacing power, for the presentation may be at once arresting and sympathetic. It is said of Dickens that when he visited the falls of Niagara he experienced a feeling of great peace. But there is a moment of suspense while our aesthetic sympathy is put on its trial, due to an absence of familiarity which may occasion a feeling of disappointment or it may be a sense of self-depreciation. We are taken at a disadvantage for the moment by the daring expression of the Ideal in the presentation, and we may call this a slight shock if we please. But it must be understood that a hostile attitude in Nature is not essential, though she does reserve her dignity. The negative moment may vary between the sympathetic reaction we feel in seeing a sunrise and the violent sense of power to triumph in our own annihilation.

Perhaps one of the finest instances of the Sublime as

arising out of a purely sympathetic admiration, is the lunar rainbow in Browning's *Christmas Eve*. The imagination of the poet, exhausted in the effort to realise the beauty of the rainbow as it sprang like a spectral creature, dauntless and deathless, across the sky, subsided in the white light of pure, spiritual energy, and the vision of the outward sense passed into a vision of the mind :

> " Thus at the show above me, gazing
> With upturned eyes, I felt my brain
> Glutted with the glory, blazing
> Throughout its whole mass, over and under
> Until at length it burst asunder
> And out of it bodily there streamed,
> The too-much glory."

An example of the lower limit is the dignified reserve in language which makes up sublimity in style, its power to dispense with fulness of diction and perfection of form. The following passage is characteristic of Hebrew prose : " Now Naaman, captain of the host of the King of Syria, was a great man with his master, and honourable, because by him the Lord had given deliverance unto Syria : he was also a mighty man in valour, a leper" (2 Kings v. 1). There is no adversative particle in the Hebrew to indicate the transition of thought. The narrative intimates the infirmity of Naaman in a quiet, unobtrusive manner that is all the more impressive. It emphasises the difference of contrasted features by taking their unity for granted. This indifference to form reaches its highest point in the silence of Ajax to Ulysses, which as Longinus remarks is more sublime than any speech.[1] When now we

---

[1] *The Sublime*, ix. ; *Odyssey*, xi. 543.

extend the range of the negative moment so as to include the minimum of inhibition, we see how large a class of phenomena come under the Sublime. We have already noticed some of these instances in the preceding chapter. If the Beautiful is that whose specific character is adequately expressed in sensuous form, the Sublime is found where the Ideal visibly goes beyond the expression ; and sublimity arises not in contempt of the form but in the exercise of our aesthetic sympathy, which is able to trust the wisdom of the Ideal when it consents to dwell in this unlikely appearance. Never is it more sublime, says Schiller, than when the Ideal seems awanting.[1] And the more sublime our own nature is, the more immediately sympathetic will the presentation be, for we are already uplifted by culture and self-discipline to the exalted level of this difficult expression. To one who is already sublime, like Faust, sublimity is beautiful :

"To me are mountain-masses grandly dumb:
I ask not, Whence ? and ask not, Why ? they come."[2]

This is the merit in Schopenhauer's exposition. He makes the Sublime the same in principle with the Beautiful, and traces the degrees in which sublimity is accentuated and intensified. The influence of Kant here as elsewhere in his system is very marked; but, unlike Kant, he mediates moral Will through Nature in the Sublime, and shows how it is able to be a factor in Aesthetic. And, generally, he has done for this part of Kant's theory what Schiller did for the Beautiful. But it is in his own peculiar method, and also his

[1] *The Aesthetical Education of Man*: Weiss, p. 49.
[2] Taylor's translation, p. 310.

aesthetic theory follows so naturally from his metaphysics that it cannot be explained to advantage apart from his system.

What Kant called the Supersensible is designated Will by Schopenhauer. In itself it is a Will that neither affirms nor denies, existing without ground or principle, the mystical One of the Vedas. To become directed and purposive it must be represented as Appearance, and this means that it becomes object of knowledge. So Schopenhauer calls the world of Appearance the objectification of Will. Now the individual for whom the world exists as objective Will is himself part of this world. Although in itself indivisible, groundless Being, the supersensible Will exhibits an intelligible, reasoned order in the graded scale of existence when it takes form in an object-world, and is related to these typic forms of existence as harmony to the single voice.[1] And in this ascending order, brain and nervous system stand among the very highest expressions of Will. But since the individual in his bodily being is part of the world as objectified Will, his knowledge will be conditioned throughout by all the lower forms of existence which harbour in his individual nature. Human knowledge is therefore characteristically impure, being always subservient to the lower grades of Will as they come to us in sensation. It represents things as artificial unities of parts which co-exist with necessity or succeed each other in a certain order, never as real unities of being. Consequently we have to make this distinction, that the world as objective Will, or the world as it is represented in knowledge, is not a direct and perfect

[1] *The World as Will and Idea*: Haldane and Kemp, i. p. 206.

organisation of the Supersensible but indirect and inadequate. But there are also direct objectifications of Will, complete organisations of the blind Supersensible, and these are the real kinds or types of existence which Schopenhauer identifies with the Platonic Ideas: "As soon as knowledge, the world as idea (*Vorstellung*), is abolished, there remains nothing but mere will, blind effort. That it should receive objectivity, become idea, supposes at once both subject and object; but that this should be pure, complete, and adequate objectivity of the will, supposes the object as Platonic Idea (*Idee*), free from the forms of the principle of sufficient reason."[1] Are these specific forms accessible to knowledge?

Before we proceed further we should notice that the German has two words for 'idea.' The translators have preserved the difference in meaning by writing the Platonic Idea with a capital. The technical rendering of *Vorstellung* is representation, but 'idea' in English Philosophy has been always associated with a concrete perception or image while *Idee* (Idea) denotes the universal; for example, Burke says: "if they may be properly called ideas which present no distinct image to the mind."[2] To answer the above question, whether the specific forms of existence are accessible to our knowledge, we must observe a distinction in our faculty of knowledge corresponding to that which we have just observed in the world of objective Will. Knowledge fed and governed by sensation is always the perception of things related in a necessary way, for sensations do not come to us haphazard but under rule

---

[1] *The World as Will and Idea*, i. p. 234.
[2] *Sublime and Beautiful*, Part v. § 7.

and measure. But besides this body-principle of knowledge to which Schopenhauer gives the name Sufficient Reason, there is a much more primary and ultimate relation, and that is the simple relation of subject to object, the mere fact of a representation in consciousness (*Vorstellung überhaupt*).[1] All that is needful for the exercise of this pure knowledge is to abstract from its subservience to Will as it is indirectly and badly expressed in our individual being. Pure knowledge is the state of freedom from our personal being with its pragmatic tendencies, when we are pure, will-less subjects (*willenloses Subjekt*).[2]

It is easy to see the close identity of this form of expression with Kant's explanation of the aesthetic state as a kind of knowledge in general, and it is this disinterested state which in Schopenhauer takes the place of aesthetic perception. It is hardly necessary to observe that its corresponding objects are those Platonic forms, which are complete organisations of the Supersensible. Outside the world of Appearance, the Supersensible is nothing because it is anything; it is groundless Being. But Appearance does not give coherent meaning to the Supersensible; it rather breaks up its indeterminate unity into a multiplicity of blind, impulsive tendencies, which war with one another without ceasing and without any final purpose to justify them—the mechanical attraction of physical bodies, the *élan vital* in plants and animals, and the impulse to action in man. Hence the misery of human life, which makes it that the first and only crime is to be born. Only in the Ideas (*Ideen*), the specific

[1] Eng. Trans. i. 227; German, Leipsic, 1844, p. 198.
[2] German, p. 201, Bk. III. § 34.

characters which are independent of the particular forms, is the Supersensible perfectly reduced to harmony and brought to peace.

Schopenhauer criticises Kant for having made the Supersensible completely unknowable. He insists that it can be known when it is the object of aesthetic intuition or will-less knowledge.[1] Thus a double change has taken place: "Since now, as individuals, we have no other knowledge than that which is subject to the principle of sufficient reason, and this form of knowledge excludes the Ideas, it is certain that if it is possible for us to raise ourselves from the knowledge of particular things to that of the Ideas, this can only happen by an alteration taking place in the subject which is analogous and corresponds to the great change of the whole nature of the object, and by virtue of which the subject, so far as it knows an Idea, is no more individual."[2] The contemplation of the eternal forms is a sympathetic intuition based on identity of natures, for outside the world of Appearance the supersensible Will is the same in the subject as in the object.[3]

In this contemplation the subject loses himself and comes into peace. It is the satisfaction in the Beautiful which is won without effort. This happens when the subject is occupied with those forms of Nature or Art whose content is in harmony with its sensuous expression. There are few or no contingencies to obstruct the passage of our sympathy, for that object is beautiful in which the stress of Nature's elemental

---

[1] *The World as Will and Idea*, i. p. 226.
[2] *Ibid.* p. 228.
[3] *Ibid.* p. 233.

Will is laid to rest. But there are also forms which do not yield so readily to such facile contemplation. Because they are themselves beset and hedged about with Nature's blind effort which guards their secret, their accidental form, unsympathetic to the pure Idea in themselves or us, provokes to activity the elemental Will of Nature as it is organised in our body. And being thus drawn into conflict with the hostile presentation, our will-less knowledge is in danger of being engulfed in the pragmatic interests of our personal being. From this thraldom it can only be delivered when by a violent effort we exert our will against our will, and refuse to be drawn into this strife with Nature. Then sublimity arises. Refusing to take up the challenge, we steadily penetrate the forbidding appearance until it yields the secret of its inward being to our disinterested knowledge and we have pleasure in its contemplation. Our emotion is sublime because we are lifted up above our personal being and its inevitable strife with Nature.

In this brief account of Schopenhauer's theory, it will have been noticed how the Sublime and the Beautiful are interpreted by a single principle. In both it is the inner teleology that is the object of aesthetic pleasure, and we are able to enjoy the contemplation of the sensuous form because we ourselves exist in our supersensible character. There is only a difference of method. While in the Beautiful we come into this state without a struggle, we attain to the Sublime by "a conscious and forcible breaking away" from the hostile relation of the object to our will. But this does not affect the community of principle in both, which at least ensures that the Sublime is a genuine part of Aesthetic. There are degrees in the Sublime according to the strength or weakness of the effort by which it is distinguished from the Beautiful. As an instance of the weakest degree, the following example may be given : " If, in the dead of winter, when all nature is frozen and stiff, we see the rays of the setting sun reflected by masses of stone, illuminating without warming, and thus favourable only to the purest kind of knowledge, not to the will ; the contemplation of the beautiful effect of the light upon these masses lifts us, as does all beauty, into a state of pure knowing. But, in this case, a certain transcending of the interests of the will is needed to enable us to rise into the state of pure knowing, because there is a faint recollection of the lack of warmth from these rays, that is, an absence of the principle of life ; there is a slight challenge to persist in pure knowing, and to refrain from all willing, and therefore it is an example of a transition from the sense of the beautiful to that of the Sublime."[1] He gives other instances of rare beauty. I shall only mention what he says of solitude in Nature : it is a test of our intellectual worth to endure the state of pure contemplation in a region where there is nothing to engage our will, which is always in a state of want either of striving or attaining, and where we are tempted, in our incapacity, to abandon ourselves to the vacuity of unoccupied will and the misery of ennui.

It is only by recognising such a principle of graduated indifference to harmonious expression that we can effect a real synthesis between the Beautiful and the Sublime and bring them under a common name. It

[1] *The World as Will and Idea*, i. p. 263.

may be, however, that we should be prepared to find two forms of sublimity, one of which is not aesthetical, and separated in their less extreme forms by inappreciable lines of transition. We should not be anxious to show that every form of the Sublime is aesthetical, for there are many which are not aesthetical and yet are sublime. King Lear is sublime when he defies the elements. He rises above the thunder-storm, he accepts the challenge as a very little thing, but there is nothing aesthetical in his emotion. It is only as a dramatic representation that Lear can be aesthetical, when he together with the raging elements becomes an object for the spectator; and we can judge him as sublime because we are able to free ourselves from practical interest, which he could not do. To be aesthetically sublime in and for himself, he must become the storm as it passes over the trembling forest in its fury or lashes the deep into tempestuous foam. I have a distinct recollection of sublime emotion when witnessing a thunder-storm on the Brocken. But it was not aesthetical, for the elements of Nature suffered in comparison and dwindled into ostentatious display of mechanical forces. This is nothing more than the triumph of our moral nature over the natural forces which make the cattle tremble, and is very different from the aesthetical peace a Wordsworth would have felt in his sacramental fellowship with Nature.

But Kant has made it impossible to unite the Sublime and the Beautiful under a common principle, because he has defined the Sublime in terms of those extreme forms which lend themselves most readily to a purely moral interpretation. We have already noticed how he approaches a synthesis in the conception of Nature as a symbol of the Supersensible, and also in the recognition of a process of subreption; but these are found to be little more than a *façon de parler*. There is a remaining principle, however, tending in the same direction, on which he lays some emphasis and which ought to be examined. It is the idea of Security. Terrible Nature is attractive, he says, provided we are in security. There is no actual fear but only "an attempt to feel fear by the aid of the imagination." The quality of our emotion is not affected by this apparent want of seriousness, because it is not our actual experience of life that matters but the consciousness of our supersensible destination.[1] This seems to be his meaning, and it is plausible enough. We are reminded of Schopenhauer's 'volition in general' (*Wollen überhaupt*). Schopenhauer also insists that there must be no actual danger: "if a single real act of will were to come into consciousness, through actual personal pressure and danger from the object, then the individual will thus actually influenced would at once gain the upper hand, the peace of contemplation would become impossible, the impression of the sublime would be lost, because it yields to the anxiety, in which the effort of the individual to right itself has sunk every other thought."[2] He means that our exaltation is consciously maintained by a constant recollection of effort, which is not a particular act of our will but the elemental sense of opposition between us and Nature. It is the aesthetical consciousness of will as completely dissociated from our personal striving and idealised in being identified with

[1] Bernard, pp. 125-6 and 136.
[2] *The World as Will and Idea*, Eng. Trans. i. pp. 261-2; German, p. 229.

the universal will of humanity. In this way the moral consciousness is passed through Nature and becomes aesthetical. But this interpretation has nothing in common with Kant's true position and is only a happy accident. Indeed, when we examine it closely, we find that it is a return to the formalism which we discovered in his theory of the Beautiful. The principle by which he has been guided in both instances is, that whenever Aesthetic is free it ceases to be earnest, and that when it is earnest it has lost its purity and becomes dependent. He shows this formalism in another passage, where he says that we must not think of the stars as inhabited worlds or as physical bodies moving in elliptic orbits, but as a spangled canopy: nor of the ocean as peopled with the denizens of the deep, or as the source of clouds, or as the means of transit between the continents of the globe, but just as it strikes the eye.[1] This would be a very empty feeling and quite unworthy of his serious, wistful experience of the morally Sublime. The writer of the eighth Psalm, who looked up to the heavens, had much deeper thoughts than those; the moon and stars were at least framed by the fingers of God.

It is the beauty of morality, then, that Kant mistakes for the aesthetical Sublime, as Baumgarten would speak of the beauty of knowledge; it is what we might call the aesthetical resonance of moral feeling, not the aesthetical expression of a moral disposition. In a stray passage he seems to make a considerable advance. He says that moral feeling is so far cognate to aesthetical that it can represent moral action as sublime or even as beautiful, without losing in purity.[2] But we must be

[1] Bernard, pp. 137-8.   [2] *Ibid.* p. 133.

guided in our interpretation by the total impression we have received from his work. With the most sympathetic intentions we cannot help thinking that this statement is quite different from the position, that in the Sublime or Beautiful the moral consciousness is reduced to aesthetic form. Kant's definition of the aesthetic consciousness as a disinterested, which for him means impersonal, feeling of satisfaction, does not include, and therefore does not affect, the personal consciousness of character. The moral feeling of which he speaks as being closely akin to Aesthetic, is only a generic form which is indifferent to its content, like Socrates' sail in the *Parmenides*; it is the afterglow of self-conscious virtue. If the moral consciousness is to enter into Aesthetic at all, it must exist in us in some such instinctive way as Wordsworth believed it to exist in Nature:

> " Through primrose tufts, in that green bower,
>   The periwinkle trailed its wreathes;
> And 'tis my faith that every flower
>   Enjoys the air it breathes.
> " The budding twigs spread out their fan
>   To catch the breezy air;
> And I must think, do all I can,
>   That there was pleasure there."[1]

For Kant the moral consciousness must always be wide awake. He reaches his highest point in establishing a close connection between aesthetic feeling and moral culture. He had already attained to this level in his early *Observations*, and he never gets beyond it.[2] It is the lower limit in Schiller's *Aesthetical Education of Man*.

[1] *Lines written in Early Spring.*   [2] Hartenstein, ii. p. 239

The Sublime might be called the test in aesthetic theory. Its importance is seen in its decisive bearing on the relation between Beauty and Expression. If we hold with Lessing that expression must always be subordinate to Beauty so that Laocoon must not open his mouth too wide, we confine Aesthetic to a very narrow field. There is a beauty of spirit as well as of form—for example Maeterlinck's plays, to take a recent instance. The beauty of form is the essential condition of all expression. But while the beauty of spirit will not conflict with this formal symmetry, it demands its own individual expression which the beauty of form may never have dreamt, and is such stuff as dreams are made of. In the following passage from George Eliot's *Romola*, expression is made subordinate to beauty of form: "a perfect traitor should have a face which vice can write no marks on—lips that will lie with a dimpled smile—eyes of such agate-like brightness and depth that no infamy can dull them—cheeks that will rise from a murder and not look haggard." This view could be defended on the ground that it is the character of a perfect traitor to dissemble his own nature and counterfeit another. But this is only as it appears to the ordinary eye. Art has no use for such a creature, and will express in the features not only the perfect dissemblance but also some hint of the fact that it is a dissemblance. If now we look at such a painting as "The Two Usurers" by Marinus van Romerswael (London National Gallery), we see two men whose souls are carved upon their faces, the one secure from threats or dint of pity, the other agonising in the grasping greed for gold. Both are ugly and repulsive, but although there is no immediate beauty of form, there

THE CRITICAL PHILOSOPHY 217

is beauty of expression; their soul flows from their features, and this spontaneous, undisguised portrayal holds our admiration "like the red blood spouting from a vein."

This question was important for Kant had he cared to take it in this way. For beautiful objects are the first intimation on the part of Invisible Nature that it is in sympathy with our limited intelligence. This accommodation, upon which all natural science rests, is what Kant calls the Technic of Nature. In view of those natural forms whose significance is not exhausted in their mechanism, it is essential to our further understanding of Nature that we should regard her as working on a definite principle. We think of her as an artisan who fashions and moulds his material with conscious purpose. Otherwise we should be in a hopeless predicament, because our Understanding has no categories for those contingent forms. The Beautiful and the essence of Life escape a mechanical explanation. In the absence of such definite knowledge as a mechanical explanation can give, we must have some assurance that Nature knows what she is doing, and indeed we could not carry our mechanical explanation nearly so far as we do if we were not buoyed by this subjective principle. Certainly this persuasion does not make our knowledge of objects more intensive, for knowledge ends with mechanism and beyond that limit we are in the night where all cows are black. We may say, for instance, that the blood is carried into the lungs that it may be oxidised and diffused again throughout the body for the purpose of nutrition; but this teleological explanation throws no light on the efficient cause of its circulation. Yet if our knowledge is not intensified it is extended, and if we cannot say precisely what things really are, we can classify them, which is a great matter.

Now the Beautiful is a visible evidence and not merely a hypothetical assurance of Nature's sympathy with our intelligence; it is that quality in objects which facilitates the knowledge of their specific character. It will therefore be in the interest of our subjective principle if the range of these objects can be extended as far as possible, and this can only happen if we are willing to define Beauty in terms of expression. This will enable us to secure the testimony of those phenomena which in themselves are a positive denial of the purposive disposition of Nature, the phenomena of the Sublime, the ugly, the unsightly and unformed, and all the darker features of experience.

But this is not the course Kant has followed. He acknowledges that the Sublime is contingent to the second power, neither lending itself to interpretation by the scientific Understanding nor by the teleological function of Reason. And so he thinks that "the concept of the Sublime is not nearly so important or rich in consequences as the concept of the Beautiful."[1] But in neglecting this advantage, Kant believes that we are introduced into a more fruitful field of discovery. For in the untowardness of those forms which seem to call in question the adaptation of Nature to our minds, we are thrown back upon ourselves and strike upon a higher harmony, the sympathy of our minds with the Supersensible. If the Imagination sacrifices its freedom, it acquires "an extension and a might greater than it sacrifices"; for instead of being the instrument of

[1] Bernard, p. 104.

THE CRITICAL PHILOSOPHY 219

Understanding as in the Beautiful, it becomes "the instrument of Reason."[1] And if the Sublime does not recognise the subjective specification of Nature as a working principle which only makes Nature explainable so far, it is because it assumes the *de jure* conformity of all Nature to the highest and most ultimate purpose, the moral destination of man. Thus the Sublime is indirectly a further influence of the supersensible Thing; for if Nature in her beauty is influenced in favour of our Understanding, in her sublimity "Reason exerts a dominion over sensibility" in order to extend its outlook into the Infinite.[2]

Hitherto we have been obliged to develop Kant's theory in slow stages. In proceeding to a final appreciation, we must now try to give a clear idea of his position.

Kant considered that in Beauty and Sublimity there are two kinds of teleology which are at last complementary. The harmony of our mental processes is a subjective indication that Nature is, positively or negatively, in sympathy with our minds. But in the Beautiful the harmony is due to the play of Imagination and Understanding, and this means that Nature is only adapted to our knowledge. Now in pure knowledge there is nothing truly infinite; its object is rather the unending. Infinity dawns upon the scientist who is engaged with incalculable quantities only when his moral consciousness is awake. For his imagination, under the rule of scientific Understanding, makes no effort to realise infinity, being able to give it a figure by means of numerical schemata. Such is the limited nature of the mental powers which are active in the

[1] Bernard, pp. 136-7.   [2] *Ibid.* p. 130.

Beautiful. The procedure of the Understanding does not indeed appear as this bad infinite in the aesthetic form, because it is the genius of the Beautiful to present the unending as immediate completeness, and it gives satisfaction because the Understanding has ceased from its wandering. But this does not affect the nature of the faculty itself, and what we have presented in the Beautiful is not Infinity but the crystallising of a false infinity. The superiority of the Sublime, in Kant's view, is that in it for the first time the Infinite dawns upon us, for it is the Imagination and the moral Reason that are in play.

It was essential to Kant's theory of the Sublime as a negative experience which is not aesthetical, that the Understanding should be omitted; for according to his theory we are not reconciled to Nature as known to the Understanding, but Imagination fabricates a new world under the controlling influence of Reason. It is the presence of this latter power that distinguishes the Sublime. But it calls for some words of explanation, for throughout the discussion Kant is confusing Reason as the unconditioned Understanding and Reason as the moral faculty. Primarily, of course, he means the Practical Reason, and it is quite clear that in the Sublime this is the dominating and final sense in which it is used.[1] But he also appears to take it as the faculty of the unconditioned, the Theoretic Reason of the *Dialectic*, as is evident from the prominence he gives to the idea of infinity. This confusion is due to the subtle way in which the *Gemüthskräfte* and the *Erkenntnissvermögen*, which are ostensibly a single specification of the former, run parallel to and into one

[1] See Bernard, pp. 151-2.

another. As Judgment, which is only a subordinate element in the higher faculty of Knowledge, came to be identified with the higher faculty of Feeling, so the Theoretic Reason, itself a subordinate element in Knowledge, becomes germane to the Will or moral Reason. And after all, in spite of their apparent difference, there is a very close connection between them. For Theoretic Reason is the faculty which seeks to realise extensively in knowledge the same completeness (*res completae*) which moral Reason apprehends intensively in practice. The latter, firing at close range, either misses fire or strikes with deadly aim ; the former, firing at long range, is dispersed like small shot over a wide area. It is only an over-refined subtlety that would distinguish too nicely the *Gemüthskräfte* from the *Erkenntnissvermögen*, and it is an equivocal merit in Cohen's book that he seems to assume their identity, at once making Kant's meaning more intelligible and his method harder to appreciate. There is no doubt that Kant's methodological intention was to restrict the Reason in the Sublime to its theoretic use, as a specification of the cognitive faculty.

In the Beautiful, then, the content is limited. It is the perception not of infinity but of an infinite finite, an inexhaustible Nature but still unmediated Nature, an indeterminate concept of Nature but still a concept, the immediate consciousness of Nature only as it is adapted to knowledge. It is in the Sublime that the Infinite first appears in its true nature as spirit. For the harmony of Imagination with Reason is a subjective indication that Nature is purposive to our highest destiny, not indeed directly and positively for then this final end of Nature would be evident to our knowledge, and in our immediate consciousness of this end as known the Sublime would also be beautiful. Now we see clearly and for the last time the double error in Kant's Aesthetic. The Beautiful is formal, without specific meaning, because it is exclusively intellectual and is not affected by the spirit of our mind. It is an idealised Understanding. There is no final end in Nature for knowledge, and however far we carry out the process, we never get any nearer to the heart of things. The immediate consciousness of this unending teleology is much the same as the ideal sum in arithmetical progression. The secret of our pleasure in this formal Beauty is its premature completeness, its anticipation of discursive processes, but it does not follow that we have a deeper insight into Nature. The immediate consciousness of infinite extension does not make our perception more intensive. It is only the unending processes of Nature crystallised in certain of her forms, very pretty like a glass marble; but it has nothing spiritual, the breath of Art has not breathed upon it. Again, in the Sublime it is our spirit and not our Understanding that is affected by Nature whose final end, inconceivable for knowledge, is consummated in the consciousness of our immortal destiny. But this consciousness of Nature is not aesthetical; it is spirit without form as the Beautiful is form without spirit. The sublime faculty has no aesthetic Understanding to perceive the final end in Nature, and must therefore think it outside of Nature in the formless void of an Imagination whose light is extinguished. In such exalted feeling, Nature has no community with man's spiritual being.

The cause of this double error is Kant's radical separation of the mental powers. He did well to prevent all confusion of Volition with Cognition, and by doing so he ushered in the dawn of a new day for ethical theory; he did well also to maintain a distinction between Feeling and the other faculties, and in doing so he laid the foundation-stone of aesthetic theory for all time. But Kant carried this separation into the root and destroyed the primordial unity of human nature. He ignored the fact that while these faculties are separate as explicit elements in consciousness, they lose their distinctness in the elemental unity of mental life: the intellective consciousness has a moral nature, instinct with spirit, and Beauty must possess the Infinite; the moral consciousness likewise has a nature that is intellective, instinct with form, and our sublime Reason must shape itself in Nature.

But although Kant does not succeed in transforming the moral consciousness into an aesthetic factor and hardly suspects that it is possible, he really does succeed with knowledge. And faults in theory must not affect the merit of his intention. If he denied a soul to Beauty, it was in order that Goodness might live: a needless sacrifice, for the moral consciousness pre-existed in a form much more akin to aesthetic feeling than to its own specific function. Kant himself was aware that the Ideal which he found in the moral consciousness is the soul of Beauty and what alone could make it precious. But in his theory of Genius he goes much further. It is Nature in the subject, the supersensible substrate of all his faculties, that utters itself in Genius; and evidently this cannot mean the ethical personality but the Man of Humanity, not his character but the totality of his nature. It is the supersensible substrate of his Humanity which, as Cohen says, holds itself responsible for the harmony of all the tendencies of consciousness.[1]

There is the further consequence that Aesthetic cannot be subjective in the sense that it is a more abstract interpretation of Reality. For Aesthetic is the most concrete expression of our elemental disposition. We do not commit ourselves to the statement that it is more original, in the sense that it precedes and conditions the emergence of Knowledge and Morality. We must not be misled by Schiller's poetic fancy when he says that virtue was loved and vice rejected before Solon's laws were made.[2] It is quite a plausible theory that, before our moral nature became self-conscious, it already contained the end of its development instinctively; if its content was meagre, less precious than the exposed and naked sense of self-conscious virtue in its ungainly growth, its eyes not yet being opened and innocent of good or evil, it had at least the form of its consummated perfection in the fruit, the innocence of its own goodness. But this ingenuous state is as little aesthetic as it is moral. It is simply the condition of a "living soul." We must distinguish the physical theory of the Play-impulse from the imaginative theory. The former is among the very earliest factors in the development of child-life as also in the race, but in this function the play-impulse is only another name for the consciousness of motion. Aristotle observed that the most rudimentary form of sensation in animals, namely Touch, is a discriminative activity by which the objects of nutrition are accepted

[1] *Kants Begründung der Aesthetik*, p. 263.
[2] *Die Künstler*, iv.

or rejected, and this primary attitude of consciousness is inevitably bound up with the consciousness of motion. The play-impulse as we find it in the child is a purely physical motive, the discharge of surplus energy, like the roaring of the lion in the forest when he has nothing else to do. But this is surely not the same as the play with images of things or the delight in seeing for seeing's sake. The world of the child is altogether a world of play in the sense that the distinction between Appearance and Reality has not yet emerged, while Aesthetic is based on the conscious implication of this distinction. But, on the other hand, Aesthetic is at once more original and concrete than either Knowledge or Morality; for while these are particular functions of consciousness, Aesthetic is the original disposition itself in its totality raised to a higher immediacy. It is the same elementary state but informed and enriched by the contributions of Knowledge and Morality, as the trunk of the tree grows with its branches and draws its nutriment partly from them and partly from its own root. The ever-recurring question whether Aesthetic should be moral or intellective, is the same as if we should ask whether the tree can contain its own branches. If Aesthetic is affected by Knowledge and Morality, it is not in the form of raw impressions but as light and atmosphere are transmuted into the sap of the tree.

Now Kant's view, strictly understood, means that the farther we are removed from outer presentations, our consciousness becomes less and less intensive: Aesthetic is subjective the more it loses contact with Reality. The theory is an echo of his doctrine of Inner Sense as a form of consciousness which is not schematic. Subjectivity first appears in the Beautiful. The pleasure is not the consequence of sensation but the concomitant of aesthetic reflexion, and consequently seems to lose the thrill of sensation and sensuous charm. We are still, however, in the realm of Appearance. But in the Sublime, subjectivity becomes outrageous. We soar upwards into the void where there are no objects of Appearance but incoherent figurations of a blind Imagination. Yet there is no candid reader who will seriously believe that this is an adequate statement of Kant's meaning. In Reflexion, of which Aesthetic is the typical expression, he finds something more than the neutral attitude of Science; it is the Personal in man. It could not therefore be other than subjective, but for Kant it is the richest plane of experience and objective in its own right, though it cannot be measured by the standard of Science. It is in the Sublime, regarded as a further development of the moral Ideal, that we receive this deeper impression of Kant's meaning; and while we acknowledge that in his exposition the gulf between Nature and Freedom is widened, we are bound to admit that in principle he effects a reconciliation between them. This principle is expressed mainly in the profound conception of subjective teleology as the felt harmony of our mental powers, and may be studied in the two Introductions, especially the first, and also in his theory of Genius.

An attempt may be made in closing this first part of the *Critique of Judgment* to indicate a solution of the final problem, how, in spite of their subjective character, the judgments of Reflexion may be considered as even more objective than those of Science. According to Weber's law, the intensity of sensation varies in a constant ratio with the increase or diminution in the presentation-stimulus. For our purpose it does not matter whether we reject this quantitative theory and hold with M. Bergson that there is no minimum increment of sensation. The fact remains that the intensity of sensation diminishes in the degree that presentations are withdrawn. But this is only true up to a certain point. Increase the presentation-stimulus to its maximum and sensation disappears. Thus we have two very different orders of zero, that which registers the total absence of presentation and that which registers the maximum of stimulation. There can be no hesitation in deciding which of these applies to Aesthetic. Notwithstanding the ideal character of the world of Art as removed from the first rude contact with Reality in sensation, there is no diminution but an access of vitality. Therefore our zero must be the maximum. Aesthetic feeling is not the negation of sensibility but the transmutation of sense-affection into a new order of sensation. What gives the appearance of objectivity to sense-perception is just the partial and limited range of the presentation-stimuli. Their number is so modest that we are incapable of rejecting their addresses and readily give ourselves up to their entertainment. A few guests are always engaging and compel our devoted attention. But what do you do when the whole world calls at your house? You begin to think of your own soul. It is not the absence but the prodigality of presentations that exhausts our sensibility and oversteps the maximum. Now think of the whole world knocking at your senses, and you will readily conceive how you may be conscious of no sense-affections, just as we do not hear the motions of the heavenly bodies after the fancy of the Pythagoreans, and still have an intensive consciousness. Kant's degrees in Subjectivity are our degrees in Reality. Aesthetic is for him an original faculty of intuition which is independent of the distinction between subjective and objective, thought and sense, because its object is the supersensible substrate of Nature "which lies at its basis and also at the basis of our faculty of thought."[1]

[1] Bernard, p. 117.

CHAPTER VII.

TELEOLOGY OF NATURE.

WE now turn to what seems to be a very different subject of study. But if we keep in mind Kant's original intention, the transition to the Teleology of Nature is quite easy. It is sufficient that we should have pleasure in discovering purposive connections, to bring this discriminative activity under a common principle with Aesthetic. For although the pleasure in either is of a different kind, it is characteristic of a mental procedure common to both, in which the mind is more interested in its own processes than in arriving at any definite conclusion. Each is a form of judgment which does not define an object but illustrates the way in which the conscious subject is affected. This is what Kant means by Reflexion. If we are pleased to call it a judgment, we must remember that it is not logical but psychological; for in place of a predicate whose meaning is fixed and explicit, there is only an inarticulate feeling or affective description. A thing is beautiful only so long as it contains something which cannot be defined; and living forms, in like manner, lose all their sacredness and charm, when a mechanical interpretation is sufficiently convincing to influence our judgment and to destroy the sense of wonder in which Philosophy takes its rise.

No doubt, connected with the difference in the kind of pleasure, there is a very marked distinction between the objects of Art and Teleology. In common language we speak of beautiful objects, although they are not beautiful in themselves but as representations in consciousness. Aesthetic pleasure is not the perception of a quality in the object but the sense of harmony in our mental processes. Or if we still prefer to use the language of common sense and say that the object is itself a harmony of elements, it is nevertheless true that its purposive form only comes to self-consciousness in us. The beautiful object indeed exists outside of us, but conceived as a common object it has no aesthetic interest. If now we turn to living forms, we are confronted with things which continue to hold our interest while they also exist independently, and indeed because they do so. Therein lies the difference between Aesthetic and Teleology. Even the objects of Science are the creatures of our Understanding,—their extension, rigidity and motion are subjective constructions; and whatever their independent basis may be, they do not exist as objects in themselves, for object means synthesis and synthesis is the work of mind. For the sake of brevity we might adopt J. S. Mill's convenient evasion and say that they are 'permanent possibilities of sensation.' How much more will the objects of Aesthetic, which is a still more independent activity than Understanding, be the peculiar creation of our mind? Our processes of imagination, feeling and thought *are* the objects themselves, and consequently the pleasure we feel is quite distinctive. We have aesthetic satisfaction only when objects yield up their natural existence and impersonate our inner life.

But in observing living forms, our admiration is sustained by the thought that the object has an independent being, and we enjoy the excitement of our own processes, not because they are a finished symphony as in aesthetic pleasure, but just because they are incomplete; it is pleasure in a harmony that is realised progressively. Our own processes are interesting only because they are the transcript of a purposive form which is intensely interested in its own activity. We may now express the distinction in Kant's technical language: " we can regard *natural beauty* as the *presentation* of the concept of the formal (merely subjective) purposiveness, and *natural purposes* as the presentation of the concept of a real (objective) purposiveness."[1]

But even this difference of province between Aesthetic and Teleology need not put us off the track. For although Teleology is the experience of our affective states in essential connection with real objects, in the long run it is not less subjective than Aesthetic. It does not profess to determine anything conclusive about these objects. It is true that all Science is built up by teleological observation, and Kant himself devotes more attention to Teleology as a system of heuristic principles than is consistent with his original purpose. But he is quite positive in his opinion that the experimental sciences never give a final result which is different in kind from our mathematical knowledge of Nature. However far the biological sciences may carry their investigations, they do not come any nearer to the secret of a living form. Undoubtedly the sciences greatly extend our knowledge of Nature, but they are still working from the outside with quantities and measure-

[1] Bernard, Introd. p. 35.

ments; and if, as Kant says, the end of Nature must be sought outside Nature, the door is foreclosed against them. He means that there can be no science of ultimate ends corresponding to our knowledge of relative existence. And since Metaphysic has the ultimate for its object, it can never be a positive science but only the science of the limits of human reason.

In teleological reflexion we do not define the exhaustive unity of existence in a living form, but, to use a phrase of Mr. Bradley, give "illustrations of its latent qualities." For although a thing exhibits purposive activity and may therefore be regarded as an End of Nature (*Naturzweck*), we are not at liberty to say that its existence is an End of Nature.[1] The end which it embodies is limited to the organism and is not by any means self-explaining. All that we have said is that there is present a relative End of Nature. We are using little more than a figure of speech when we say that an organism is a natural purpose, for this it could only be if it were also a natural product. But if we try to answer this latter question we fall into confusion, for it is meaningless to speak of a product unless we know something about the mode of production. We say it is a product of Nature and do not even know what Nature is.

It is true that we do see Nature organising herself in her products, and Kant himself thinks that we are nearest to the truth when we describe Nature as "an analogon of life."[2] But this is not encouraging: for it either means Hylozoism, the conception of Nature as living substance, which contradicts the very being of matter, spontaneous generation being an idle fancy for

---

[1] Bernard, § 67, p. 283. [2] *Ibid.* p. 279.

Kant ; or it means the conception of Nature as informed by a soul, which is equally improper, for Nature is made into the instrument of a soul which governs it but does not bring it into being; or, finally, this latter theory may take the deistic form that the soul, existing from without, fashions the world out of an independent substance which it does not make. As he says in a further passage, to think of Nature as an intelligent being would be preposterous, and to place another intelligent being above it as its architect would be presumptuous.[1] For the reason that we cannot prove the existence of God, we are also unable to speak of a natural product with any degree of intelligence. In order to speak of a natural product it is not enough to think of it as manifesting a purpose of Nature in its inner structure, for this is limited to the life of the organism and gives no hint of Nature's complete design ; we must be able to give the full reason for its existence as a reciprocal part of a world-organism. This would be to determine with precision the final end of Nature, and this we cannot do without a scientific knowledge of the God who made it, which is impossible.

Kant gives the example of a blade of grass.[2] A blade of grass is an organic form of Nature and therefore something which no mechanical interpretation can ever explain. It is no mere concursus of fortuitous atoms. Even to make it thinkable at all, we must introduce the idea of design. So far, then, as its internal structure is concerned, it may be regarded as a natural purpose. But our fatal mistake is to jump from this purely subjective idea of design, which is a necessity of our Reason, to its actual existence, as if what we think ought to be must

[1] Bernard, p. 290. [2] *Ibid.* § 67.

be in fact. It is the same criticism as Kant makes on the ontological argument for the being of God. How do we know that there is any final end in Nature at all? Indeed our certitude diminishes as the evidences of design increase; for each fact of teleological observation leads to another by which it is cancelled, and we are carried forward in an unending progression from which the idea of a final purpose fades away. Thus, while the blade of grass bears the evidence of design in its structure and cannot have sprung up by accident, it offers no indication of the reason for its existence and we must seek the final cause outside of it. Let us say, then, that it is needful for the ox. But the ox is not in itself an end of Nature and again we must be satisfied with a relative explanation. We can say that the ox is needful for man as a means of subsistence. But no amount of scientific knowledge can offer the reason for man's existence, though he is the most highly developed of all organic products. The end of existence only becomes more ironical as the adaptations appear more wonderful. To take another example from Kant, the Laplander finds many conveniences marvellously suited to the maintenance of life in these inhospitable regions: the reindeer which can subsist on a dry moss which they scratch from under the snow, enable him to have intercourse with other races of men; sea-animals provide him with food and clothing, and with their fat and the wood floated in by the sea his huts are warmed. This is very instructive, but it gives no conclusive proof of a divine purpose in Nature. For neither do these conveniences exist exclusively for the Laplander, although he happens to make use of them, nor does he contain a reason in his own being why he should be thus provided.

If men are to live there must be the means of livelihood, but it is not by any means clear why men should exist at all. As Kant rather wittily remarks, the case of the Laplander is not an evidence of purpose and harmony, but rather of their absence in the constitution of the world; for it is only disagreement and strife that could have dispersed mankind into such inhospitable regions.[1]

Teleology therefore in Kant's view makes no pretension to Science. Though it deals with objects which have an independent reality, it is subjective like Aesthetic. Its use as a scientific principle in building up our experimental knowledge of Nature is only a secondary result and not its proper function, which is to determine not the mechanical relations of objects but the total unity of their existence, their purpose or end. Now Science is so far exhaustive in its achievement, and Teleology would likewise be Science if it could discover with the same precision the final causes of things. But we have seen that it can never do this. In Science our judgments are objective because our thoughts about objects obtain necessity in sense-perception. But in Teleology our thoughts are only possibilities which cannot be verified in actual presentation. We can have no sensation of an end. So while the judgments of Teleology may indeed be necessary truths of Reason, they are not necessary truths of Science. They are economic devices of Reason to help our memory and to save us from being confused in the multitude of scientific principles, by giving them the lead in a single direction towards which they converge and meet in a point. By the discovery of common elements, the multiplicity of scientific kinds is reduced

[1] Bernard, § 63.

to a comparatively small number of higher genera (*entia praeter necessitatem non esse multiplicanda*). These genera are capable of being further differentiated by features which are only found in a certain number of the species included under the genus, and thus the number of genera is increased on a new basis of distribution (*entium varietates non temere esse minuendas*). But Reason will not rest until it has reduced all these genera with their sub-genera to a single, comprehensive unity, and this is effected by carrying the principle of differentiation to an unlimited extent until the plurality of genera melts away and gives place to a single genus. For by increasing the diversity, it is found that the sub-genera or species hitherto obtained are not fixed but continuous with one another. And although this approach of Reason to a final unity is always asymptotic, it is understood in the interest of systematic knowledge that no species is absolutely separated from another; it will always be possible to discover between any two a third whose difference from either of them is less than their difference from each other, and so prove their affinity (*non datur vacuum formarum*).[1]

In consequence of these three maxims of Reason, namely, Homogeneity, Specification and Continuity, the general principle follows that there are no first and original differences separated from each other by an empty interval, but that all the manifold genera are divisions in a single, supreme genus. It is natural that we should think of this final point in which the various principles meet, as a stable fact of Science; and if man were to be taken as the apex of the manifold genera, he would not only be able to give a reason for the hope

[1] *Appendix to Dialectic.*

that is in himself but also to substantiate the existence of all the lower forms as ends of Nature in their relation to him. Teleology would then have scientific value and man's immortality might rest on other than moral grounds. Modern thought favours this point of view and has reversed the order in Kant's statement. As Dr. Ward would put it, Science is not objective and ultimate but reflective, while it is Teleology that interpretes the real constitution of Nature. Science is only a conceptual description of facts, and for its boasted necessity there is not a trace of evidence except what we project into Nature out of our own heads, causation being nothing more than what Mill said it was, uniform antecedence. It seems that Hume was not so far wrong after all. But the modern attitude to Teleology is different. The ends which we read into Nature are valid and objectively true because they are a creative interpretation of Nature.

We shall not stay to examine this position further. But it is right to say that the difference between Kant and his critics is in great part a matter of words. We have reason to think that the Subjective in which Teleology finds its place, is for Kant more real than Science; but he reserves for Science the title to knowledge and denies it to Teleology, because in its determinate, mechanical relations Science has the completeness and finality of a limited achievement. However, we must at present accept Kant on his own terms. This point to which reflective Reason decoys the laws of Understanding is no proved fact of Science but an illusion, a *focus imaginarius*, like the naïve belief that objects reflected in a mirror are actually behind it.[1]

[1] *Appendix to Dialectic*: Meiklejohn, p. 395.

He is quite emphatic in the *Critique of Pure Reason* that these principles are not derived from the actual nature of objects but from the interest of Reason in the completeness of knowledge.[1] They are not constitutive but reflective, not interpretative but descriptive. They are not properly concerned with objects at all, but only with the way in which they are illustrated in the consciousness of ourselves. Teleology is therefore reflective like Aesthetic. They are different because they are on different planes and are occupied with different aspects of Nature, the former through reflexion on concepts, the latter through reflexion on representations.

This is the implicit intention of Kant's Teleology. Its primary significance is not logical but affective. It is the play of concepts as Aesthetic is the play of representations. In neither of these forms of judgment do we look for a predicate which specifies the scientific nature of objects, so much as for an affective Idea which carries their resonance in the consciousness of our own processes and is marked by a feeling of pleasure. This is their common attribute and the only justification for having brought them together as modes of Reflexion. But there are so many strands in the discussion that we lose sight of this original motive in a complicated analysis. Kant himself seems to forget all about it and shows a greater amount of interest in the metaphysics of Biology, so that we who have been hitherto engaged in the analysis of Fine Art now find ourselves thinking of Darwinism and kindred problems. He had already discussed Teleology at sufficient length in the *Dialectic*, being

[1] *Ibid.* p. 408.

more intent on the criticism of its misuse than on the recognition of its positive function. What he ought now to have done is to develop this positive side so as to show its affinity with Aesthetic. But throughout the *Critique of Judgment* and the two Introductions we hear the same old song as in the *Dialectic*, with the exception of a few sporadic strains.

There is, of course, a new element introduced into Teleology in the *Critique of Judgment*. In the *Dialectic* Kant is only concerned with what may be termed Formal Teleology, because it surveys things with a view to their symmetrical arrangement in a logical system; and it does this on the principle that Nature specifies the laws of Understanding, which really mean mechanical causation, into more minute applications throughout her whole empire. This procedure of Reason carries the belief that Nature will be found constant to her character as governed by necessary laws, even when we press the causal conditions to their farthest limit which is manifestly beyond the reach of knowledge. It is no other than Mill's Uniformity of Nature with his supplementary doctrine of Probability.

This is the logical disposition of Nature, though it must not be supposed that it is the empty analysis of an arbitrary premiss. Kant explains in the original Introduction that it rests on a transcendental principle which has its ground of expectation in Nature herself; it is not the Logic of the Syllogism but the Logic of Nature.[1] This does not alter the fact, however, that the system of Nature obtained by inductive hypothesis is logical, for Nature is never given to us

[1] *Über Philosophie überhaupt*: Rosenkranz, i. p. 590, note.

as a completed whole any more than she is given as beautiful, and therefore Induction like Art is a teleological determination of Nature. Not seeing the end, we endure "as seeing Him who is invisible," and are only able to realise it in a logical anticipation. Accordingly, we are not surprised to find Kant saying that the end or ends, by whose help we imagine to ourselves the independent series of causal conditions not only as completed in themselves but also as uniting in a final direction, do not exist in the things of Nature; it is solely in the thinking subject they reside, for the behoof of his reflective faculty.[1] It is called formal Teleology because it is a necessity of our Reason to regard Nature as governed throughout her extent by a systematic Idea, and because it does not dogmatically assert that there is a purposive activity in Nature herself. For as Stadler admirably expresses it, the laws of Nature are always mechanical and it is only their relation to each other that is not mechanical. When we say that a particular thing is contingent, we must not mean that it cannot be mechanically explained; for how could we ever recognise that it fell outside the universal order of Nature unless it were a possible object of experience with causal conditions? Every fragment of appearance must have causal relations, even the most complicated fact must be presented as a sum of effects; otherwise it is no object of experience.[2] What we want to know is how these innumerable threads of causal conditions, which no memory can hold, are related to each other and whether they unite in a common direction. The

[1] *Ibid.* p. 594.
[2] August Stadler, *Kants Teleologie*, pp. 63-4.

THE CRITICAL PHILOSOPHY 241

hypothesis of Reason is absolutely necessary for the sustained activity of Understanding, for without this systematic Idea of determination according to end, Nature would be a torso even as mechanism and the supposed necessity of the categories would have merely subjective validity. As Kant says in the Introduction, without the principle of Formal Teleology "the Understanding could not find itself in Nature."[1]

What is to be noticed in this entire procedure of Reason is that nothing further is determined in the constitution of Nature herself. Formal Teleology rather emphasises the mechanical order of Nature and gives sureties for its continuous and unquestioned application. The novel feature in the *Critique of Judgment* is that Nature is purposive, not simply as a logical system in the interest of our Reason but in the organisation of her own products. These organic forms are much more than a complex of mechanical processes, and are only intelligible if we regard them as the immediate products of a Nature which organises herself in them. We should expect this new field of observation to react in a very marked way on the teleological judgment, to the extent of creating a new type of Reflexion. For there is the greatest possible distinction between a Nature of mechanism, which is only figured as purposive with a view to completing and sustaining its original character, and a Nature which is herself purposive in her products. The former exists as a system altogether in our teleological reflexion, but the latter is in parts of her domain quite independent of our interpretation and is herself purposive. This at least is how the case seems to

[1] Bernard, p. 36.

stand. And Kant makes the rather unexpected statement that this Objective Teleology "has nothing to do with a feeling of pleasure in things."[1] Surely this is taking very high ground. It shows at least how clearly Kant meant to distinguish the two fields of teleological observation. He freely acknowledges that in Formal Teleology the discovery of a higher principle under which several heterogeneous laws of Nature may be combined, is the ground of a very marked pleasure, although hardly anyone except a transcendental philosopher is capable of this admiration;[2] and if we do not always have this feeling, it was certainly present at one time. But in the case of things which are themselves real organisations, it would seem that our own interests are silenced in the presence of a being which enjoys its own existence, and we surrender the pleasure we might have in our processes of observation to the neutral attitude of the scientist who merely registers the harmonious activity of the organism. Thus the difference between these two provinces of observation does not affect the nature of Kant's Teleology in the slightest degree.

Two courses were open to him: either the subjective factor in the judgment is practically negligible, as appears from the statement just quoted in which the feeling of pleasure is excluded, and then Teleology becomes an objective judgment of Science and ceases to be a form of Reflexion altogether; or its reflective character is retained, not because of, but in spite of, its objective province. His critical temper will not

---

[1] Bernard, Introd. p. 34. Cp. *Über Philosophie überhaupt*: Rosenkranz, i. pp. 602-3; Hart, vi. p. 392.

[2] *Über Philosophie überhaupt*: Rosenkranz, i. p. 595.

THE CRITICAL PHILOSOPHY 243

tolerate the first alternative, for he is bound to maintain that Metaphysic can never be Science. Just as he had exposed the false application of Formal Teleology in the *Dialectic*, he must now show that no form of judgment which goes beyond the causal connections in experience can have more than subjective validity. He therefore explodes the illusive certainty to which we pretend in our interpretation of organic life, quite in the manner of the *Dialectic*, and finally proclaims that what he himself calls objective, material, internal purposes are only predicates of Reflective Reason. But this is just Formal Teleology over again, and the judgment has gained nothing from the character of this new field of observation. We simply pass through the world of organic life and, like a diver whose eyes are shut under the water, rise to the surface as wise as we were before. We can now appreciate Stadler when he says that the Reflective Judgment in its entirety is identical with the regulative Ideas of Reason, and that the only peculiar and novel feature in Reflexion is Aesthetic.[1] At first we should be naturally inclined to agree with Dr. Frost, who holds, on the contrary, that they are not the same, for Reflexion is meant to provide deeper categories corresponding to those of the Understanding. But Stadler is speaking from the actual results of Kant's exposition, and Frost admits that he is quite correct,[2]

---

[1] "Wo immer Kant von einer eigentümlichen Urteilskraft spricht, er damit die ästhetische meint, und dass er keineswegs gedacht hat in der teleologischen Urteilskraft ein neues, von der Kritik der reinen Vernunft noch ungekanntes Vermögen aufzustellen." *Kants Teleologie*, p. 29, cp. p. 36.

[2] *Der Begriff der Urteilskraft bei Kant*, p. 115.

as indeed it is only too easy to prove his position from statements in the two Introductions, which are quite explicit in its favour. But if this is all we have to learn, we have spent our labour in vain. The teeming forms of life emit no response to our efforts to understand them, but shrink into their crevices before the fatal sneer of Criticism ; and all that we have for our part is a judgment which is neither scientific nor reflective, but a hybrid form of judgment which determines nothing either in the object or the subject. For Criticism is perfectly justified in reducing organic life to the same level as the field of observation in Formal Teleology. Organisms must be perfect mechanisms above all else, and any flaw in the mechanical functions is fatal to the life. The heart beats, the blood circulates, with the same purposeless, insensate motion as the stamps in the battery of a gold-mine. As Kant says, without mechanism organised beings " would not be natural products." [1] They are a system of mechanical processes which we can follow and understand. What we cannot understand is the system itself, which gives a meaning and a purposive direction to those processes which no mechanism could initiate. An organism is as true to its mechanical character as an engine which is controlled by an external agent, although the controlling power is not without but in the organic processes themselves. Consequently our teleological observation of an organism is essentially the same as when we round off the purely mechanical world of Nature into a completed system by the help of final Ideas. Organisms, therefore, from our point of view, are not generically distinct from the totality

[1] Bernard, p. 342.

THE CRITICAL PHILOSOPHY 245

of mechanical Nature as empirically contingent for our Reason; they are particular illustrations of what is essentially the same problem, and though outstanding are not peculiar.

But the question which becomes increasingly insistent in the *Critique of Judgment* is precisely how far the standpoint of the Kantian Criticism is justified. If we accept the position that the mechanical interpretation of Nature, as the essential implicate in the conditions of knowledge, is the first and indispensable basis of all Science, we need not look for anything higher even in Organic Nature than a Formal Teleology—the synthesis of mechanical relations in the unity of a *logical* system. But the priority of a mechanical interpretation is not by any means a proved position, notwithstanding its significance for Epistemology. Nor are we therefore required to deny the intimate association of Epistemology with the Metaphysic of Nature. For our part we see no reason to reject Kant's fundamental principle that all Science of Nature must be based on the fact of self-consciousness. Even Pluralism, in spite of its antagonism to Kant's theory of knowledge, may be said to accept his principle: with the characteristic qualification that the emphasis is placed on the conative rather than on the cognitive aspect of self-consciousness. But Kant's peculiar analysis of self-consciousness admitted of only two alternatives, which excluded the counterpart in consciousness to that aspect of Nature which is most insistent in its demand for explanation, and which is universally regarded as higher than mechanism in the scale of values, namely, the organic. These alternatives were, the interpretation of self-consciousness as a mystical unity and as a determined succession represented under the form of space. And since the former was quite undetermined in content and therefore useless as a category of interpretation, Kant adopted the latter as the representative schema of Nature. There was no middle way. Hence his theory of knowledge that the mathematical and physical sciences are established by analysis of the nature of self-consciousness. But though the conditions of knowledge require that there shall be necessity in Nature, they do not decide one way or another as to what the nature of this necessity may be. We are quite free to suppose that mechanism is only an abstract aspect of a deeper Reality, which includes mechanism as a factor but which is not itself mechanical. As we shall presently see in the following pages, Kant's theory of Nature in the *Critique of Judgment* requires a conception of mechanism which is something more than just mechanism itself. The consequence is that Formal Teleology loses its significance; for what Kant represents as a logical system of mechanical relations, is really a system of relations which are not merely mechanical and therefore a system which is not merely logical.

Kant's error was to suppose that Teleology is only the indefinite extension of a mechanical whole: the latter, which is always relative, becomes a teleological whole when it is rounded off by a logical complement. The completed teleological whole is thus the logical equivalent for what is meant to be a completed mechanical whole, and is therefore a Formal Teleology. Now, as Mr. Bosanquet has recently remarked,[1] there is a striking resemblance between a mechanical and a teleological whole: both are approximations to the

[1] Proc. Arist. Soc. 1912, *Purpose and Mechanism*, iii.

type of timeless existence. Of course a mechanical system such as an engine exists in time, but time does not exist for it to any appreciable degree. As a constant repetition of identical relations, the engine is equally significant at any given moment, succeeding repetitions contribute nothing to its perfection as a system. Its functioning has nothing corresponding to memory—the assimilation of the past to the present with a bearing on the future, and therefore the engine exists only in numerical moments which have no individuality in time. On the other hand, at the opposite extreme, a perfect teleological whole may also be regarded as timeless; for, as a complete realisation, it transcends the temporal process which is essential to a finite purposive whole. It would thus be quite easy to suppose that Mechanism and Teleology are identical in nature, the latter being simply an indefinite extension of the former. But Kant hardly recognised that the very idea of extending the system must alter its whole character. His own conception of regulative Ideas which imperatively demand completeness of explanation (*res completae*), requires a different interpretation of Teleology. Why must we demand completeness for the relative mechanical whole, unless this latter itself exhibits a *tendency* towards completeness and is therefore in its nature conative? Is this not what Kant himself means by his rather unexpected announcement, that, having once discovered a true instance of teleology in organisms, we must eventually extend the organic conception to the whole of Nature? Nor is this interpretation of Teleology inconsistent with its apparent independence of time. For still its timelessness is not that of an abstract logical unity but of a unity which must be regarded as somehow conative. For, as Mr. Bosanquet further observes, perfect realisation implies satisfaction, satisfaction is inseparable from the notion of value, and the appreciation of value can hardly be divorced from conation. Even as absolute, Teleology does not exclude the individuality of its moments. The connection of perfect realisation with conation may seem paradoxical enough, but it is not by any means inconceivable. And, without going back to the Platonic and Aristotelian conception of pleasure unconditioned by want, we find the contradiction realised in Kant's aesthetic theory. Although he conceived of aesthetic experience as essentially immediate, he could yet find room within this immediacy for a kind of causality by which the mental powers maintain themselves: not as if the aesthetic state were in its nature incomplete, but simply to indicate that excellence of activity can never be devoid of power;[1] it is a state of complete realisation which is unceasingly engaged in realising its own excellence, or in Kant's words, it is purposiveness without a purpose. He therefore refused to connect Aesthetic with the reproductive function of Imagination, and placed it in the medium of Productive Imagination where time seems to exist in the form of a conceptual play rather than of a sensuous representation. Accordingly, a teleological whole can only be understood on the analogy of individual experience. We are not therefore pledged to say that it has individual consciousness; we only need to assert that it

[1] "And, O heavens, can we ever be made to believe that motion and life and soul and mind are not present with absolute being? Can we imagine being to be devoid of life and mind, and to remain in awful unmeaningness an everlasting fixture?" Plato's *Sophist*, 249.

has at least that individuality of being which is implied in eternal and complete unity with self. And if a perfect teleological whole is in its nature conative, *a fortiori* a finite teleological whole, that is, an organism, must be explained as a system of real purposes and not as an appearance which is due to the discursive application of a logical end.

Accordingly, the difference between organic and inorganic remains to be explained. In the one case mechanical Nature does nothing to further its own interests, it lodges no claim to systematic uniformity; it is we who have to bring its case to chancery and plead its cause. But in the other, Nature is assertive and needs no counsel to speak for her. For though we see no more than a complicated mechanism at work in a living being, and can have no determinate perception of an end or purpose as we do have of necessary changes in causal sequence, it enacts a purposed plan in every phase of its activity; we are quite sure that there is more than mechanism there, although we cannot give it a name that has any intelligible sound in the language of mechanism, just as the conception of end has no meaning for a Haeckel. Yet there is nothing in the teleological judgment to register this change. Our pulses do not quicken nor is imagination kindled, there is no intimation that we are in the presence of the living; nay, we are even told that this kind of observation has nothing to do with a feeling of pleasure.

Thus Organic Teleology is neither scientific nor 'reflective' for Kant. He indeed calls it 'reflective,' but that it is not 'reflective' is quite evident from his statement that it has nothing to do with a feeling of pleasure. The explanation of his perplexing attitude is that he could see no means of connecting Reflexion, or the consciousness of subjective purpose, with objectivity. Judgment for him must be either purely subjective—hence the false subjectivity of his aesthetic theory, or purely objective—hence the false objectivity of mechanism and its consequent priority in his theory of knowledge. But since Organic Teleology must be in the first instance subjective—for the behoof of our reflective faculty, and since it must also take some cognisance of the objectivity of its province : Kant was fain to institute a hybrid hypothetical judgment which resembles a blend of Science and Reflexion, but which really determines nothing either in the object or in the subject. While this hypothetical predication pretends to be 'reflective,' though it has nothing whatever to do with Reflexion, it practically reduces Organic Teleology to the universal postulate of Uniformity—the conception of a formal purposiveness of Nature *without which the Understanding could not find itself in Nature.* The principle of Uniformity were well enough if it were an elastic conception which admits of different levels of coherence, and if it were left to Nature herself to decide what kind of coherence will be forthcoming in any given instance. But when the principle is understood, as Kant understood it, to mean that there is one fundamental type of uniformity and one only, namely the mechanical, that Nature is therefore coherent only in the sense of an invariable repetition of identical relations without the slightest difference of quality : the door is foreclosed against us ; whatever type of coherence other than mechanical which Nature may present, must be regarded as an inexplicable accident which is due not to Nature but to the nature of our

Understanding. Organic Teleology consequently resolves into the analysis of organisms strictly as effects, not of organisms as themselves causes : it is Teleology considered solely as an ancillary instrument of Science, which is not also the explication of a higher type of coherence in Nature ; it is Teleology exclusively as a means of explanation, not as a fact which itself requires to be explained. If we wish to vary our language and say that, in view of those natural products which are not mechanical, Nature is most happily conceived as an *analogon of life*, Kant has no objection—provided we do not run into Hylozoism ; or we may adopt a psychological instead of a logical idea and think of Nature as acting on the analogy of our practical causality. But although these expressions may be more picturesque, they are nothing more for Kant than alternative statements of the mechanical principle of Uniformity. Nature is not allowed to speak for herself. Organic Teleology is consequently an external reflection[1] on a given Nature, it is not in any sense a *reflexion*[1] as we have understood the term in connection with Aesthetic. It can only be a form of Reflexion, in the technical sense we have given it, if it is the predication of a real quality which is at the same time reflected in the consciousness of ourselves. In other words, Teleology as a 'reflective' idea is not a contingent inductive hypothesis, for it is Nature in us that determines the particular kind of coherence or uniformity which this 'reflective' idea should lead us to anticipate. This is the psychological aspect of Teleology on which we have

[1] The difference in spelling is intentional, in order to conserve the technical sense of the word in the *Critique of Judgment*. *Vide supra*, p. 33, note.

insisted as Kant's real problem in the *Critique of Judgment*. The emphasis is to be placed on the contribution of objects to our perception of them : what we think of them is bound up with the way in which we are affected by them; our teleological observation takes its peculiar character from the nature of the objects themselves. And, in so far as it has a coherent content, our 'reflective' observation is also logical ; but it is by the Logic of inner development that it is governed, and not by the Logic of external reflection on a given material.

Certainly a strong case may be made in Kant's favour to show that he did appreciate the distinction between Formal and Objective Teleology. Dr. Walter Frost, for instance, rates Reflexion higher than Formal Teleology because it brings an intensive insight into objects, while Formal Teleology only makes a demand for larger objects and a larger outlook. We are far from denying the truth of this opinion, and hope to use it with advantage in the proper place. Thus the highest reach in the Objective Teleology, to take it in its net result, is the interpretation of organisms as the spontaneous products of a Creative Understanding, the conception of which is based on the analogy of our own practical causality. This is a thought which is infinitely higher, more illuminating, and more precious as it is more human, than the greatest pretension of Formal Teleology which is the interpretation of Nature, not as the immediate product of an Author, but of an indeterminate cause in which it is 'eminently' contained. As Kant says, "the transcendental and only determinate conception of God, which is presented to us by speculative reason, is in the strictest sense *deistic*."[1] Therefore

---

[1] *Transcend. Dialectic* : Meiklejohn, p. 413.

the Objective Teleology is a deeper insight into Nature than Formal, as the immanence of Theism excels the artificial transcendence of Deism.

This is readily conceded. But the more intensive the predicate the farther is Kant drawn away from his proper study, which is not to interpret organisms as effects but as themselves causes. An intensive predicate does not constitute Teleology into Reflexion unless this intensity is reflected in the consciousness of ourselves. Reflexion is something more than inductive hypothesis, if by inductive hypothesis we mean an invariable principle of uniformity which is restricted to a single type of coherence. It is only in the theory of Aesthetic that Reflexion maintains its distinctive character, and there is absolutely nothing in the Teleology of Nature to save it from confusion with the ordinary, systematic or Formal Teleology which is just the specification of Causality to the nth power. Judging by results, then, Stadler is justified when he says that Reflexion is nothing different from the regulative function of Reason in the *Dialectic*,— excepting Aesthetic, which alone introduces a new principle. The process of Induction is described in the *Critique of Pure Reason* as Reflexion is later defined in the *Critique of Judgment*,—the qualification of a particular which is given and certain by a merely problematic idea;[1] and the maxims of Reason, Homogeneity, Specification and Continuity, are called the maxims of the *Urteilskraft*.[2] The Teleology of Nature, in Kant's treatment, is simply an extension of Formal Teleology, and so the *Critique of Judgment* closes with the same

[1] *Appendix to Dialectic* : Meiklejohn, p. 396.
[2] Bernard, Introd. pp. 20 and 24.

impression of disappointment as the Book of Job, in its present melodramatic and spurious conclusion.

Perhaps we may seem to be forcing an interpretation of Kant which his expositors will not recognise. But in no other way is it possible to give a plausible explanation of the connection between Aesthetic and Teleology, and I believe they were originally united in Kant's mind in a very real way. His main achievement in the Teleology of Nature is not by any means to destroy, but to sift in order to place on a more secure basis, the argument from design. The critical review of Kant's Teleology such as we find in a book like Dr. Kennedy's *Natural Theology and Modern Thought*, shows a curious want of insight. Kant's objection to the argument was that it degraded God to the level of an architect. Otherwise he holds it as deserving of respect, being "the oldest, the clearest, and that most in conformity with the common reason of humanity." He thinks that it would be utterly hopeless to destroy the irresistible conviction to which it rises: "the mind, unceasingly elevated by these considerations, which, although empirical, are so remarkably powerful, and continually adding to their force, will not suffer itself to be depressed by the doubts suggested by subtle speculation; it tears itself out of this state of uncertainty, the moment it casts a look upon the wondrous forms of nature and the majesty of the universe, and rises from height to height, from condition to condition, till it has elevated itself to the supreme and unconditioned author of all."[1] It was held that the form of things, the arrangement of means and ends, is contingent, being foreign to the matter which was regarded as eternally necessary. Kant

---

[1] *Transcend. Dialectic*: Meiklejohn, p. 383.

replied that God is then limited by the matter whose necessary being lies outside of His creative power. In order that He may be a creator and not an artificer on the analogy of technical Art, matter must be equally contingent. For to say that matter with its purposive forms is contingent for our knowledge, is to admit the probability that it is the spontaneous product of a creator whose ways of working we cannot conceive. All apodictic certitude must be confined to the mathematical form of things and is not to be entertained of matter and its purposive modifications, which can only appear as inexplicable accidents to our intelligence. The only certainty we can have in regard to these is hypothetical.

But this criticism rather strengthens the argument from design, for he has extended the borders of certitude beyond the mathematical and introduced it in a qualified form into the realm of contingence. He has shown that Metaphysic can be Science if only its necessity is hypothetical. Kant's so-called scepticism amounts to nothing more than the hypothetical element in all modern Science: "he is *unbelieving*, who denies all validity to rational Ideas, because there is wanting a *theoretical* ground of their reality."[1] We need not allude to his *Natural History and Theory of the Heavens*, which breathes a spirit of religious adoration his critics may seldom enjoy, as it falls within his pre-critical period. We have only to cite another short treatise which appeared three years after the *Critique of Pure Reason* was first published, where he evinces the same devout belief in a beneficent Creator.[2]

---

[1] Bernard, p. 411.

[2] *Idee zu einer allgemeinen Geschichte in weltbürgerlicher Absicht*: Hart, iv. pp. 147-8.

But although Kant has displayed his critical acumen to great advantage, he has made no contribution in his Teleology of Nature to the study of Immediate Experience, which is the proper and only domain of Reflexion. He has indeed extended the boundaries of Science, though he must retain a distinction in name between the mathematical and hypothetical. But according to his own finding, there is a very decided limit to this extended Science, and we are constrained to ask if we have not been on the wrong road. Its hypothetical results are not different in kind from mathematical certainties, the interpretation of organic life by the Idea of end being just the specification of mechanical processes as forming a systematic unity. Moreover, Kant admits that the whole teleological procedure is due to a defect in our intelligence. It is because we cannot perceive an organic unity without discursively apprehending its elements in their discreteness, that we must prefigure our perception of the whole in the conception of its end or the idea of what it would be like if we could immediately perceive it. So far are we from acquiring a deeper insight by this method, that we disrupt the original unity of organic life into end and means, idea and existence, and consequently fail to receive a direct impression of its nature. It is only to manufactured things which we ourselves can make that the conception of end may be applied with advantage. But in the instance of a living thing which never is completely but always is to be, the conception of a final end may be a false anticipation which destroys the perception of its immediate unity. We must choose, then, between the following alternatives: either Kant was not justified in co-ordinating Teleology with Aesthetic under a common principle, or else

Teleology is something more than a logical method. If the latter of these is accepted, the system of Nature determined by Teleology cannot be merely empirical— a system of concepts organised into an artificial unity which is not reflected in experience but only furnished out of our methodological interest. If, as Kant himself believed, the aesthetic consciousness is an *a priori* apprehension which has more affinity with sensation than with logical process, Teleology should also be equipped with an intuitive *a priori*; otherwise it cannot have a genuine community of function with reflective experience. To put it concretely, the activity of the scientist who makes a true induction, is not exhausted in the formation of judgments and in trains of reasoning : there is something in his mind which precedes and conditions the inductive process itself, and that is the entire attitude of consciousness which Kant would call reflective—the catholic unison of the mental powers which constitutes aesthetic experience. And just because it is Nature in the subject that is expressed in this fundamental harmony of mental function, the proleptic ideas with which the subject seeks to interpret Nature in his teleological method, must be an *a priori* insight into Nature which is transcendental and not a merely logical *a priori* which is simply another name for empiricism. The remainder of this chapter will be given to a more minute study of the Teleology of Nature, to ascertain whether and how far it is able to bear this interpretation.

A complete scheme of Kant's Teleology is not helpful; it rather discourages the reader from entering into the matter at all. However, a spectre is most easily laid by walking through it. For our purpose, it is convenient to take the main division as into subjective and objective. But under the subjective are included two very different kinds of Teleology, Formal and Aesthetical. They both define the state of the subject alone, the one being a play of notions, the other of representations. Otherwise they are not subjective in the same sense. Kant characteristically identifies formal and subjective, and we have already seen how this is exemplified in his theory of Aesthetic. But we also showed how Subjectivity, even on Kant's principles, has a content of its own which is anything but formal. In so far as Art expresses an Ideal, its problem is the individual, for the Ideal is an Idea embodied in individual form, and this puts Aesthetic on a level with Objective rather than with Formal Teleology. Stadler correctly keeps them apart as distinct types.[1] Then follows what is most important for us at present, the Objective Teleology. But this is again subdivided into formal and material, the same distinction as we have just made and which Kant should have made under the heading 'subjective.' What he calls objective-formal are geometrical figures; they are formal because they are capable of many relations and constructions which are not essential to their existence as a determination in space, for instance, a circle. Finally, the other subdivision, objective-material, admits of a further distinction, inner and relative.

We do not seem to have gained much by this exhaustive dichotomy. It is sufficient to say that Kant's main concern is to establish a difference in kind between organic teleology which is self-contained, and all other types whose purpose is only relative to other

[1] *Kants Teleologie*, 112.

things. What he calls relative-objective-material is not really different from the formal type of Teleology. The superficial distinction between them is that what is formal only applies to the purely mechanical aspect of things which have no purposive intention in themselves, while relative teleology is called material because the things to which it applies do exhibit adaptations which contribute to the existence of things and not merely to the unity of our knowledge. Kant gives the instance that the sand deposited by the sea is excellent for growing pines. But these adaptations can be adequately explained by mechanical causes without supposing any design. Indeed it would be ridiculous to think that the deep sea had nothing else to do than to look after the growing of pine-trees; the growth of pines is quite contingent to the action of the sea, for sand can be left in large quantities without growing pines. Why should we credit the sea with a self-conscious purpose, when we know that it is itself an effect of a larger cause, the history of the earth?

Relative teleology, then, is really formal, because the purpose it appears to carry as contributive to the existence of things can be demonstrated to be an effect of mechanical causes, and it is only we who suppose designed adaptation. It can only be material and therefore something more than formal, if that to which it is contributive is itself a purpose of Nature,[1] for then it would be means to a real end of Nature and not to a figment of our fancy. But we know of no such real end in Nature even among organic beings, for "to judge of a thing as a natural purpose on account of its internal form is something very different from taking

[1] Bernard, pp. 271, 346.

the existence of that thing to be a purpose of Nature."[1] If we look away from the self-contained teleology in organisms and consider their relation to the environment, we find that they are pieces of Nature like everything else. They are of a day and perish in a day. Their purpose is cut before it is fulfilled by the abhorred shears which "slits the thin-spun life." Even man, the highest of the creatures, is not excepted from the ravages of Nature, nor is he treated with more respect. Kant recognises only one genuine type of Teleology, and the saving feature which marks it off from those which are relative, contributive, conditional, is its inner adaptation. If we abstract from the relation to environment altogether in which there is no suggestion of final purpose, we find in the organism an adaptation of means to end which is self-sufficing within the limits of its life.

The result, then, of the entire scheme is to establish a broad distinction between external and internal Teleology. The former can only have the relative validity it claims if that for which it is useful is itself a final purpose of Nature, and this can never be demonstrated; but the internally purposive "is bound up with the possibility of an object irrespective of its actuality being itself a purpose."[2] This internal Teleology is quite distinctive and cannot be confused with what is only relative. The first broad specification of natural laws is into organic and inorganic. Although in Kant's opinion our judgment is equally formal in both, the objects themselves are radically distinct. And we should notice here that the expression, Objective Teleology, is confusing. He

[1] Bernard, p. 283. [2] *Ibid.* p. 346.

only uses the term 'objective' to characterise the province of Judgment and not the judgment itself. What is distinctive in an organism is not a greater complexity of relations but a new kind of relation. The structureless plasma is a single organ without differentiation, while the crystal is a complicated formation; but the plasma has what the crystal has not, reaction and assimilation. In an organism the parts are reciprocally cause and effect; it is a new kind of causality.

This important finding, however, does not seem to enrich Philosophy. It has only brought us an enigma. Organisms are unthinkable, he says, unless we regard them as purposes of Nature; but there is no question here of final cause, for it is only as "considered in themselves and apart from any relation to other things" that we must think of them as natural purposes.[1] How they can also be natural products will remain for us a mystery, until we are able to show that there is a necessary relation between the environment and their purposive organisation. Darwin's brilliant hypothesis of natural selection is very far from demonstrating necessity in this relation. The variations which present themselves arise contingently, and we have no means of knowing if these and no others should be forthcoming. The structure of a bird is perfectly adapted for flight, but there is no ultimate necessity in this particular adaptation: "Nature, viewed as mere mechanism, *might* have shaped and connected the parts in a thousand other ways, without stumbling upon the unity which such a principle demands."[2] But accepting it as an enigma,

[1] Bernard, p. 280.
[2] Caird's translation, *Kant*, vol. ii. p. 478; Bernard, p. 260.

it is the only genuine instance of a real purpose that we know; and although we do not understand this new principle on which Nature organises herself in her products, we are justified in seeking to extend it to the whole of Nature in the belief that nothing is in vain.[1] In Kant's words: 'the concept of natural purpose inevitably leads to the idea of entire Nature as a teleological system; and in view of this example which Nature gives in her organic products, we are entitled, nay called upon, to expect that there is nothing in Nature and her laws that is not ultimately purposive.'

We are now confronted with one of the unsolved problems in the Critical Philosophy, which has puzzled its expositors not a little. If the conception of natural purpose be applied beyond organic forms to every object of experience, it remains undecided whether this should mean the discovery of a thorough-going mechanism or a complete teleological system in the whole of Nature. Kant can be interpreted in favour of both positions. Dr. W. Ernst thinks that the relative priority of Mechanism and Teleology in the *Critique of Judgment* is a *non liquet*.[2] I think we are able to entertain a more positive opinion. In like manner, Pfannkuche can find no clear solution in view of the criticisms offered and the misunderstandings which have arisen.[3] He admits that the discovery of an ultimate mechanical interpretation lies in the trend of Kant's thought, but that all his explanations are in favour of an External Teleology which can hardly be different from the old rationalistic procedure except in its conditional character. The first

---

[1] Hartenstein, v. § 67, p. 391; Bernard, p. 284.
[2] *Der Zweckbegriff bei Kant und sein Verhältnis zu den Kategorien*, p. 68.
[3] *Der Zweckbegriff bei Kant.* . *Kantstudien*, Bd. V.

actual result of Kant's Teleology was to destroy the easy optimism of Rationalism. We are at liberty to organise our knowledge into a unity as far as possible but not to introduce any specific end into Nature. Now if Kant intends that we should apply this specific principle which is exemplified in organic life to all objects of experience, he is certainly going beyond the Formal Teleology of inductive science. But I do not think that he would acknowledge this interpretation. Pfannkuche appeals to the discussion on the antinomies in support of his view. There Kant says that we must explain Nature on mechanical principles, but that when these fail, as they do in the case of organisms, we have instructions to interpret these forms and *eventually the whole of Nature* by the principle of final cause. Pfannkuche considers that this implies something more than the indefinite extension of mechanical principles which Formal Teleology is meant to provide, because inorganic Nature is already adequately explained on mechanical grounds, and therefore the application of final cause can only mean some kind of special Teleology. But this is just what is not true. From the moment we enter the *Dialectic*, it becomes evident that Mechanism is quite insufficient to give a complete explanation even of inorganic Nature without the help of Teleology as a heuristic principle, and that the objects of experience are only necessary within the limits of a wider contingence. Besides, Kant distinctly says in the passage to which Pfannkuche refers, that though this principle obtained from organisms is certainly useful, it is not indispensable in our judgment of inorganic objects " for Nature as a whole is not given as organised."[1] I therefore think

[1] Bernard, p. 310.

that Kant did not seriously intend organic purpose to be taken as a principle of External Teleology, but as an additional maxim of Reflexion to help us in our researches into Nature.

The truth is that, at an earlier period, Kant had entertained something like this view to which his language in the *Critique of Judgment* certainly lends countenance, and its traces still remain. At that time his interests were mainly scientific, and he was content to assume certain connections of ideas which his critical reflection afterwards rejected. In 'The only possible proof for the being of God' (1763), he is evidently criticising two well-known theories which he afterwards explicitly mentions in the *Critique of Judgment*. These theories, which prevailed in the eighteenth century, were Occasionalism, which goes back to Cartesian principles and Preformation, which was formulated by Leibniz. On the first view, the appearance of every new species or variety in a species was the occasion of a divine act; on the second, there was no such thing as a new formation, but simply an unfolding of parts which were preformed from all eternity and already existed in all the complexity of their later development,— though very small, like diminutive models.[1] This theory of Preformation went by the name of Evolution (*Auswickelung*). In the *Critique of Judgment* Kant exposes its false pretensions and shows how a better name would be Involution or emboxing (*Einschachtelung*).[2] It is not a real evolution, but an unfolding of what is already completely involved. Preformation is therefore no advance on Occasionalism. For it is all the same whether a divine

---

[1] See Schultze, *Kant und Darwin*, pp. 35-7.
[2] Bernard, § 81; Hart, v. p. 436.

THE CRITICAL PHILOSOPHY 265

act is invoked for these new formations at the time of creation or in the course of development. Indeed, Kant thinks Occasionalism has the preference, for it restricts the interference of the supernatural to the forms which actually come into existence, while Preformation must provide supernatural agency for every possible variety whether they come to maturity or not.[1] Preformation does call in the aid of natural science to explain the growth and transmission of the preformed characters, but it is not less supernatural; for the distinction between the two theories does not lie in the degree of immediate divine activity employed but solely in the time of interference.[2]

The real issue, then, is between Occasionalism and genuine Evolution, or what is a still more apposite term, Epigenesis. Kant was not the author of this theory, which still remains as the essential basis in the modern doctrine. According to Schultze, it was first announced by Caspar Friedrich Wolff in 1759. Epigenesis means that an organism is not simply the growth of a tiny preformation as a literal evolution of already perfect parts, but an accretion of successive new formations which previously had no existence at all in the embryo; or, as Kant would express it, it is not an educt but a product. Yet Kant does not mean to exclude the supernatural. The advantage which he commends in Epigenesis is that it involves the least expenditure of the supernatural. In Preformation, which is a maximum Occasionalism, every species of animal and plant is eternally created by God, and the only natural feature in this supernatural production

[1] Bernard, p. 344.
[2] *Der einzig mögliche Beweisgrund*, u.s.w. : Hart, ii. p. 158.

is the simple transmission and growth of the original characters. But in Epigenesis the production of the variations in a species is natural just as much as the transmission of the original tendencies, and it represents Nature not merely as evolving but as self-producing.

Darwin later essayed to show how this is possible by 'natural selection.' Kant's sympathies, however, were quite averse from materialism. Though he conceives of the production of species as natural, he does not so regard their origin. He indeed said in his 'Natural History of the Heavens,' *Gebet mir Materie, ich will eine Welt daraus bauen!* But this is only with reference to the inorganic world, for in the same context he challenges anyone to show how from given matter even a worm can be produced.[1] The question for Kant was whether every individual in a species is immediately created by God, or whether only the original individuals are indeed divinely created yet endowed with a power, inconceivable to us, of producing their kind in accordance with natural law, and not of merely evolving them as educts.[2] The first alternative he rejects under the name of Occasionalism, the second is the theory of Epigenesis which he favours. He thinks that there must have been a first divine disposition of plant and animal life (*ersten göttlichen Anordnung*) in which the seeds of later tendencies are found, not as individual but as *generic* preformations.[3] And further, in order to restrict the range of supernatural agency, these

---

[1] Hart, i. pp. 219-20.

[2] *Der einzig mögliche Beweisgrund*, u.s.w. : Hart, ii. p. 157.

[3] *Der einzig mögliche Beweisgrund*, u.s.w. : Hart, ii. p. 158; Bernard, p. 343.

THE CRITICAL PHILOSOPHY

original individuals must be reduced to the smallest possible number.

On this principle of seminal tendencies or generic preformations, he explains the races of men as a teleological organisation of Nature. He rejects the idea of local creations of races, and maintains that, in spite of their differences, whites and negroes are sprung from a single stem. While he anticipates what is important in the modern theories of adaptation and natural selection, he will not hear of contingent variations which are the distinctive feature in the Darwinian hypothesis. He defines a Race as constituted by constant, hereditary characteristics which are unfailingly transmitted, and he will not allow us to speak of it even as a particular species; otherwise genus and species would solely denote what is incompatible with a common stem.[1] He means that these hereditary characteristics are not specific, for that would involve Preformation or Occasionalism, but generic differences which were originally united in mere tendencies (*in blossen Anlagen*), and which are gradually developed and separated out in the course of propagation.[2] A Race is a variation of the type, but it must not be regarded as produced by a contingent act of Nature. He therefore proposes to substitute for the word Race a technical term which will indicate this meaning of variation; it is *Abartung*, which denotes the hereditary variations generically contained in the common stem, as distinguished from *Ausartung*, which denotes complete deviation from type. For this latter he can find no place.[3] As he says in his 'Races of

---

[1] *Über den Gebrauch teleologischer Principien in der Philosophie*: Kirchmann, p. 153.

[2] *Ibid.* p. 152.   [3] *Ibid.* pp. 150-1.

Men': "an animal species, having a common stock, contains no different kinds (for these just mean differences of derivation); but their deviations from one another are called *Abartungen* if these are hereditary. The hereditary marks of derivation, if they tally with their parentage, are called *resemblances*;[1] but if the hereditary variation no longer exhibits the original stem-formation, it should be called *Ausartung*."[2]

Kant's own way of dealing with what we should call contingent variations is as follows: if the variant characteristics which are compatible with a common stem are necessarily hereditary, a Race is constituted; if they are not necessarily hereditary, it is a Variation.[3] He thus throws the burden of explanation upon Teleology, for it is the original tendencies that must explain when and where the variations shall be hereditary or not; just as he believes that the varieties among men of the same race are, in all probability, designedly (*zweckmässig*) reposed in the original stem.[4] His theory of evolution may be summarised in the following passage from the 'Races of Men': "This providence of Nature in equipping her creatures by means of hidden, inner provisions against all manner of future conditions, that they may maintain themselves and adapt themselves to differences of climate or soil, is wonderful; and by the wandering and transplantation of animals and plants, it produces kinds which are to all appearance new, but which are nothing else than

[1] He is thinking of half-breeds like the Moors.
[2] *Über die verschiedenen Racen der Menschen*: Hart, ii. p. 436.
[3] *Über den Gebrauch teleologischer Principien in der Philosophie*: Kirchmann, p. 153.
[4] *Ibid.*

constant variations (*Abartungen*) and races of the same genus, whose seeds and natural tendencies have been developed only occasionally throughout long periods of time in diverse ways."[1] Kant anticipates the *impasse* which a mechanical theory like Darwinism is bound to encounter, by making the mechanism of evolution finally subordinate to a teleological principle. What is developed by external causes, such as climatic conditions, are seeds (*Keime*) or natural tendencies which were given in the act of creation.

This is undoubtedly a teleological view of Nature, organic and inorganic. Although, as Schultze says, Kant's Anthropology is completely in favour of our derivation from the ourang-outang, it is only the external causes of production that are natural. The generic preformation or seed placed in the original disposition of the species, is metaphysical, and comes, like the soul in Aristotle's psychology, from without. We must not forget that Kant has unmistakably expressed his opinion more than once that matter is utterly dead, and the disposition of original seeds in a lifeless matter is unquestionably an External Teleology. As a maxim of Reflexion, Teleology would only mean that we may or must interpret Nature as purposive, but we should not be authorised to determine any specific purpose in Nature such as we do find in the present instance. Organic life comes into being on occasion of an original creative act, and so we may call his position a minimum Occasionalism.

But although Kant does not make any essential change in his theory of organic evolution, he can hardly be said to hold the same metaphysical implications in

[1] Hart, ii. pp. 440-1.

his later writings. In 'The only possible proof for the being of God,' he rejects the three proofs and advances a new one, which, from the idea of other beings and their logical possibility, infers the necessity of an existing something as their ground.[1] This, of course, is nothing new and is thrown over in the *Critique of Pure Reason*, as it well might be, for it is simply a restatement of the ontological argument. It shows that Kant was content to reinforce the existence of God as an *a priori* certainty arising out of the mere conception of possible existence, by an *a posteriori* regress from the purposive relations in existence, which are consequently regarded as external predicates of inorganic Nature.[2]

In the *Critique of Judgment* all this is altered and therewith a subtle change enters into Kant's view of the origin of species. He is no longer prepared to maintain what is exactly the position of an intelligent theist to-day who is anxious to reconcile Theology with Darwinism, but advances towards the view that matter is brought into existence by the same creative act as endows it with life; or, to take it from the other side, that matter is a divine creation and may therefore contain in its original constitution the purposive combinations of organic life. It is true that up to the last he thinks that living matter is an impossible conception,[3] and he shows no favour to hylozoism. But that is only because we cannot see into its hidden ground, and for this reason we are for ever precluded from pretending to a theory of matter. We are free, however, to use the indications which Nature has given us in speculating on her super-

[1] *Erste Abtheilung*, see p. 126; Hart, ii.
[2] *Ibid.* see p. 135, last paragraph in *Erste Abtheilung*.
[3] See Bernard, p. 304.

sensible substrate, and to cherish without proof the conviction we are empowered to entertain. As in the instance of Practical Reason, we are at least safeguarded by a negative certainty. Just because we cannot perceive the inner constitution of matter, it is impossible to demonstrate that the origin of life may not lie in the mere mechanism of Nature: "it is left undecided whether or not in the unknown inner ground of nature, physico-mechanical and purposive combination may be united in the same things in one principle."[1]

This does not mean that the distinction between Mechanism and Teleology is removed, nor does it affect the sincerity of Kant's warnings that we must not mix the two modes of explanation. Although an intuitive Understanding would see no difference between them, the difference as it appears to us will still exist even for that Understanding. There is occasion for much confusion in this intricate connection of ideas, and it can only be avoided if we distinguish Causality from Mechanism. I agree with Frost as against Stadler that in the antinomy, where this question arises, the distinction is not between Reflexion and Causality but between the maxim of Finality and the maxim of Mechanism, both of which are forms of Reflexion.[2] Causality means the perception of necessary change, and this remains fundamental throughout as an *a priori* certainty. But beyond the field of immediate perception, it only obtains as an 'analogy of experience,' and its application to unperceived Nature is therefore always problematical. This hypothetical Causality is the maxim of Mechanism, which is as much a heuristic principle in empirical research as

[1] Bernard, p. 296. Cp. p. 313.
[2] *Der Begriff der Urteilskraft bei Kant*, p. 108.

the maxim of Finality. The difference is, that while Causality is quite assured of its necessity within the narrow limits of immediate perception and has no misgivings, the maxim of Mechanism advances trembling in the dark, not knowing what may turn up, and is quite prepared to find maggots springing into life spontaneously from a dead body. In Mechanism as a maxim of Reflexion, the ultimate nature of Causality is treated as an open question and remains quite undetermined.

Yet I feel that we are taking our results too easily in what is a very complicated analysis. It is hard to elaborate a consistent opinion out of Kant's own writings, nor are his expositors in agreement. It does seem contradictory to prohibit confusing or mixing Mechanism and Teleology as methods of explanation and at the same time to suggest their ultimate identity. If they are only aspects for us men of what is really a single intuition, it should not greatly matter if we are careless in our use of them. Their common element will surely draw them together in spite of our efforts to keep them apart. But a complaint of this kind will not arise when we have grasped Kant's proper meaning. In two of his smaller writings he makes a clear distinction between two uses of Teleology, one of which alone is entitled to our serious consideration; and it is the other and false Teleology, I think, that he has in mind when he warns us against a confusion of principles. It must be remembered that Teleology in the first instance is a purely empirical procedure. The ends of Nature are found solely through experience. We cannot see *a priori* why there should be ends in Nature as we can quite well see *a priori* how there should be

THE CRITICAL PHILOSOPHY 273

a connection of cause and effect. This at least is Kant's opinion.[1] What saves the judgment from being a worthless hazard is the connection of our moral consciousness with these empirical concepts. Now it is quite plain that this kind of judgment may easily lapse into the crazy teleology which says, in the jesting spirit of a Voltaire, that we have noses in order that we may wear spectacles, unless the intelligent sanction of our moral consciousness is present. And since Teleology, in so far as it is limited to empirical conditions, can never adequately define the first cause of purposive connections, we must "expect this complete explanation from a *Pure Teleology* which can be no other than that of Freedom, whose principle contains *a priori* the relation of a Reason in general to the totality of all ends and can only be practical."[2] We are safeguarded in our teleological reflexion by a sense of obligation which delivers our thoughts from being contingent speculations. In the structure of the eye, for instance, as adapted for sight, we must imagine a certain necessity which is anterior to and independent of its particular, physiological formation. In the instance of a stone we feel no such necessity, for it may be used for breaking on or for building or for many other purposes, none of which is final. But of the eye we judge that it *ought* to be adapted for sight, although its structure is quite contingent for our judgment and might be adapted for sight in a thousand other

---

[1] See *Über Philosophie überhaupt*: Rosenkranz, i. p. 609; *Über den Gebrauch teleologischer Principien in der Philosophie*: Kirchmann, p. 172.

[2] *Über den Gebrauch teleologischer Principien in der Philosophie*: Kirchmann, p. 173.

ways unknown to us; and this sense of obligation "can be determined just as little through merely physical, empirical laws, as the necessity of the aesthetical judgment through psychological laws."[1] It is therefore only the empirical use of Teleology, unsanctioned by Practical Reason, that Kant will keep distinct from Mechanism, for no Teleology of this kind can supply the want of physical theory. Without mechanical explanation we are always uncertain about the actual causes, no matter how clear our supposition may be.[2] But when it is a genuine teleological judgment, its relation to Mechanism is very different. Then Teleology is not only in place but must always be present even in our observation of inorganic Nature, and must have the precedence. It is no longer a question of co-ordination, but Mechanism must always be subordinate to teleological reflexion.[3] Kant means that induction and deduction, synthesis and analysis, are both essential in every explanation, and Teleology takes the lead because the regress from effect to cause is conditioned and instructed by an ideal progress.

It is so far settled, then, that there is nothing in the distinctness of Mechanism and Teleology as principles of explanation to preclude their fundamental identity. What lies behind both and unites them is the supersensible substrate of Nature, which takes the place of a theistic God in his theory of organic evolution. For although he still conceives of the ultimate Ground

---

[1] *Über Philosophie überhaupt*: Rosenkranz, i. p. 610.

[2] *Über den Gebrauch teleologischer Principien in der Philosophie*: Kirchmann, pp. 145-6.

[3] Bernard, § 78, pp. 331-3.

as an intelligent Being, he does not now think of this Being as designedly disposing the orders of Nature and endowing them with life. On the contrary, we do not demand "that there should be actually given a particular cause which has the representation of a purpose as its determining ground," and it may be that organic products should find their ground in Nature's mechanism,—"a causal combination for which an Understanding is not explicitly assumed as cause."[1]

This is put very clearly in the essay 'On the use of teleological principles in philosophy,' only published two years earlier (1788). We can only understand how an organism is made by using the analogy of our own technical activity, which is a mixture of Understanding and Will. It is nothing more than an analogy, however, because we cannot make an organism as we can make objects of technical art. The real cause of an organism, therefore, must lie outside experience as a causality of which we have no example; and the nearest approach we can make to such a conception is that of a Being whose activity is purposive but which has not the ground of its determination in an Idea. But since the conception of a Being, in itself purposive and acting without specific end or aim in view ("aus sich selbst *zweckmässig,* aber *ohne Zweck* und Absicht zu wirken "), is quite fictitious for us, we must either give up all attempt at explanation or still think to ourselves an intelligent Being ; not as if we considered that such a ground-principle is impossible, but because the conception of an intelligent Being is the only support we can find in our thought for the otherwise unthinkable conception of a ground-principle, which

[1] Bernard, § 77, p. 320.

is in itself purposive but excludes final causes from its activity (*Ursache mit Ausschliessung der Endursachen*).[1] The notion of intelligence which is inseparable from the conception of acting according to purposed ends, is not introduced for its own sake but only for the sake of a conception which contradicts the notion of intelligence; the supersensible substrate is a Being which has no ideas as motives for its creative acts, and is presupposed as indeterminate Ground (*Grundkraft*) rather than as cause. It may therefore be that there is no real basis for what we observe as teleology in Nature, and that nothing more is needful for explanation " beyond the mechanism of causes working blindly."[2]

This, however, does not mean that Kant has finally displaced Teleology in favour of a rigid mechanism. If we read § 77 of the *Critique of Judgment* we shall find that the Mechanism which Kant approves as an ultimate mode of explanation, is something much more than just mechanism itself. It means that the parts are explained by automatic analysis as the parts of a real whole which is given in perception with them, as would happen to a divine mind,—a very different thing from the conception of discrete parts out of whose mechanical aggregate a whole is constructed. We have to notice in Kant's Teleology a similar result to what we already found in his aesthetic theory. While according to the view we have taken, he does not reduce Aesthetic to intellectual processes in terms of which it is explained, but conceives of it as a higher plane of mental activity in which knowledge is a limited and specialised direction; he now interprets Mechanism in

[1] Kirchmann, pp. 171-2; Hart, iv. pp. 493-4.
[2] Bernard, p. 287.

terms of a *Grundkraft* which transcends the distinction of Mechanism and Teleology, instead of explaining organic Nature on strictly mechanical principles. It is Nature conceived as purposive without a purpose, a process which to all appearance is mechanical but which unfolds itself in marvellous wise and moves indeed to an event we can surmise and applaud, yet without forecasting or express intention. This theory, which will sound somewhat novel to students of the first *Critique*, can only be named an idealistic naturalism or 'creative evolution.'

Perhaps it may seem a little hazardous to urge this point of resemblance between Kant and M. Bergson in view of the sharp contrast which the latter has made between Kant and himself. But so far as I know, M. Bergson makes no serious reference to the *Critique of Judgment* and confines himself exclusively to the *Critique of Pure Reason*. Is it too much to contend, as our short study has essayed incidentally to show, that the third *Critique* effects a real modification in Kant's theory of knowledge? Let us just think what Kant's position means at the point we have now reached. It is true that his accredited view moves between a timeless supersensible and phenomena juxtaposed in abstract time. But a mechanism working blindly and yet fruitful of reasonable consequences is certainly not the abstract relation óf cause and effect, and much less is it the timeless identity of mechanism and teleology in the divine mind. It is clearly an existence which is more than quantitative: on the one hand, it is not a mere mechanism whose parts are simply repetitions of an identical relation, for it springs spontaneously from a Ground which is purposive and must therefore be itself individual in' each moment of its existence; and, on the other hand, it is not an empty teleology which, as the realisation of a predetermined end, eliminates real change, but an accretion of real parts in which the end, unknown even to the Ground, is progressively revealed. Now, as M. Bergson has observed, Causality for Kant has " the same meaning and the same function in the inner as in the outer world." [1] He means that inner experience keeps time with the outer process, and that while our experience is really a continuum of interpenetrating elements which are never external to each other, Kant has made our experience conform to what is only a single and ultimately false tendency in experience, the externalising function of the intellect in space-relations.

But this simple statement does not cover the whole ground. Just as we have observed in Kant's final theory of Teleology a conception of existence which is more than that of quantity, whose parts, over and above their formal character as repetitions of abstract causation, have an individual character as purposed elements which can never be repeated, we have now to recollect a corresponding change in the subject. Kant conceived of the inner life as divided into two orders, both of them, strange to say, in the same medium of Time, the Imagination. Of these the schematic order is subject to the law of determined succession, the other is vaguely defined as an Inner Sense, and if we are able to have that determined succession in consciousness which is necessary to the maintenance of our own identity, it certainly does not constitute a coherent perception and is only a fleeting awareness. So much is this the case that, as we saw

[1] *Time and Free-Will*, p. 232.

THE CRITICAL PHILOSOPHY 279

in Chapter IV., the contents of Inner Sense are more of a conceptual play than a sensuous succession in Time, although they are affections of the very and only faculty of Time and are expressly described as sensuous. But in the Productive Imagination, which is to all appearance a timeless faculty, a new causality is sprung upon us without warning to take the place of the reproductive function which Kant had denied to it. By means of this causality the volatile contents of the Inner Sense are transported into coherent forms, which we can recognise as enduring unities with all the perfect finish of immediate creation. He speaks of the aesthetic state as maintaining and strengthening itself by an inner causality, in virtue of which we are able to linger over the Beautiful as something more than an inconsequent conceptual play.

Now the peculiar feature of this theory is the way in which Kant has combined, in a single process, the timeless nature of indeterminate intellective functions with the quality of schematic coherence but without the characters of abstract Time as they are found in our perception of the external world. I am not forgetting that Kant's prevailing expressions convey the idea of a negative, formal consistency without any real content; but it is equally clear that concrete coherence lies in the line of his thinking. It is just because he has no terminology for a real duration which is other than that of external perception, that he is forced to deny coherence to the Inner Sense. The puzzle in his theory of Aesthetic is created by the search for an order of Productive Imagination which will be in Time and yet not in that determined order of necessity which controls our sense-perception. For Kant there is no such thing as a perception of Time itself, and therefore the schema of

Causality is not a mode of Time, for this would mean a determinate consciousness of Time, but a mode *in* Time. But in Aesthetic there must be no necessity in Time, for then the Beautiful would be indistinguishable from objects of Science. There is only left to Aesthetic, if it will be anything at all, the alternative that its symbolic schemata are modes *of* Time and therefore a more or less durable consciousness of Time.[1]

But it is all the more disappointing to find that for Kant the ultimate identity of Mechanism and Teleology in real existence is a hidden Ground, completely unknown to the subject, notwithstanding the fact that on his own admission the nature of this Ground and of the subject is the same, namely, purposive reality without a purpose. Our main contention throughout this study may be put in the form of a question: why should the *Critique of Judgment* have been written if Teleology is to gain nothing from the theory of Aesthetic? The classic reason Kant offers for this failure is the discursive nature of our Understanding. This remains to be examined.

The proof is contained in the difficult and important § 76-77, which really contain the crux of the argument in the Teleology of Nature. It turns on the difference between the human mind and what we are able to conceive as divine. Our defect is shown in the presence of two heterogeneous factors, sensuous intuition and

---

[1] See the discussion in the *First Analogy*: Meiklejohn, p. 137. Notice how Kant says that succession and coexistence are modes *of* Time, and then corrects himself a few lines further on, but only with reference to coexistence. To be consistent he should have made the same correction in the case of succession, as is evident from the glaring contradiction in this sentence, where he says that Time is not affected by change and that its parts are all successive.

thought. We know when we are in touch with fact, our thought runs against something hard and becomes perception. And we also know when we are not in touch with fact but are moving in airy circles of possibility. According to Kant, actual fact (*Thatsache*) means sensation with the solitary exception of the Idea of Freedom, which is a fact although it has no adequate intuition corresponding in sense-perception.[1] Apart from this exception, for it does not interest us now, we may say that without sensuous perception we have nothing left but the bare sense of possession, and our supposed objects pale into the mere " representations of a problem." It is our misfortune that we have more thoughts than we can make into objects and are neither god nor beast. For a god the possible is itself actual, and we can suppose that for an animal all perceptions are necessary—at least if all animals are the same as Mr. Bradley's dog, for whom there is but a single possibility : what is, smells ; what does not smell, is not.

But the simple consciousness of possession is no slight acquisition. In the *Dialectic*, Kant recognised principles of Reason which never have immediate relation to a sense-object and yet are synthetic with a suggestion of objectivity. Their function is to organise the concepts of Understanding as it in turn organises into unities the manifold of sensation.[2] In our Reason we recognise a power to think our thoughts about objects as if these thoughts were real objects themselves, and although we never expect to find a correspondent in sensation to this high thinking, we cannot over-estimate its importance. There is no such thing in fact as pure

[1] Bernard, § 91, pp. 405-6.
[2] Meiklejohn, pp. 213-4 and pp. 394-5.

earth, pure air or pure water, but these are real objects for Reason as sensibility is real for the Understanding, and are necessary abstractions for determining the share which each of these natural elements has in any given objects.[1]

Now there were four chief Ideas of Reason recognised in the dogmatic metaphysics, God, the Soul, the World and End. To the first three there is nothing adequately corresponding in perception: in order that our conception of the world may be actual, we should have to see the whole world at a glance, and of course that is impossible; again, we cannot run against our own souls and *ricocher* as if they were external bodies—we are only going round them; and of the first of these, namely, God, our conception is entirely problematical. But in the instance of End, Kant changes countenance, for it is peculiar to this Idea that a corresponding intuition is actually given in organisms. At this point we might naturally think that metaphysic has at last vindicated its claim to science, for there is one Idea of Reason which is immediately related to experience and so becomes a necessary perception. But we are at once pulled up by the fatal docetic formula, 'as it were.' According to Kant an Idea of Reason is only synthetic for the thoughts, and not for the objects, of Understanding. Both Understanding and Reason are synthetic functions on different planes of experience, which at their nearest point of contact are divided by a film of sense. And although an intuition corresponding to the Idea of End is given in organisms, it is only the Understanding that can see it.

This is what Kant means by the somewhat doubtful

[1] Meiklejohn, p. 396.

assertion that we cannot perceive teleology in Nature as we do mechanical causation.[1] There is at least this to be said, that while experience would be impossible if there were no mechanical necessity in Nature, we are not able to say how far the absence of natural purposes would affect the possibility of experience. In an organism as object of sense and therefore as judged by the Understanding, nothing is perceived beyond a complex of mechanical processes; and when Reason asks the questions, 'what is it doing and where is it going?' we have ceased to think of it as mechanism. The perception of Reason comes too late. It is as if we were looking at an object through two different pairs of eyes, which are as unrelated as the perception of a mechanic and an artist. Reason, who is wearing glasses heavily smoked, is peering over the shoulder of Understanding, and enquiring with the suspicious alertness of Maeterlinck's Sightless, 'What is that, what is that? Why don't you tell me? I am sure I saw something.' To which the Understanding laconically replies, 'Compose yourself, my dear fellow, it is nothing for you; it is only one of my little men.' The moment we try to use a principle of Reason as a principle of Understanding, its synthetic quality resolves into the vague function of an Understanding in general (*eines Verstandes überhaupt*).[2]

[1] "Dass es in der Natur Zwecke geben *müsse*, kann kein Mensch *a priori* einsehen; dagegen er *a priori* ganz wohl einsehen kann, dass es darin eine Verknüpfung der Ursachen und Wirkungen geben müsse." *Über den Gebrauch teleologischer Principien in der Philosophie*: Kirchmann, p. 172; Hart, iv. p. 494. Cp. Bernard, pp. 311-2 and p. 327.

[2] Hart, v. p. 418; Bernard, pp. 319-20.

Now we go a step further. Not only are principles of Reason inapplicable to objects of sense, the principles of Understanding are in a similar case. When we read in the *Critique of Pure Reason* that there are synthetic principles of Understanding, we must remember that they only become synthetic, formative, creative, because vision has been lent to them from without in sense-affection. As we saw in Chapter IV., Kant favours the suggestion that the pure conceptions of Understanding are true of things as they really are, while schemata, the applied conceptions of Understanding, present things only as they appear. In their unconditioned form, the principles of Understanding are indistinguishable from those of Reason, and like them are analytical, without immediate relation to experience. As applied in experience they are forms of synthesis, but they are not synthetic in their own right, as may be seen from the unsatisfactory character of experience. The unity which Understanding gives to objects is not the perfect universal it is capable of thinking, but a unity which it is obliged to construct by reproducing the parts of existence in a determined order. The consequence is that we only see aggregate unities and discrete successions, never the soul of things. Had the Understanding a gift of vision all its own, we should be able to see with the children in *Blue-bird*, the soul of flinty rock blue as sapphire, the souls of the Hours tripping out of the clock or Bread tumbling out of his pan. A principle which is synthetic in its own nature can only be found in the Ideas of Reason, for they are not limited by sensation and are therefore free to produce their objects in the simple perception of their unity. But then they have no application to experience, and so far as objects of sense are concerned they are really analytical; for while the whole is real enough, the parts are ideal. For an opposite reason, there is no principle of Understanding which is synthetic in its own right; for while the parts are real enough, their totality is supplied by the Ideas of Reason and is merely ideal. A genuine synthetic principle means such a creative insight into the whole nature of a thing as that Being has who, in the simple perception of its unity, is able to produce the complexity of its structure. In Kant's words, "we see into a thing completely only so far as we can make it."[1] To the same effect Lord Kelvin is reported to have said, that he could not be satisfied that he had explained any natural process until he constructed a working model.

It is as a consequence of this analytical nature of thought that our Understanding is discursive. When we speak of thought as an analytic unity, we mean that it is incapable of analysis, its parts being so completely transparent as to be non-existent. A real whole is reciprocally conditioned by its parts, but this analytic whole is unconditioned and has no immediate relation to particular instances in experience. The particular is therefore contingent for the universal of Understanding, it has a multiplicity of possible relations which are quite undetermined for this universal. In the simple fact of knowledge, on the other hand, the universal and particular are both immediately given in the individual perception and the contingency is not apparent. But that is because only those relations of the particular presentation are allowed to enter consciousness as are necessary for the consciousness of our own identity.

[1] Bernard, p. 291.

Here we return to Kant's original doctrine of sensation. What is determined is not the particular itself in its exhaustive relations, but the particular as it must appear to us if we are to have a necessary perception of it. If we now proceed beyond the simple needs of immediate perception, we find that we have no universal to cover the multiple relations of the particular which do not enter into the consciousness of ourselves. This is just how we feel in thinking of an organism. A knowledge of its mechanism is given in the simple fact of perception, because without causal necessity in perception we would not be conscious of our own identity. But although we can surmise the end in an organism, we can never be sure that our judgment is final, we have no necessary perception of its ultimate unity. If our Understanding were intuitive, every nuance in the structure of an organism would be immediately perceived as self-explaining. This Intuitive Understanding is the Mrs. Harris of philosophy quite as much as the Supersensible Thing. Since the universal of our Understanding is not synthetic, we cannot perceive the whole as cause of the parts but as their effect, and therefore cannot have an *a priori* perception but an *ex post facto* idea of the whole. In Kant's technical language, we must proceed from the universal to the particular. Since the particular given in perception is contingent and we have no corresponding universal to determine the multiplicity of its possible relations, we must first think it in the most general terms, then advance from this unspecified thought to a more conditioned, until we arrive, if we are able, at an adequate conception which will commend the particular to our intelligence. We thus proceed from the analytic

THE CRITICAL PHILOSOPHY 287

universal. This is the discursive nature of Understanding.

It will be noticed in this account that Kant makes a sharp contrast between discursive and intuitive. Our Reason, in itself intuitive, is only capable of perceiving bare unities, not individual things. It consequently becomes discursive when applied to a particular which it does not itself create. It has a stock of ready-made suits, all empty, formal, pathetic in their simulation of the individual, which it essays to fit, one after the other, on the presentation. It usually happens that during this discursive process, the presentation walks away. The Understanding, which is the business faculty we use in daily life, is wise; it builds the suit on the person of the presentation. The universal and the particular are immediately given in the individual perception. It is only when our thoughts are applied in the form of schemata, or conceptions specially adapted to presentations, that they become intuitive. Kant, then, appears to think that in the schematic consciousness the discursive process comes to an end. On the contrary, it is in the schematic consciousness that the discursive process is initiated, sustained and completed. It is true that our thoughts, like the waves of the sea, are more or less contingent modes of mind, whose meaning is as elusive and unspecified as the crest and oval rings on the breakers, and flow discursively over the surface of the deep until they peradventure break upon the shore. But they are motived by the tide. We never think to any purpose without schemata. No matter how abstract it may be, our thought is always intuitive in nature because it is dynamic, having an original tendency to imaginative form. Kant said, our thought is discursive because it is unconditioned; we say, it is intuitive because it is conditioned. Schemata are not by any means confined to the Applied Understanding. Kant himself recognised that there are schemata of Reason. The Ideas can only think their Ideal of systematic unity by the energy of some dynamic form of thought, and this is the idea of a maximum;[1] or if we will think of something even more attenuated, the idea of a Supreme Intelligence comes before our minds under the schema of a thing in general.[2] These he calls analogous or symbolic schemata, and so far there is some ground for this distinction between the schemata of Reason and Applied Understanding. For however strong our tendency may be to think the being of God or the maximum unity of existence, our thinking never arrives at a completely determinate concept; the tendency towards imaginative form is inevitably arrested, and just when we think we are coming at it, our thoughts disperse into vacuity. But the ground of difference which Kant supposes to underlie these distinct orders of schemata is quite fictitious. In his opinion it consists in the fact that the schemata of Understanding have a necessary reference to Time, whereas the symbolic forms of Reason have no implication of Time at all. This does not prove anything. The reference to Time in schemata is nothing more than the feature of change which is essential to the fact of self-consciousness, and this implication of Time is quite as real in the symbols of Reason. For Kant admits that "we may have a determinate notion of

[1] *Appendix to Dialectic*: Meiklejohn, p. 407.   [2] *Ibid.* p. 411.

a *maximum* and an absolutely perfect."[1] But a determinate notion we cannot have unless we are balancing and recovering ourselves in the yielding medium of consciousness, and this implies some displacement in Time.

The theory which we are now criticising is deeply embedded in the history of thought. Aristotle, thinking from an opposite standpoint, held the same mechanical opinion as Kant of the relation between sense and thought. He indeed speaks of the Passive Reason as perishable, but he does not therefore mean to identify it with the soul of the lower powers as Zeller seems to understand him. It is the discursive processes that are perishable, and these are not themselves affections ($\pi\acute{a}\theta\eta$) of Reason but of that "which has Reason in it in so far as it has it,"[2] that is, images embodying universals. In itself, Reason is incapable of being affected and is unmingled ($\dot{a}\pi a\theta\grave{\eta}s$ $\kappa a\grave{\iota}$ $\dot{a}\mu\iota\gamma\grave{\eta}s$).[3] By being passive he only means that it is reduced to potentiality. But when Reason becomes active, as it may be supposed to exist in the divine mind, the discursive processes have fallen away.

Both Kant and Aristotle hold that discursive is inconsistent with intuitive thought. We are prepared to go a certain length in consenting to this opinion. The discursive nature of thinking signifies, that nothing of sense or imagination can have any meaning for us unless we are thinking of something else at the same time; consciousness is apperceptive. Were our Understanding intuitive, we are told that each individual perception would be immediately self-explaining. But, unfortunately, this Intuitive Under-

[1] *Ibid.* p. 408.   [2] *De Anima*, 408 b.   [3] *Ibid.* 430 a.

standing is unable to answer for itself, and it is not by any means decided, in our opinion, that even in the divine mind there is not something corresponding to our discursive thought. At all events, we refuse to countenance the idea that our thought has only an accidental relation to sensuous experience. In Kant's schematic consciousness, thought and sense are only united *de facto* and the same is true of Aristotle's theory. But we can also point with Kant to a higher plane of our experience where they are united *de jure*, in the aesthetic consciousness. As Hegel says in his Philosophy of Art, it is not that Sense may be tolerated as a medium, it is rather that Reason must be degraded into a symbol and cannot appear except in sensuous form. In his conception of mental Play, Kant has given conclusive proof that thought is inherently perceptive, and that therefore schematic consciousness is original to the nature of mind and not the accident of a psychological device. The discursive nature of our thought does not argue a defect in our intelligence, for the discursive process is instituted and maintained by what is truly divine in us, the dynamic energy of thought. It may be desirable that our thought should be improved in the direction of becoming more intuitive and less discursive, but that its discursive nature should be eliminated altogether is a doubtful proposition. Even for the divine mind immediacy may not exclude mediation. It may argue a superficial intelligence in a deity whose mind does not admit of more and less. If Kant's Intuitive Understanding can see at a glance, so to speak, it is only because He has no ideas, no discriminating preference in the vast universe of His resources. Certainly we do not think of a

THE CRITICAL PHILOSOPHY 291

discursive transition in the divine mind as happens with us, but we can imagine some qualitative sense of change. In so far as we have anything divine in us, we need not blush to own discursive thought. What lies at the back of all our thinking, except when our apprehension is completely implicit, is the Schema; it is that transcendental element of thought which is felt before it is noticed,[1] preceding and informing all perception.

In conclusion, we have still to explain why the schemata of Understanding should appear to be so much more effective than those of Reason. While the schemata of Reason float with extended wings in the pure ether of *Theoria*, the schemata of Understanding stick their claws into the pulp of sense and prey on garbage. The latter have the advantage of a more immediate contact with Reality. While Reflexion is said to be transcendental and *a priori*, it only organises Nature into an empirical system; but the Understanding has an apodictic knowledge of its province and its *a priori* is absolute. Perhaps the following suggestion, somewhat on the lines of the conclusion to Chapter VI., may throw some light on the problem. It is in the nature of thought that it should have a certain amount of generality and so be able to embrace many different particulars. Our thought can therefore attend to one of these only as it thinks it through the others. But in simple perception the apperceptive function, which is not different in kind from the discursive nature of reflective thought, is limited. We do not need or wish to do more than perceive, and the amount

[1] For this expression I am indebted to a suggestion in F. H. Bradley's acute article on Immediate Experience : *Mind*, Jan. 1909.

of suggestion and memory-processes called into play is no more than what is needful for simple perception. In Reflexion the apperceptive function is intensified. Presentations are not simply to be perceived as they ought but as we should like to perceive them, and for this a far greater amount of suggestion and recollection is required. But the result is not less actual, it is more actual. Every atom of sensation is spun into a web of apperceptive gauze until the merely actual disappears and the actual with increased significance takes its place, the world of Art and Life. The more the beauty of a thing is seen and felt, the more does it stand out from the frame-work of the actual, suspended in splendid isolation by its own invisible thread; the more we draw the ends together in a living being, the more do its organs lose their exclusive independence: they have ceased to exist as merely actual parts in their discreteness and have become distinctive elements in a system of ideal relations. A living body is no longer an aggregate of impressions, but a real whole productive of its parts.

CHAPTER VIII.

AESTHETIC AND TELEOLOGY.

THE discursive method of our thought does not disable us from apprehending living Nature. On the contrary, our Understanding with its modicum of intuition is peculiarly fitted for assimilating this plane of perception. In Aesthetic our ideas displace each other with such a facile motion—and not less in the Sublime where the aesthetic process may originate in a violent dislocation—that the discursive transition melts into a frictionless continuum like the ether. It is not on that account a timeless or unreal process, but the self-mediation of immediate experience. But in Teleology the discursive process must be more explicit, because we are subject to a different kind of constraint due to the influence of living beings, which we do not feel in Aesthetic. The wisest course, then, for the Understanding is to abase itself before the aggressive presentation, and ponder discursively what it has to say in a kind of personal intercourse. We can adopt George Meredith's expedient of finding out all we want to know, by asking questions without expecting a reply. The least significance Teleology should have for us is that, like Art, its object is the individual and not the generalisations of abstract induction, which is all the meaning Kant put into it. Every true induction is a discursive process shot through with momentary flashes of insight, which reveal the individual nature of the thing examined. The cumulative judgments of a scientist who devotes years to the study of a spider, have the emotional quality of artistic divination : with this difference, that while representations occupy the foreground in the artistic consciousness, which is unthinking, they form the background in the active consciousness of the scientist to explicit conceptual relations.

This is the chief distinction between Aesthetic and Teleology. The judgments of both are forms of what Kant has called subjective teleology, that is, they are purposive as psychological processes of ours quite apart from any predicate of purpose. But while the aesthetic consciousness is exhausted in the subjective feeling of harmony in a play of unthinking representations, a harmony which is capable of infinite expansion, Teleology is a conceptual play which, in its very nature as conceptual, must refer beyond the process to an object which has a different kind of independence from that which we recognise in objects of Art. The predicate in a teleological judgment is at one and the same time a purposive feeling and a concept of purpose ; and the subjective teleology is not exhausted in our feeling of harmony, because it is the emotional transcript of purposive activity in a being which enjoys its own existence. While we recognise the objects of Art as individual with an independent, abiding existence, our pleasure consists precisely in the fact that the product of an independent will so easily yields to our interpretation. But our interest in organisms is stimulated and strengthened by the thought that they do not yield up their independent existence. Teleology is not simply the reflection of our personality, but Nature enacts our freedom in her living forms.

It was this independence in the organism that stood as a stumbling-block in Kant's way. His final criticism was that we cannot understand an organism because we cannot make it, and that therefore the application of our own practical causality as a means of explanation must only be analogical. This limitation to our knowledge constituted for him the difference between the mathematical and biological sciences. He thought that the only things we can know with certainty are extensive magnitudes, because, as Geometry shows, we literally produce representations in space *a priori*. His view of intensive magnitude or degree in sensation does not really affect his position, and is hardly more than a corollary to the preceding principle. It is fundamental for him that "sensation is just that element in cognition which cannot be at all anticipated."[1] And the only element in sensation which we can anticipate, is that to which we can give a mathematical ratio. It is true that he speaks of intensive magnitude as if it were an individual quality, apprehended in a single instant of sensation. For example, we perceive by the muscular sensation of lifting that a brick and a stone, of equal size, have different intensive magnitudes. It would thus appear that we can have a knowledge of objects which is not quantitative. But in order to be *a priori*, it must be a sensation which can be measured in terms of space, for example, the number of feet a body with specific intensive magnitude will fall in a given time. When Kant speaks of intensive magnitude, he is thinking of the quality of a quantity and not the

[1] Meiklejohn, pp. 126-7.

quantity of a quality. We have no right to infer from his statement that we perceive intensive magnitude as an individual quality, that we can also anticipate different qualities in sensation to which we cannot give a mathematical ratio. He denies that we can have an *a priori* sensation of an end, or the intensive unity in an organism. His mathematical ideal of knowledge is the necessary correlate to his mathematical view of mental life, as a succession of elements in abstract time, represented under the image of position in space. He can hardly be said to have regarded consciousness as organic : it was either an empirical representation of parts external to each other, or else an analytic unity. It is not therefore wonderful if he should have thought that we cannot have a necessary perception of an intensive unity, which is neither mathematical nor mystical.

In reply to Kant we should say, that we can understand the organic better than anything else for the reason that we know nothing so intimately as ourselves. And we have this intimate knowledge of ourselves because our personality is something we cannot make, as if it were a living thing which exists independently of our self-consciousness, and which is therefore able to react on our knowledge of it and check our surmises about it. The only real kind of knowledge is obtained in a discursive intercourse punctuated by flashes of intuition. In the same way, an organism is a thing of which we can have real knowledge because it is something which we cannot make. If we wish to vindicate the validity of the historical and biological sciences against a mathematical ideal of knowledge, we must first recognise the individual existence of their objects. Of geometrical figures we may be said to know nothing real, in so far as we are able to produce them. They are only models which we construct of natural forces and their relations to each other, such as the elliptical motions of the heavenly bodies, which we do not make. It might be objected that we do understand a natural law when we are able to produce an illustration of it in a working model. But all that we understand about it is only what we ourselves have put into it. Our so-called mathematical certainty is just what precludes us from ever knowing how far our conception is true. As Kant himself said in the preface to the second edition of the *Critique of Pure Reason*, what we know *a priori* in things is only what we ourselves put into them.[1]

In so far as we may be said to have mathematical certainty in our knowledge of anything, there is either nothing in it to be known, that is, it is not an individual thing but a centre of endless relations, or we know nothing real about it. If we are able to explain a fact of history like the French Revolution, precisely as the effect of certain causes, we have missed its significance as an individual event, an act of cosmic will, and explained it away. We do not forget that natural forces are realities which we do not create any more than organisms, and it is a plausible inference that we should be able to have a real knowledge of them too. For all we know, they may be what Schopenhauer believed them to be, manifestations of Will, and therefore realities which are capable of reciprocating our consciousness of them. But it is just because they suffer themselves to be measured with mathematical precision and do not question or disturb

[1] Hart, iii. p. 19.

our *a priori* peace, that we can never have a real knowledge of what they are in themselves. As matters now stand, we certainly know a great deal more about personality, notwithstanding its obscurity, than we know about the ultimate nature of mechanical forces. The Individual is the only thing that stands up to our scrutiny, and it is the only thing of which we can have real knowledge because it is the only thing that has a self-subsisting centre of reality which is not dissipated by criticism. There is nothing else in Nature of which we can have real knowledge because there is nothing else in Nature with which we can have personal intercourse in a reciprocating consciousness. The living, or if not the living itself, that which refuses to be measured by mathematical standards and subsists as the act of creative will in History or Art, is the only thing that gives a sense of security to our self-consciousness because it responds. The phenomena of quantity keep us completely in the dark, the only answer we receive is the mocking echo of our questioning spirit: 'we are what you have made us and no more.' It is the response that gives reality to our knowledge, it is the one touch of Nature that makes the whole world kin.

Now Kant admits that a Teleology of Nature is possible and that we can have at least some hypothetical knowledge of organic forms, but it is by a negative process of subreption similar to what we already found in the Sublime. The conception of a natural purpose would be quite unintelligible except to a being who is capable of acting from ends of Reason. The conception of ends in Nature is therefore a psychological idea imported from our moral consciousness and attributed to Nature. And we can never be sure if it is not we rather than Nature who are originally responsible for the purposive manifestations of organic life. Like the Indian who wondered, not that the froth should foam out of the beer-bottle but that it should ever have got in, we are prone to imagine that what we think to be traits of character and will in organisms, exist in Nature as they appear to us.[1]

It is right, then, that we should not rashly choose our ground but first apply the thought of living purpose, which we find in ourselves, to those organic forms which are able to sustain it. Although we may confidently think of persons as having a nature like our own, it is a precarious inference that animals and plants have anything corresponding to a moral consciousness; it is possible that their appearance of purposive activity may be sufficiently explained as mechanical functions. At the meeting of the British Association in 1908, Mr. Francis Darwin gave an interesting address on a kind of memory-knowledge in plants and lower forms of life. The plant which raises its leaves with the dawn and depresses them at dusk, continues to do the same when kept in total darkness; flowers that are sweetly fragrant during the night, also exude their grateful odour during an eclipse of the sun. When we consider that the natural causes of their several functions are absent, we are forced to think of these phenomena as due to a kind of association of ideas which implies memory. But we are still in the region of conjecture. We can never be sure that our proleptic idea of purposive causality in an

[1] Bernard, p. 224; Schopenhauer, *The World as Will and Idea*; Haldane, iii. p. 78.

organism is a fact of Nature. In Kant's opinion, there is only one Idea of Reason which is a fact independent of experience, and that is Freedom. Man is in himself an unconditioned end of Nature, for he contains the highest purpose to which Nature can be subordinate.[1] We do not see all things already put under him, but "the earnest expectation of the creation waiteth for the revealing of the sons of God." Man is the only animal who bids defiance to Nature's rule and chooses his own destiny. He is what Professor Ray Lankester calls him, Nature's rebel.[2] The animal kingdom was made subject to vanity, being ruthlessly governed by the principle of natural selection; Nature bids die all who fail to reach the required standard of efficiency. Only man has the courage to answer Nature's challenge with the will to live: "I shall not die but live, and declare the works of the Lord."

Thus the highest Idea of Reason for Kant is the Idea of Personality. The only certain end in Nature is the end of human life, and it is therefore our moral consciousness alone that gives the sanction to Teleology. As subordinate to man, all the purposes of Nature, internal and external, may have a relative meaning and truth. But in themselves they have no independent substrate of reality, and we can only judge of them reflectively by an external teleology to which there may be nothing corresponding in themselves. When Kant says that the thought of teleology in organisms is due to the discursive nature of our Understanding, he evidently means that their whole significance consists in their relation to a self. The unity is in themselves but not for themselves, as a

---

[1] Bernard, pp. 360-1. [2] *The Kingdom of Man*, pp. 26, 40.

stone may be said to have a unity of form, or what Aristotle calls an external entelechy. They are conscious but not self-conscious. In Dr. M'Taggart's words, they are not able to withstand the unity of the Absolute Idea which is an abstract description of the human spirit.[1]

Although Kant strongly affirms the relative validity of the categories of abstract science, which Dr. M'Taggart as strenuously denies, he would agree with him that the biological categories are not a true description of Reality but are due to the zig-zag movement of our thought as expressed in the law of Contradiction, or in Kant's own terms, to our discursive Understanding. But as Mr. Bosanquet has shown in his important article on 'Contradiction and Reality,'[2] contradiction is one thing and negation is another. Dr. M'Taggart has not sufficiently noticed this distinction. Contradiction is a vanishing factor and diminishes in the higher reaches of experience, where the elements are opposed not so much in earnest as in play. But this does not touch the question whether there may not be an original and abiding discursive factor in all our thinking, even when it approximates to the intuitive. Kant's fundamental error consists in having assumed as the type of real existence, an ultimate unity which is incapable of further analysis and which excludes not only evanescent oppositions but also original distinctions. The consciousness of Freedom is such a reality, and that is why he is able to call it a fact independent of experience. His position is that finite existence is for a self but Reality for itself, or in Mr. Bradley's phrase, that Reality is

[1] *Studies in Hegelian Dialectic*, p. 143. [2] *Mind*, Jan. 1906.

experience. The only difference is that what Kant conceives as a higher immediacy in the analytic consciousness of Freedom, Mr. Bradley conceives as a lower immediacy in Sentience. The former is a subject which is its own object, the latter an object which is its own subject. But, on their own admission, both these realities are ideal limits which have nothing to do with experience. Kant admits that it is absolutely impossible to procure a single case in experience with complete certainty, in which the maxim of an act, ostensibly done for duty's sake, has rested solely on moral grounds and on the idea of duty.[1] Mr. Bradley, again, cannot find a single piece of experience which is not vitiated by relation to a self, and consequently swollen with a merely ideal content like a face stung by a bee; just as Kant's consciousness of Freedom transcends, Mr. Bradley's object which is its own subject falls below, the margin of experience, and then it becomes a lost quantity.[2] Mr. Bradley desiderates a quiet encounter with a fact outside of experience, where he may shun publicity and the exaggerated reports of the upper world :

" Foliis tantum ne carmina manda,
Ne turbata volent, rapidis ludibria ventis."

One is reminded of the tramp who remarked on being convicted of drunkenness, that he must have had a glorious time of it last night judging from what the policeman told the magistrate.

This position that Reality is immediate experience, which is really the basis of modern Pragmatism however indifferently disposed to this school its

---

[1] Hart, iv. pp. 254-5.
[2] *Appearance and Reality* : see especially chap. xxvi.

authors may be, begs the whole question. Clearly we can only start from experience, but if we also equate Reality with it, we are for ever disabled from answering the inevitable question how far experience itself is real. And the logical result is solipsism. This is what happens with Dr. M'Taggart. He would fain find his personal monads consenting to a mutual correspondence, but if there is no feature of negation in the immediate unity of self-consciousness, how can the monad ever get beyond anything other than itself? It is certainly a pious and noble reflection, that if we could see clearly enough our minds would see a nature like our own in everything.[1] But this does not mean for him that everything bears the image of the heavenly, but that everything which is not able to bear this image is nothing at all. For by everything he does not understand every chair, every crystal, but that there are personalities behind them.[2] Whether there is a spirit hiding behind each group of chairs, or whether it may have a dash of crystals into the bargain, or whether finally there must be no μετάβασις εἰς ἄλλο γένος, we are not told. But why should we be so anxious to force our own nature on everything? If this is the kind of heaven to which these thinkers are travelling, where every corner is packed with experience, where there is no room to stand and nothing to sit down on, we at least are desirous of a better country. We want more room.

It is the same tendency we find in Kant. In so far as organic forms have no consciousness of Freedom, they have no supersensible substrate but an external entelechy, and their purposive appearance is an accident

[1] *Studies in Hegelian Dialectic*, p. 143.   [2] *Ibid.* p. 222.

of our thought. Consequently, the sole basis for a Teleology of Nature is our moral consciousness, and it has no valid application except to persons; in a secondary way, by a kind of subreption, it may be applied to animal organisms in order to assist our Understanding.

There seems to be some doubt, however, as to whether this is Kant's real position. We should not wish to raise a critical point at this late stage, but it is important as it focusses the two different methods of interpreting the *Critique of Judgment*. Frost stands for the position we have taken, that Teleology requires the help of Practical Reason.[1] Stadler, on the other hand, is of opinion that this is not necessary, the Theoretic Reason being alone sufficient to account for Teleology. Then it follows that Mechanism is unbroken throughout as an exhaustive method of explanation, and Teleology is only called in as an auxiliary principle to complete this explanation. Wundt and Basch apparently endorse this interpretation.[2] But, as Frost pointedly observes, if it were really the case that Teleology is only a supplementary principle to Mechanism, how could Kant speak of an antinomy between them?[3] It is certainly true that Stadler has decided support in Kant's writings. It is very significant that in the original Introduction all judgments are divided into theoretical, aesthetical and practical.[4] In this passage, Teleology has no distinctive place at all in the system of philosophy. And near the end of the same essay, there is a whole page which is

[1] *Der Begriff der Urteilskraft bei Kant*, pp. 105, 116.
[2] *L'Esthétique de Kant*, p. 143.
[3] *Kants Teleologie.* Kantstudien, Bd. XI.
[4] *Über Philosophie überhaupt*: Rosenkranz, i. p. 600.

completely conclusive. There Kant says that what is distinctive in Reflexion is the aesthetical judgment alone, while Teleology follows the lead of Reason and does not need to base itself on any special principle.[1]

In view of these statements, which constitute a real difficulty, it will perhaps be sufficient to say that at least they need not be taken as representing Kant's final view. Stadler was evidently misled by Rosenkranz's statement in the introduction to his edition of Kant's works, that the writing in question first appeared in 1794, four years after the *Critique of Judgment*.[2] It has now been ascertained that the *Über Philosophie überhaupt* was written in its original form before the *Critique of Judgment* appeared. The fact seems to be that Kant had prepared an Introduction which he afterwards laid aside. This manuscript was the original Introduction in an extended form. When he saw the need for a more succinct statement, he characteristically wrote out an independent essay without caring to revise or elaborate what he had already written. This is an accredited feature of Kant's style. In the same way, the *Prolegomena* is a second and independent treatment of portions of the *Critique*; and the *Dissertation* of 1770 was not revised but embodied without change in the *Transcendental Aesthetic*, although it maintains a radical opposition between Sense and Thought which was foreign to Kant's critical purpose. Meanwhile, Kant had given the original manuscript to J. S. Beck to use at his discretion. Beck made extracts which he published in 1794, and these extracts make up what is known to us as the *Über Philosophie überhaupt*. Now

[1] *Über Philosophie überhaupt*: Rosenkranz, i. p. 614.
[2] Rosenkranz, *Werke*, i. Vorrede, p. 37, note.

Stadler was under the impression that the *Über Philosophie überhaupt* was a recast of the official Introduction.[1] But the fact seems to be that the official Introduction was a recast of the *Über Philosophie überhaupt*. Kuno Fischer dates the original manuscript as far back as 1787,[2] while Erdmann puts it down to 1789.[3]

It is not, then, the case that this work, which contains the principal evidence for Stadler's position, gives Kant's last words on the matter. It was in the closing years of the eighties that Kant first tried to effect a connection between Taste and Teleology. The first work in which this connection is systematically developed is the *Über Philosophie überhaupt*, and he is so exclusively occupied with this particular problem in that work that he loses sight of Organic Teleology. At least, he has little more to say about it than he had already said in the *Dialectic*. If now we turn to the essay entitled 'Concerning the use of teleological principles in Philosophy,' which was published about the time the *Über Philosophie überhaupt* was originally drafted (1788), we find that Organic Teleology is definitely based on a new principle, namely, our practical faculty of Reason, both pure and applied. The significance of this double use of Practical Reason will be explained immediately. But Stadler is not to be put down so easily. He is familiar with every passage in which Kant connects Teleology with Practical Reason. His contention is that this new principle is not necessary. In so far as organisms are only considered as effects, Stadler is correct. The relation of the organism to

---

[1] *Kants Teleologie*, p. 44.
[2] *Kant und seine Lehre*, ii. pp. 412-5.
[3] *Kants Kritik der Urteilskraft*, p. 341 ; Einleitung, s. xvi.-xvii.

its cause, however peculiar and enigmatic it may be, completely falls within the systematic teleology of the *Dialectic*. As we saw at the close of Chapter I., we may introduce a new principle in the shape of a psychological idea imported from ourselves, and think the Cause of Nature, organic and inorganic, as artisan. But although this may be more picturesque than the idea of Nature as a logical system, it is not necessary, and is only of use in helping us to complete that system. This is the point of Stadler's contention. Without receiving any hint from our moral consciousness, Theoretic Reason already instituted a logical Teleology of Nature, which is quite indifferent to the circumstance that some of Nature's objects are organic; for the classification or specification of Nature as a system of ends, according as we start from the particular or the universal, is not derived from the constitution of objects but from the speculative interest of Reason in the completeness of knowledge.[1]

So far Stadler's argument is conclusive. As was pointed out in the preceding chapter, Kant has not fulfilled our expectations of his new principle. The psychological idea of Nature as conceived on the analogy of our practical causality, ought to mean a very different conception of Nature from that of a logical system. But this psychological idea does not tell us anything new about the constitution of Nature: its sole significance for Kant is that of an additional heuristic principle in the extension of Nature as a mechanical system. There are some indications, however, that Kant was prepared to take his new principle in earnest. If in its aesthetic application this principle is responsible

[1] *Appendix to Dialectic*: Meiklejohn, p. 408.

for a real purpose in the subjective mind, it ought also, in its scientific application, to sanction a real purpose in Nature as something more than the external reflection of our discursive Understanding on Nature. Now, in his later theory of organic evolution, Kant suggests the much deeper view of Nature as a creative process in which mechanism is a subordinate factor; and this conception of Nature would answer somewhat to the psychological idea of his new principle. And further, in what seems to be a distinction between an organism considered as effect and an organism considered as itself a cause, he recognises the need of basing Organic Teleology on the moral consciousness, instead of explaining it as being due to the discursive Understanding. The significant consequence is that the conception of organic Nature is largely due to an attitude of mind, namely, the conative, which, unlike discursive Understanding, depends for its validity on the reality of natural purposes. I have noticed that Kant distinguishes the two ways in which an organism may be regarded by a very subtle difference. We have already observed the thorough distinction which he draws between technically practical, and morally practical, Reason. When he is thinking of the cause of organisms, he appeals to our technical Reason which is a mixture of Understanding and Will. ("Wir kennen aber dergleichen Kräfte, *ihrem Bestimmungsgrunde nach*, durch Erfahrung *nur in uns selbst*, nämlich an unserem Verstande und Willen, als eine Ursache der Möglichkeit gewisser ganz nach Zwecken eingerichteter Produkte, nämlich der Kunstwerke.")[1] What is important in the application

---

[1] *Über den Gebrauch teleologischer Principien in der Philosophie*: Kirchmann, p. 171; Hart, iv. p. 493.

of technical Reason is not the organism so much as the architect.¹ But when he is thinking of the organism as itself a cause, he seems to appeal exclusively to our Pure Practical Reason as the means of explanation.

Two decisive passages may be noted. Kant says that the inner teleology in an organism " is not analogous to any physical, *i.e.* natural, faculty known to us ; nay even, regarding ourselves as, in the widest sense, belonging to Nature, it is not even thinkable or explicable by means of any exactly fitting analogy to human art." ² The significance of this passage is negative. It excludes the use of technical Reason to explain organisms as themselves causes. The following passage, of which I give a paraphrase, contains a positive statement, and insists on the use of a faculty which is not natural but supersensible : ' While we can quite well see that there must be a nexus of causes and effects, it is impossible to say *a priori* that there are ends in Nature. Therefore the use of the teleological principle in Nature is always empirically conditioned. It would be the same with the ends of Freedom if our motives came to us from Nature, and were formed simply by comparing natural needs and inclinations with one another. But this is not the case. Practical Reason has pure *a priori* principles which specify the end of Reason *a priori*. This is the true finalism. Consequently, if the use of the teleological principle can never sufficiently specify the ultimate ground of teleological connection in natural purposes, because it is limited by empirical conditions, we must expect this complete explanation from a Pure Teleology which can be no other than that of Freedom, whose

[1] See Bernard, pp. 290-1.   [2] *Ibid.* pp. 279-80.

principle contains *a priori* the relation of a Reason in general to the totality of all ends.'[1]

It must be confessed that we seem to be making the most of a poor case. But I think everyone who has read Kant with close attention will acknowledge that, while he has confused these two aspects of Organic Teleology, he intended to keep them apart. Were it not for our moral consciousness, there would be no Organic Teleology and no really new principle. Such ends as Nature presents to us would remain what they are, empirical observations of which we can make nothing, if our moral consciousness did not encourage us to take them seriously. Our moral personality is the only clear instance of a self-contained end, therefore of a natural purpose, and it is from this instance in ourselves and from it only, that we are able to think of other purposive appearances as having inner teleology.

Thus the final outcome of the third *Critique* is Ethical Teleology. If our moral consciousness institutes Organic Teleology, it also determines its limits. Wherever the Idea of Freedom fails to apply, Organic Teleology ceases to be a certainty and becomes a subsidiary speculation. Kant's ostensible reason for this restriction is that we have an intuitive perception of Freedom as a fact in ourselves, which we can therefore apply to a society of persons who are able to sustain this Idea. The implication is that since we have no *a priori* intuition of biological unity, our judgments on organisms must only be analogical. But this is an unreasonable assumption. Our discursive thought is

---

[1] *Über den Gebrauch teleologischer Principien in der Philosophie*: Kirchmann, pp. 172-3; Hart, iv. pp. 494-5.

THE CRITICAL PHILOSOPHY

good enough, provided it is a reciprocating consciousness. As Kant himself acknowledges, this trumpery Idea of abstract Freedom has no existence in fact. The consciousness of Freedom may be an immediate certainty, but it is not therefore an unmediated perception. We come into the consciousness of Freedom through our discursive intercourse with persons in a society of Ends. What George Meredith says tentatively of Nature in the *Egoist* may be said of our moral personality, that it is not so much a fact as the effort to master a fact, in a progressive culture. Kant's mistaken assumption is the error in all Intellectualism, a one-sided criterion of interpretation as reposed in a pre-conceived unity. In every case this dogmatism makes no serious attempt to explain the diversity. In Plato it is non-being; in Spinoza, all determination is negation; in Leibniz, truths of fact are ideally truths of Reason, but they only become intelligible by an arbitrary choice of the Best as if the essences of Reason existed prior to the divine Mind; for Mr. Bradley it is mere appearance, so that in its highest manifestation as personality, "*he*, as such, must vanish";[1] Dr. M'Taggart confesses that we must come to a halt somewhere in our system, and that whereas there is much which is far from being individual and has a non-spiritual appearance, we must be content to leave it unexplained; a confession which, after so brilliant a display, is almost as remarkable as Hume's.[2]

The history of philosophy is a fair indication that we are on the wrong road when we insist on an unconditioned unity as capable of interpreting the diverse forms of existence. As I have heard Professor Stout

[1] *Appearance and Reality*, p. 419.
[2] *Studies in Hegelian Dialectic*, chap. v.

say at the meeting of the Aristotelian Society in Birmingham, 1909, we are not to seek for a unity which will interpret the diversity, but a unity which the diversity can adequately interpret. That is to say, our consciousness of Reality must be reciprocating, and it is because the organic facilitates this kind of consciousness that it is more easily within the reach of our understanding than anything else. One recalls what St. Augustine said about plants making advances to our knowledge of them, by inviting our admiration. Kant thinks that it is we who project everything into the organism. But our thought becomes coherent precisely in the measure that the organism reciprocates our consciousness of it.

Kant, however, was aware to some extent that if the conception of Nature as organic must have the sanction of our moral consciousness, our moral consciousness must be reinforced by our consciousness of Nature as organic. Apart from his familiar position that the validity of Ethics involves, as an essential hypothesis, the subordination of Nature to a moral purpose, he expressed himself more particularly with reference to the problem of Teleology in the passage we have just paraphrased, and which we now continue: 'Granted that this pure Practical Teleology is destined to realise its ends in the *world*, it ought not to neglect ensuring the possibility of these ends as effect, and to do this both with reference to the *final causes* given in the world and also the organisation of all ends as the effect of a supreme world-cause; in short, it must not neglect to substantiate Organic Teleology and also Transcendental Philosophy, or the possibility of Nature in general, in order to ensure objective reality to the ends of Practical Reason.'[1] The ends of Freedom can only be realised if Nature will glow with some spark of fire in her grey ashes and discover a real kinship to our moral personality. The ends of Nature, of which we have only a dim presentiment in empirical observation, but which Freedom devoutly elaborates into a system of Ethical Teleology, are not of Freedom's making. They are favours of Nature, and without this concession on the part of Nature, Freedom would go darkling. Moral culture is impossible except in a world which is itself informed with a moral intention. The deep without must answer to the call of the deep within. Already in her Beauty, Nature becomes responsive. But in organic forms there is a nearer approach to the nature of man. We have not only the picture but the fact of Freedom; organic Nature is the instinctive enactment of our ethical personality, or the realisation of moral ends in a natural way.

But Kant goes much farther. The moral earnestness in virtue of which we appeal to Nature as a system of real purposes, is only an accident of our practical faculty, as the discursive method of thought is a defect in our intelligence. In a Being whose Understanding is intuitive, the distinction between 'ought' and 'is' does not exist, because the possible is itself actual.[2] From this it should follow that if the manifestations of purpose in organisms are delusions of discursive Understanding, our Practical Reason is responsible for the fictitious belief in moral persons, and the Idea of personality is as much an external entelechy as the Idea of biological

[1] *Über den Gebrauch teleologischer Principien in der Philosophie*: Kirchmann, p. 173; Hart, iv. p. 495.
[2] Bernard, § 76, p. 317.

unity. Perhaps Kant hardly realised the far-reaching consequences of this admission, which is the root of ethical scepticism.[1] With the identification of Theoretic and Practical Reason, as it was developed by Fichte, morality ceases to be unconditioned and becomes phenomenal like the knowledge of sense-perception.

This ethical nihilism is the worst form in which the conception of an Intuitive Understanding could be presented, and is a very doubtful speculation. It is stated in an extreme form by Mr. Bradley when he says: "most emphatically no self-assertion nor any self-sacrifice, nor any goodness or morality, has, as such, any reality in the Absolute."[2] We do not say that the conception is altogether fictitious. The motiveless morality which Schiller saw typified in the Greek statues, represents a real attitude in the life of sainthood. Holiness is more than virtue. It is the state of soul which knows all imaginable forms of evil but will not image any of them, the state of sublimation in which the soul maintains its calm above the earth-storm of the will. In our unsanctified morality the will is only exercised in self-defence, at random ventures, and it is little better than an accident if we come off victorious; it is a negative reaction to an external irritant rather than spontaneous expression. In Holiness the will is watchful and wakeful, the issue is foreclosed, the way of the battle determined, before the suggestions of evil arise. He is indeed noble who wins a victory over temptation in the fierce struggles of the will, but at the best it is a grudging victory. Much nobler is he who, like Perseus on his winged sandals, rises above temptation's level and engages with the dragon from above.

[1] Cp. Dorner, *Kantstudien*, iv.   [2] *Appearance and Reality*, p. 420.

Now this exalted state is anything but motiveless. It requires a far greater expenditure of effort to maintain this level than to keep our ground in the struggles of the will. For the same reason, I do not think that obligation loses its meaning even for the divine mind. The existence of moral evil would be a hopeless enigma unless it had its ultimate ground in the nature of God. As Theaetetus said to the Stranger, this may seem to be a "terrible admission." But if we say that obligation is confined to the finite mind, we are positing something which God does not understand, and therefore something by which the absolute nature of His being is limited. To be absolute the nature of God must contain the element of finitude, and in such a way that His finite nature shall not be regarded as evanescent appearance but as a permanent feature of His existence. This is the truth expressed in the Christian doctrine, that the Son retains his humanity in His state of exaltation. It would be impossible for men to sin unless the possibility were present to the mind of God. When we say with Plato that God cannot possibly do evil, we mean that it is His nature to be good, and we do not express anything different in the alternative statement that He is good because He wills to be good. But the simple statement that He is good just because it is His nature, altogether neglects the element of striving in the life of God. The goodness of God would mean nothing to us unless it were possible for Him to be otherwise. And if the nature of God is such that this contingency shall never happen, it is because the necessity to be good is maintained by continuous assertion of His self-hood. There is no reason, in existence or out of it, why God should not let go the rudder of the universe, except that He has chosen not to do so, and the maintenance of His eternal choice is a state of being which is unthinkable, apart from the conception of something corresponding to moral obligation.

But there is sufficient in the distinction between the intuitive and moral will as we have understood it, to destroy Kant's laborious edifice. At least we have forced him into a consistent scepticism. The moral consciousness is not a fixture any more than the discursive Understanding. The issue is so uncertain, the end of conduct which we confidently set before us as supreme and absolute, becomes so transformed into the commonplace of action, that it is possible to doubt our freedom and to regard all persons as complexes of animal functions; the moment of free choice which we enjoyed before action, resolves in retrospect into a series of inevitable causes. So much does the mere consciousness of Freedom mean for us. Freedom is not a fact sufficiently stable to support the idea of personality in ourselves or others, until it has ceased to be self-conscious. The sanction for an Ethical Teleology does not lie in the consciousness of Freedom but in a habitude of Freedom, which is much more akin to the aesthetic than to the moral consciousness itself. But we do not need to wait upon this habitude, for which a life-time may not suffice, in order to believe in personality; this habitude of Freedom already exists in us instinctively as a lower immediacy, in the original disposition of our mental functions. Our belief in personality is due to something in us which is deeper than the consciousness of moral freedom, it is what constitutes the basis of personality itself. There is the further important consequence that, since we are conscious of this basis as natural rather than as moral liberty, this fundamental consciousness of ourselves is also favourable to our belief in the existence of organic Nature, or the enactment of our moral freedom in a natural way. The moral consciousness is only an episode in the process from a lower to a higher immediacy, the lowest phase of which contains the consciousness of personality.

This problem of the relation between Aesthetic and Teleology brings our study to a close. There is a curious fascination in the way Kant brings together these different attitudes of consciousness. Our principal source is the original Introduction. In this essay, Kant defines his position in two completely contradictory statements. On the one hand, it is said that the introduction of the *Urteilskraft* into the system of philosophy, rests wholly on its peculiar, transcendental principle, that Nature specifies her causality in accordance with the idea of a system.[1] Teleology of Nature is therefore the sole justification for Reflexion. On the other hand, it is argued with equal emphasis, that the aesthetical judgment is the only distinct and peculiar element in Reflexion.[2] In so far, then, as Teleology has a place at all in Reflexion, it is because of the aesthetic principle. But it is in this antinomy that the solution lies. These two statements are necessarily abstract and untrue because they are independent expressions of a single fact. Aesthetic and Teleology are complementary attitudes of consciousness which stand to each other in the relation of content to form. The content in Reflexion is the consciousness of harmony in our mental states, the form is the principle which makes this harmony possible,

[1] *Über Philosophie überhaupt*: Rosenkranz, i. pp. 612-3.
[2] *Ibid.* p. 614.

pure teleology or the principle of adaptation in general. Thus, in a passage which Stadler regards as a slip of the pen, Kant is able to say, that the aesthetical judgment alone contains the principle of adaptation without which Understanding could not find itself in Nature.[1] Stadler very naturally considers that this is a confusion of aesthetical with systematic Teleology and an oversight on Kant's part.[2] But I think he meant it. Undoubtedly, the connection of the teleological principle with the aesthetic process was made easy for Kant by his predecessors, and it may quite well be nothing more than a confusion. What we should call beautiful Art was confused in Leibniz with technical skill, and this explains why a moral end or purposed intention clings to Aesthetic in the subsequent philosophers.[3] The principle of Teleology is Technic, the conception of Nature as artisan in the disposition of her laws, and of course this conception has nothing immediately to do with beautiful Art. It is exactly the same in sense as the τεχνίτης Λόγος of Irenaeus, and indicates the original meaning of the Greek word, technical or industrial Art. But the use of the same word, *Kunst*, to denote both beautiful and technical Art, made a confusion easy. Kant is by no means free from this ambiguity and takes advantage of it. There is a deeper justification, however, for the connection of Aesthetic with Teleology, which cannot be explained away as a confusion of terms. Kant's meaning in the above passage is that the essence of the aesthetic disposition of our faculties consists in their *formal* harmony, that is to say the harmony, not of particular representations,

---

[1] Bernard, Introd. p. 36.   [2] *Kants Teleologie*, p. 113.
[3] Erdmann, *Hist. Phil.* ii. p. 198.

but of the faculties themselves as unspecified content in a particular representation : the harmony, therefore, of Imagination and Understanding, Sense and Thought, Nature and Mind. The ground-work in Aesthetic is an *Erkenntniss überhaupt*, an Understanding in general, that is to say, the organised Imagination in general, and this can only mean the first and original application of Understanding to Nature ;[1] it therefore contains the original hypothesis that Nature is adapted to our intelligence.

But, so far, it is only the connection of Aesthetic with Teleology in general that Kant has in view. There does not seem to be any distinctive reference to Organic Teleology in this relation, and it is precisely the connection of Aesthetic with Organic Teleology that is in question. Organic Teleology is, of course, included in Formal or Systematic Teleology, for this latter means that Nature specifies her causation into new kinds of causality, such as mechanical reciprocity and organic teleology, and always in keeping with the conception of Nature as a systematic unity. Kant, however, has taught us to believe hitherto that this disposition of Nature is purely logical, and therefore quite indifferent to the particular constitution of the objects which come under its notice. It arises altogether out of the logical interest of Reason in systematic unity, and therefore what matters is not what we find in Nature but what we are able to put into Nature, so as to satisfy our intelligence. There may be a good deal left unexplained

---

[1] Kant says in the *Analytic*, that the synthesis of Imagination " is the first application, and so the condition of all other applications, of understanding to objects that we are capable of perceiving." *Watson's Selections*, p. 78.

in the nature of particular objects, but that is of no account so long as our interpretation, which is altogether subjective, gives a satisfactory result. It makes no difference to Reason that there are organisms, whose existence is so far individual and whose causality is so far independent, that they cannot be exhaustively explained as subsidiary to higher ends of Nature. It would make no difference to Reason if angels with wings appeared on its ground; Reason would soon accommodate them to its principle. Thus in Kant's view of Teleology there is no real difference between organic and inorganic, so far as our judgment is concerned. The so-called Teleology of Nature in the *Critique of Judgment* adds nothing to the regulative function of Reason in the *Dialectic*. For we are told that the predicates of Organic Teleology are reflective or logical, and therefore do not refer to real qualities of Nature. Considered as elements in a logical system of Reason these predicates may be regarded as *a priori*, because the subjective principle of teleology in general lies at the basis of all cognition; but considered as science they are purely empirical. The purpose in an organism is a purpose which is none of ours, and Kant would seem to think that the recognition of such a purpose as a real constituent of the organism, is quite inconsistent with the subjective principle of the consciousness of a purpose in ourselves. Accordingly, whenever Teleology pretends to be Science, it is disowned by the subjective principle of logical purpose and is dismissed under the ban of Criticism. The logical or reflective teleology, on the other hand, which we attribute to Nature, does fulfil a purpose in us, the unification of our knowledge in a system: it is a harmony of concepts as Aesthetic is a harmony of unthinking representations.

But now we wish to address a final question to Kant. Whence did Reason obtain this logical interest in Nature? From itself? No indeed. It is what is Nature in the subject that gives rise to the logical interest of Reason. For the consciousness of our subjective harmony is the felt knowledge of that very principle according to which Nature is specified in the organisation of her parts, and therefore the consciousness of a harmony in ourselves is based upon the implicit consciousness of a real harmony in Nature. The interest of Reason cannot, then, be merely logical, it must be transcendental. There is something deeper in us than the logical function of Reason as there is something deeper than the mere consciousness of our subjective freedom, and that is our personality, the fundamental consciousness of ourselves as natural liberty. We are now able to lay our finger on the source of so many contradictions in the *Critique of Judgment*. Kant has been using Reflexion in two different senses throughout: in the *Critique of the Aesthetical Judgment* Reflexion is transcendental, in the *Critique of the Teleological Judgment* it is logical. Thus the unity of Kant's original plan, if he had any, is completely broken. But the official 'deduction' or justification of Reflexion is given in the *Critique of the Aesthetical Judgment*, and Reflexion is there expressly identified with the conception of mental play as the basis and condition of all explicit knowledge, and is consequently entitled to an *a priori* sanction that is transcendental or immanent in experience, and not an *a priori* that is merely logical or contingent to experience. As I have said in the preceding chapter, the aesthetic consciousness, which is the typical expression of Reflexion, has more affinity with sensation than with logical process,[1] although it is not sensation. Hence the significance of Kant's derivation of Reflective Judgment from the Feeling of pleasure and pain (*Gefühl*), which he defines as a peculiar form of sensation (*Empfindung*).[2] There is no reason, therefore, why the Judgment in the domain of Organic Teleology should be denied the name of Science; its *a priori* sanction must be more than logical, that is, necessary from a particular point of view which may be quite contingent to experience, for it is only empirical in the qualified sense that it is a synthesis which is a further analysis. If, as we saw, the aesthetic consciousness may be taken as the content in Reflexion, of which the principle of pure teleology is the form, Organic Teleology, or a genuine inductive synthesis which reveals the true nature of the individual, will be a further specification of this indeterminate content which is the consciousness of ourselves as Nature, and not a purely empirical procedure.

It was surely the light of genius that led Kant, not simply to state the community of Aesthetic and Teleology, which his predecessors had rendered easy in their confusion of beautiful with technical Art, but to reiterate and insist on this relation. The real significance of his association of Judgment with Feeling is that notionless experience, as the indeterminate consciousness of a principle, conditions the application of this principle in the use of concepts. Probably this is the meaning of a baffling passage which it is almost

---

[1] *Vide supra*, p. 257.
[2] *Über Philosophie überhaupt*: Rosenkranz, i. p. 598; Hart, vi. p. 388.

impossible to render in coherent English. With the omission of certain unnecessary reiterations, what Kant says is as follows : ' Although teleology must be supplied to the judgment empirically on every occasion, still the judgment on these particular organisations of Nature obtains a claim to universality and necessity, *through the relation of the subjective teleology of the given representation to the a priori principle of pure teleology* : and thus an aesthetical reflective judgment can be regarded as resting on an *a priori* principle.'[1] The concluding reference to the aesthetical judgment is quite inconsequent and ought to stand first. What he should have said is that Teleology has the same original claim to universality as Aesthetic, because of the necessary relation between the consciousness of a harmony in our faculties and the disposition of the same according to a certain principle. There is originally a subjective element in a teleological judgment, although its predicate is found in empirical observation ; our activity fulfils a purpose in ourselves which inspires and directs our voyage of discovery. But this subjective harmony is itself the felt knowledge of a principle which must be *a priori*, because it is the principle on which the faculties of our mind are originally disposed to one another, namely, the harmony of our consciousness of Nature with the consciousness of ourselves. The teleology of Nature takes its rise in the sense of wonder, which is an indeterminate psychological process without specific predicate ; or, to put it in another way, a judgment of purpose is originally a purposive judgment

---

[1] *Über Philosophie überhaupt*: Rosenkranz, i. p. 613 ; Hart, vi. p. 400.

and therefore has the same claim to universality as the notionless experience of the aesthetic consciousness. We can have proleptic ideas of Nature which are true predicates, because Nature is anticipated by us in the consciousness of our own personality. For this fundamental consciousness of ourselves, though notionless, is not the arbitrary source of spontaneous variations whose novelty surprises Omniscience itself, as the late Professor James believed, but the felt knowledge of that very principle on which Nature is discovered to be constituted. It is intelligence in its elemental self-identity, but it is intelligence. In Hegel's words, "the nature of the universe, hidden and shut up in itself as it is at first, has no power which can permanently resist the courageous efforts of the intelligence: it must at last open itself up; it must reveal all its depths and riches to the spirit, and surrender them to be enjoyed by it."[1]

Teleology is the method of philosophy in making this unspecified content coherent and intelligible as it is reflected in the diversity of Nature. But if Teleology sets off to pick up empirical concepts on its own account, without any sanction from immediate experience, it need not expect to find anything more than a collocation of empirical elements. If we try to interpret Nature in the so-called disinterested attitude of the scientist, with an open mind, free of all prejudice and supposition, recognising only what our senses register, we shall certainly find that matter is utterly dead and moreover that life is resolved into material processes. If we approach Nature empty-handed, we shall undoubtedly go empty away. To him that hath shall be

[1] Quoted in Caird's *Hegel*, p. 195.

given. We are empowered, nay, necessity is laid upon us, to proceed in our investigation with the conviction that Nature is spirit. This may be an unreasoning assumption, but it is not unreasonable; it carries irresistible conviction (τὸ καταληπτικὸν) which, after the manner of Zeno, we are prepared to maintain with clenched fist against all the world.[1] We have the key to the interpretation of Nature instinctively in the consciousness of our own personality; for the greater and deeper part of personality is not what is consciously willed by us, but what worketh in us to will and to do, that is, the consciousness of ourselves as natural liberty; and therefore the supersensible substrate in ourselves is the same as the supersensible substrate in Nature.

In its empirical method of investigation, Teleology has inevitably lost much of its original impulse received in immediate experience, it has shed the features of its early nurture in the bosom of elemental mind. And this is not a loss in itself, it is altogether gain if it only mean that the intuition of philosophy must be supplemented by empirical science. To quote Hegel again: "Science, therefore, must work into the hands of philosophy, that philosophy in turn may translate the universality of reflection which science has produced into the higher universality of the reason, showing how the intelligible object evolves itself out of the intelligence as an organic whole, whose necessity is in itself."

On the other hand, we do not see any advantage in decrying the discursive nature of our intellect as utterly misleading. Intelligence has paid the price for its self-consciousness at a loss of instinctive insight. But we do not need to bemoan our lot. We venture

[1] Cicero, *Acad.* ii. 47.

beyond the security of Instinct in the praiseworthy effort to substantiate and extend what is intuitive in our thinking by the methods of empirical investigation. If we are thinking to any good purpose, not a shred of our thinking is merely logical. It is instituted and sustained by a transcendental feeling, in this instance the schema of Nature's conformity to our intelligence. It is only when our thinking is disingenuous or fictitious in its purpose that it is merely logical. To take an extreme instance, Hegel did not come by his great discovery of the Absolute Idea by a dialectical process, although he expounded it in a dialectical process, but by a kind of divination. Therefore even the conception of final causes, however remote it may be from the ultimate truth, need not be discarded altogether as a false anticipation. Lord Bacon's[1] statement that the inquisition of final causes is barren, and like a virgin consecrated to God produces nothing, has been nobly supplemented by the rejoinder: that although final causes may be themselves unfruitful, yet like the vestal virgins they guard the sacred fire of the temple. If philosophy will do this alone, it will do perhaps all that is needful. Nature, in grateful recognition, will yield up her secrets and complete our knowledge. There is a real danger, however, and it is here that M. Bergson's criticism applies, that the intellect in its aggressive self-consciousness should force its own anticipations on Nature. If we are convinced that Nature is spiritual, this must not mean that we are prepared to find a nature like our own in everything—the position to which modern Pluralism is committed, and that where we fail there is nothing to find. We must abase

[1] *Advancement of Learning*, Bk. III. chap. 5.

our thought to Nature's intimations "in a wise passiveness." Our consciousness of Nature must be reciprocating.

In conclusion, Kant was fundamentally sound in making Ethical Teleology rather than Aesthetic the middle term in the Critical Philosophy. Only, we should not understand Teleology as an abstract interpretation of Nature, which exploits the organic as a passing show, without individual existence of its own, in order to satisfy our intelligence and so to promote the higher culture of humanity. Moral culture may be the highest end in Nature, but that is no reason why there should not be other subordinate ends which are equally real. As was hinted at the close of Chapter II., the anomalous position of Teleology as half in and half out of immediate experience, constitutes the bridge between Nature and Freedom. The common interpretation of the *Critique of Judgment*, that Nature and Freedom are reconciled in the aesthetic consciousness, is misleading. In Teleology alone do we unite the consciousness of a harmony in our immediate experience with the cumulative perception of a harmony in Nature herself, and so render intelligible the realisation of Freedom in the world. It is not enough for philosophy to point to Aesthetic as the reconciliation of Nature and Freedom. The only real proof philosophy can offer is to be found in the process of interpreting Nature, and that is Teleology. The aesthetic consciousness has no other actuality than that of a symbol, the kind of Freedom it embodies is the deliberate refutation of moral Freedom as it is realised in the world. While, therefore, the aesthetic consciousness as symbolic expression is a real interpretation of Life, it is essentially abstract when it is substituted for the life-consciousness as the actual realisation of Freedom in Nature, and is even found to be inconsistent with moral Freedom.

It is a significant fact recorded by Schiller, that in almost all periods of history when Art flourished, society was in a state of political and moral decadence. In the golden age of Pericles, virtue was a vice on the lips of a Socrates and in the life of a Phocion; the Romans were corrupted by Oriental luxury and their strength was exhausted in the strife of civil war, before their inflexible character could assimilate the spirit of Greek Art; in modern Italy Art did not arise until the cities of the Lombard League had lost the spirit of independence. Everywhere Art founded its kingdom on the ruins of Freedom.[1] It is no reproach to Art that it has nothing to do with morality, for it already contains morality in and for itself as it is passed through the crucible of natural liberty. But it is all the more certain that Art is quite indifferent to the actual struggle of Freedom in the world, and realises the unity of Nature and Freedom by ignoring the opposition between them. If it cannot be said that Art is immoral, then it is a-moral. So long as the artistic consciousness is able to take pleasure in a representation which is indifferent to morality, it is deliberately abstracting from the life-consciousness and has very little to do with morality indeed. And although the aesthete, by reason of his indifference to the moral issue, may be free from all taint of impurity, it is clearly a very different case from the experience in which the moral consciousness is not ignored but elevated to

[1] *Letters on the Aesthetical Education of Man*, x.

unthinking goodness. Such an aesthetic consciousness recognises no distinction between what is immoral and a-moral, and is equally intolerant of either.

The complete reconciliation of Nature and Freedom has no actual existence until it is achieved through moral culture in the final destination of humanity, and for philosophy this practical determination is expressed in a teleological interpretation of Nature, whose highest end is ethical. But, for this very reason, moral culture cannot present the Ideal, for the Idea of humanity is not completely realised in the individual:—" we see not yet all things put under him." Aesthetic alone can do this in its complete immediacy as symbol. As the typical expression of our personality in its first entelechy, Aesthetic prefigures the higher immediacy of realised capacity, when that which is in part shall be done away and we shall know even as we are known. For as the ideal expression of our mental functions in their naïve simplicity, Aesthetic integrates the divergent expressions of consciousness, theoretical and practical, and resolves the opposition of whole and part, thought and sense, conception and perception, possibility and actuality, creative intuition and moral obligation. To this complete destination we hope we are travelling, and meanwhile Aesthetic is its symbol like the rainbow in the sky.

CHAPTER IX.

CONCLUSION.

WE have now completed a very summary review of Kant's Teleology, aesthetical and physical. The conclusions are well-worn and apparently of no vital interest even to the student of philosophy. But, in the close study of an author, we inevitably come into touch with the inarticulate motive of his work, and it is this deeper motive which has engaged our attention in the present study. So far as actual results are concerned, the *Critique of Judgment* is hardly a success, and must be regarded as the least satisfactory of Kant's writings. In the first place, he sought to maintain the purity of Aesthetic and at the same time to inspire it with a serious purpose; but finding that purity and purpose would not mingle, he divorced the Beautiful from artistic expression. Secondly, he pointed out the limitations to the argument from design. In this latter venture Kant has been eminently successful, and what he has done need never be done over again. But he gained his point at too dear a price. His criticism of the teleological argument turns mainly on the distinction between real or internal and relative or external purpose in Nature; and, while his exposition of organic purpose is of permanent value, he practically reduced the organic to the level of the inorganic under the

THE CRITICAL PHILOSOPHY

vague principle of Formal Teleology. From the empirical point of view he clearly recognised the irreducible difference between an organism and any other piece of finite Nature; but whenever he looked from the *a priori* standpoint, this genuine difference seemed to fade away in the dissipating function of a discursive Understanding. The result is a false theory of Inductive Science. Induction and Reflexion are characteristically defined by Kant as the qualification of empirical perception by a *merely* problematical idea : Science never comes directly into touch with Reality. This sceptical theory of knowledge has had a profound influence on subsequent speculation. It has become fashionable with present-day philosophers, who do not blush to own the consequence that the channels in human nature through which the Real may be supposed to enter and communicate itself to us are irrational. But we may be confident that so wanton an abandonment of reasonable knowledge cannot long continue to satisfy the thinking mind. It is surely a damaging contradiction that our practical and emotional nature, which is supposed to be alone capable of settling for us the riddles of the Universe, is itself *in its supposed isolation from intelligence* quite unconscious of the distinction between Appearance and Reality, and therefore incapable of even appreciating the problems which it is thought to solve.

We have reason to believe that the inner development of Kant's thought is not consistent with this sceptical basis. Evidence has been led to show that his Teleology of Nature results in a true theory of Induction. This is the first and most obvious inference to be drawn from the relation between Aesthetic and Teleology. It is to the concrete conception of human faculty which we find in Kant's aesthetic theory that this advance in his theory of Induction is directly due. Teleology can no longer be regarded as an external reflection on Nature, for the content of our judgment takes its character from the way in which we are affected by Nature. And if our judgment is *a priori*, it is because our consciousness of Nature presupposes and is conditioned by the consciousness of ourselves as Nature. The conception of natural liberty which constitutes the basis of the aesthetic *Spiel der Kräfte*, is fundamental in every expression of human faculty. This is what we have called the psychological aspect of Teleology, and, strangely enough, the designation indicates the objective aspect of Teleology at the same time that it primarily draws attention to its subjective side. To say with Kant that Teleology is only logical is to say that it is subjective or empirical.

But there is a second and even more important inference to be drawn from the relation between Aesthetic and Teleology. Reflexion as Teleology of Nature is more than Inductive Hypothesis; it is also Ethical Teleology, and it is in this latter aspect of Teleology that its connection with Aesthetic is most manifest. The highest level of 'reflective' consciousness is neither Art nor Life, neither aesthetic nor organic purpose, but Religion—a type of Science which is neither dependent for its expression on artistic symbols nor equipped with the methods of scientific observation, but which is as articulate as artistic expression and as certain in its conclusions as anything in Science. This is not what Kant means by Ethical Teleology, but unless Teleology is capable of this special and final interpretation its connection with aesthetical Reflexion must remain an enigma.

THE CRITICAL PHILOSOPHY 333

Teleology as Science of Nature has only that initial relation to Reflexion which every form of experience must have, as it is based on the fundamental conception of our natural liberty; it is not itself Reflexion, the emotional but reasonable apprehension of what is real. It is in this Ethical Teleology, and only in Scientific Teleology in so far as it is ancillary to Ethical Teleology, that the reconciliation of Nature and Freedom is found. Aesthetic indirectly contributes to the realisation of this end by its symbolic representation of man's immediate unity with himself and with Nature. The aesthetic harmony of human faculty is not yet an achieved state; it only happens in moments which, though imperishable in their significance, nevertheless pass away. It is in the teleological interpretation of human life as progressive moral culture that the incidental intuitions of Art acquire a permanent character: man's final destination is being already realised as the partial fulfilment of his complete perfection or second entelechy. And as the basic element of the first entelechy is natural liberty, that of the second will be some analogous, concrete power such as love, in St. Paul's beautiful language the cincture of perfectness, which holds in harmony every other power of heart and mind.

Now it is evident that whenever Teleology becomes a distinctive method of interpreting human life, it has changed its character. Scientific Teleology or Induction is always supplied with more or less definite empirical data, while Ethical Teleology in its distinctive aspect is characterised by their absence. There are of course empirical perceptions which indicate the moral and spiritual life, and these are quite as capable of inductive interpretation as the observations of physical science.

But the true character of our spiritual manhood is not revealed to us in this external way: the kingdom of heaven within us cometh not by observation. Introspection is the first and final method of Psychology, and the comparative and experimental methods, notwithstanding the wealth of detailed information they contribute, are only subsidiary instruments of explanation. To be assured of our immortal destiny, to secure it as a possession of which we can be as certain as anything in Science, to envisage the things that are invisible, we can no longer avail ourselves of the ordinary methods of Science. It is something far more tenuous and less palpable than emotional expression, voluntary or involuntary, or indeed any kind of sensible evidence, that procures for us this higher knowledge of our inner life and its ghostly environs. We have recently been reminded by a great authority[1] that every level of experience has logical coherence, if it is real. And I do not mean to deny for one moment that the elements of Inner Sense have a coherent content and are therefore capable of inductive synthesis. But this is somewhat beside the point. To assert that all experience is ultimately capable of coherent interpretation may only mean that it is so for a superior Understanding such as the mind of God, but not necessarily for us. There are phases of experience which may never be intellectually coherent for us, existing in the form of realised contradictions, and we can only escape the consequence that they are practically irrational by recognising a different method of coherence from that of intellectual unities. If we persist in affirming that every coherent content must be intellectual or logical, we simply

[1] B. Bosanquet: *The Principle of Individuality and Value.*

THE CRITICAL PHILOSOPHY 335

destroy the distinctive meaning of Logic and Intelligence.

At this point of our argument Mysticism is fain to enter with a gesture of approval. But it must not be supposed that we have any intention of paving the way for Mysticism. On the contrary, we should wish to reclaim for Knowledge the "cloud of unknowing" under which Mysticism has stolen a precarious shelter. Why should Mysticism be allowed to riot in phases of experience which are really susceptible of a sober Science? If Mysticism has made converts, philosophers have themselves to blame. They have not recognised, unless with disdain, the experiences of the distinctively spiritual life; and because these psychoses are judged to be incapable of logical consistency, they are swept out of court without a hearing. If our immortal destiny is a real thing, if the impalpable environs of our inner life have any actual existence, they must be the objects of a genuine Science. And though this Science is distinct from the Science of Nature because it is occupied with a different plane of experience, it is at least not less valid than the Science of Nature, for it fulfils the same epistemological conditions.

I am quite aware that the arguments which have just been advanced may appear to have little in common with Kant's discussion of Ethical Teleology. But it is not in his discussion of Ethical Teleology that our interest lies so much as in the original and profound conception of Reflective Judgment, which constitutes the motive of the third Critique—unless we take the view that the *Critique of Judgment* has no literary unity at all. Kant himself favoured a kind of mysticism. For him both ethical and scientific Teleology were regulative, and the real and only ground of certainty he could find was in an immediate conviction or practical intuition which has no scientific value whatsoever. But there are suggestions in his aesthetic theory of a moral type of knowledge which has an equal claim to validity with the Science of Nature. Then the whole of Teleology, scientific and moral, ceases to be formal and becomes a genuine interpretation of Reality.

Kant's indirect contribution to this moral type of knowledge is his discovery of a new power of Imagination. The ideal of Epistemology which we have traced in Kant's criticism, consists of a more congruous relation than is found in ordinary knowledge: the factors of possibility and actuality are homogeneous so that thought is not unduly in advance of sensation. Knowledge is imperfect while whole and part are diversely apprehended, the former intensively the latter extensively. In the higher forms of existence, which have a real intensive unity, the discrepancy tends to disappear. Aesthetical, biological and ethical unities, the three representative objects of Reflective Science, approximate to the ideal type of knowledge for which Reflexion stands: the parts can only be perceived as elements in their intensive relation to the whole. But in the lower forms of existence which fall below the category of biological unity and which have only an external entelechy, the discrepancy is more glaring: there is an unequal adjustment of sense and thought. The parts are sensuously apprehended while the unity is not perceived or imaged but imagined or conceived. The result is that when we have a clear and distinct apprehension of diversity, the unity tends to be merely ideal or practically non-existent, and consequently the diversity

THE CRITICAL PHILOSOPHY 337

itself must be prevailingly synthetic and therefore unreal; and, on the other hand, when we have a clear apprehension of the unity, we lose sight of the diversity, and the unity itself must consequently be analytic and therefore unreal.

In its most reasonable form the attitude of Pragmatism to this problem of knowledge is: that if phenomena are only artificial make-shifts, not an exact interpretation of the actual but a merely ideal expansion of the actual, we ought to limit the function of thought to those actual connections which are consistent with practical interest. The resulting experience will be a more or less satisfactory adjustment of sensation and thought; that it is satisfactory is itself a sufficient criterion of its validity. This point of view pervades the whole tendency of modern culture. The significant reality for modern culture consists of accurate correspondence to environment. We are taking in earnest the enlightenment of the seventeenth and eighteenth centuries in our demand for clear and distinct ideas.

So far this position, which may be called Scientific Sensationalism, has the same epistemological ideal as has been suggested by Kant's criticism. But it is really at the other end of the scale from the point of view of Ethical Teleology. The scientific sensationalism of modern culture professes not to understand the ethical and spiritual life as an independent reality, and regards the significance of human life as exhausted in an engrossing relation to the environment. If there is a minimum of discrepancy in Scientific Sensationalism, it is because thought is made to square with a narrow and limited expression of itself, namely, sensation: we not only take our cue from the environment but also our final conclusions.

There are thus two different interpretations of the

epistemological ideal, Scientific Sensationalism and Ethical Teleology. While the former is an adequate and perfectly adjusted response to environment, the latter accepts the environment only as the condition of its world. As Kant would say, the basis of Reflexion is not sensation but that peculiar form of sensation which cannot constitute an immediate connection with environment. The one type of knowledge may be said to begin where the other leaves off, and takes for its basis the feeling or affection of the subject in which sensation is apperceived. These two types of Science are distinct and cannot be translated into terms of each other. They are not therefore antagonistic, for they co-exist in the same individual experience. But within the same experience they constitute distinct forms of apprehension which are not meant to be reconciled or confused, however intimate their relation to each other may be: just as our senses are supplementary to each other but are none the less distinct avenues of sensation. To state the point in a concrete but somewhat narrow way, Science and Religion will remain independent worlds so long as there are elements of Inner Sense which cannot be realised in terms of Outer Sense. The basis of Science is sensation (*Empfindung*), the basis of Ethical Teleology is empathy (*Einfühlung*).

Such a distinction will be meaningless in that final stage of culture of which Aesthetic is the symbolic expression and of which Ethical Teleology is the progressive realisation. But meanwhile we are compelled to accept the distinction; and it is the duty of the philosopher to examine the conditions of a possible Science of those spiritual psychoses, which cannot be adequately conceived by the categories of Science nor

THE CRITICAL PHILOSOPHY 339

realised in the symbolic representations of Art. In his aesthetic theory, and particularly in his doctrine of the Sublime, Kant has suggested how such a type of knowledge is possible. While the aesthetic Imagination is extensive, ideational, the Sublime calls for a new order of Imagination which is intensive, volitional or mystical. It is certainly an error on Kant's part to suppose that in the Sublime the extensive or ideational Imagination is totally displaced by an intensive or mystical Imagination, for the ideational Imagination is re-instated by sympathetic reaction in so far as the sublimity is also aesthetical. Kant's doctrine of the Sublime, however, is not aesthetical, and has more in common with religious and mystical experience than with the sublime objects of Art. When the ideational Imagination struggles to grasp the intuitions of our moral Reason which are inarticulate for both Science and Art, it breaks down and never regains its footing; but at the moment when it reaches the limit of its effort, it passes over into a new phase of its activity and then it is no longer the instrument of Understanding but "the instrument of Reason." It is by this "strength of usurpation" that the moral Imagination reveals in a flash the invisible world. Although we cannot have extensive images of these spiritual realities, we can compel them into our presence by this instrument of moral Reason.

This moral Imagination is nothing else than a higher power of apperception. It will be remembered how Kant defines Reflexion as the power of comparing and holding together given representations, either with others or with the whole faculty of representation.[1] There is a

[1] *Über Philosophie überhaupt*: Rozenkranz, i. p. 589; Hartenstein, vi. p. 381.

striking parallel to this definition in St. Paul's writings. St. Paul is making a distinction between the natural and the spiritual consciousness : the natural man cannot receive nor even know the things of the Spirit because they are spiritually discerned ; but the spiritual man fathoms [1] the deep things of God, *comparing spiritual things with spiritual* (πνευματικοῖς πνευματικὰ συνκρίνοντες· 1 Cor. ii. vv. 14-15 taken with vv. 10 and 13). Following the suggestive rendering of the German version, spiritual knowledge is the method of bringing heavenly things to expression in heavenly speech. In common apperception it is the schema that initiates the cumulative tendency towards ideational form. Reason is also schematic, and when Imagination fails, it institutes an apperceptive process peculiar to itself : inarticulate intuitions by rubbing together gather significance and produce something analogous to ideational form.

There is no good reason to deny that Ethical Teleology as the apprehension of what Professor Eucken has called the independent spiritual life, is a form of true Science. It constitutes a closer adjustment of cognitive factors than anything which Scientific Sensationalism can procure. For in this higher plane of experience there is no alien faculty of Imagination to compete with the intuitions of Reason, and therefore no occasion for the discrepancy which may arise in common apperception. There is no tendency to swelling, such as can happen in the damp atmosphere of phenomena, no hyperstructure of a merely ideal content. Ethical Teleology is the highest type of Science because it fulfils the ideal conditions of Science.

[1] On basis of German version—ἀνακρίνει = *ergründet* = intensive as contrasted with extensive knowledge.

THE CRITICAL PHILOSOPHY 341

There is an obvious objection, however, which must now be noticed. It will of course be urged that there is a perfect adjustment of cognitive factors in this sublime science, simply because there are no real cognitive factors at all. There are only intuitions of Reason, empty possibilities, and there is nothing corresponding to sensation. How then can we speak of an adjustment of factors? The supposed mental synthesis can only be a bare analytic point of abstraction. But this is not true. It is frankly acknowledged that there is no element of sensation. Indeed the Imagination, which is the highest faculty of Sense, is avowedly discarded, whether in the form of scientific category or artistic symbol, as inadequate to utter the meaning of the inner, spiritual life. But let us ask ourselves what it is that constitutes cognition. It is certainly not contact with sensation; and even if a sensation could enter consciousness full-blown from without, it would not of itself provide universality which is the real criterion of cognition. For it is not objectivity that makes universality but universality that makes objectivity. Sensation as a distinctive form of sense-affection is after all a highly specialised product of thought; and the initial shock of confused sense-affection which an undeveloped consciousness may be supposed to feel and which is the nearest approximation in our developed consciousness to an external contact, is nothing more than the significant point of reference or focus of attention in a systematic world of consciousness. Judgment or cognition is the process of making explicit relations in this world at any such point of reference. Now, in the higher type of apperception there is something corresponding to sensation or affective consciousness, which constitutes the centre of attention. The inarticulate intuitions of Reason are brought to a focus, not in sensation, but in an empathy, the deep self-affection of the subject which constitutes just as truly the fulcrum for a universal predication as any form of sense-affection. This self-affecting consciousness is also the shifting centre of a coherent world, and the judgments based upon it are at least as capable of universal communication as the singular judgments of Art. An empathy is not a subjective state, it is not the after-glow of common apperception but an objective quality of consciousness corresponding to sensation. Indeed it is the least solipsistic of all mental states, for it is the deepest expression of the consciousness of ourselves as Nature, transcending the distinction between consciousness as affective and as affecting.

It is hardly necessary to insist that the interpretation of this sublime empathy which has just been offered, is quite different from that which is associated with subconsciousness. This latter, which in its fashionable use to-day is little more than a psychological name for the solar plexus or abdominal brain, is professedly irrational, while the empathic consciousness is the highest expression of a reasonable soul. And I have no serious objection to the claim that, in so far as this empathic state is reasonable, it must be intellectual or logical. On the contrary, it has been asserted that the apprehension of our spiritual life as an independent reality, is not only a form of Science but that it is the nearest approximation to the ideal conditions of Science. Still it is worth while contending for a reasonable form of apprehension which is not at the same time intellectual, for this reason : philosophers who insist on the thorough application of logical coherence to experience, will not recognise the validity of psychoses which cannot be turned out on the table and conceived as a whole of parts. It is a miserable reflection that the beliefs which are dearest to the human heart and which the common reason of mankind has never seriously doubted, have either been asserted by philosophers on a basis of scepticism which is almost worse than useless or have been brushed aside in scorn as cobwebs of the brain. Kant's proofs for the existence of God, the Soul and Immortality have been declared irrational. This is well, but what has Idealism been able to offer in their place? Nothing but a blank vacuity. The forgiveness of sins, the peace of God that *passeth Understanding*, the renewing grace of Holy Spirit, the life everlasting and the sense of continued fellowship with our dear and holy dead: these are things in comparison with which the greatest achievements of Science are illusive gain, and on these precious intuitions Idealism is silent. We are only told that everything is spiritual: an act of cognition is spiritual; fish and fowl are low down in the scale, but they are none the less objects of spiritual experience. The result is that, although a difference of levels is maintained, the distinctive meaning of Spirit has been squandered. For those who cherish such beliefs as have been mentioned, there is no shelter in the groves of Philosophy unless it be irrational philosophy, and that we do not want. We are disinherited to herd with mystics who love the way of unreason; we are fain to lend our ears to the fabulous reports from another world of so-called Spiritualism, reports which are anything but spiritual and much more nearly resemble the gibberish of forlorn devils shivering on the cold shell of Reality or the distant sound of muffled voices from behind a frosted pane; or we are left at the mercy of sub-conscious incursions which may hail from a hell as often as from heaven. We are therefore driven to maintain the validity of our beliefs if need be in spite of logical consistency. But this unwelcome course is hardly necessary, for logical consistency is itself based upon experience which is not distinctively intellectual. Our consciousness of Nature is conditioned by the consciousness of ourselves as Nature, which is not an intellectual content but indeterminate coherence. Logical coherence is a system of relations which are only necessary within the limits of a wider contingence; and although this apparent contingence is coherent in and for itself, its coherence can hardly be of the same character as that of a logical whole. The experience which is more than intellectual, the experience which assimilates Intelligence as one of its elements, does not need to wait upon a logical criterion. To insist that this empathic experience is intellectual would be as misleading as to say that thought is sensational because sensation happens to be a limited and particular expression of thought.

Without this method of indeterminate coherence, we are for ever incapable of appropriating the independent spiritual life. The scientific Intelligence, unaided by the empathy of Reason, knows practically nothing about its own ultimate hypothesis, except in the form of an intellectual torso. And Philosophy as criticism of Science is apparently content not to know any more, provided that the method of Science, that is, of logical coherence, is exhaustively applied to every plane of experience. The ultimate unity of existence is not perceived by scientific

THE CRITICAL PHILOSOPHY 345

Intelligence but conceived or imagined in the form of a heuristic principle. It is only a unity which can interpret the diversity, not a unity which the diversity can adequately interpret: that is to say, a unity which is completely coherent in and for itself and not problematically coherent as it is revealed to the finite Intelligence. This latter conception is what Hegel meant by the Absolute Idea. But so long as we insist on the universal application of logical coherence as the criterion of experience, the Absolute Idea can never be revealed to us except in the form of hypothetical reality—unless our philosophy is irrational, and then the Absolute Idea may communicate itself to us as a plurality of finite gods. The ultimate unity of existence must not simply be conceived, but perceived in a way that is homogeneous with the perception of the parts, that is, in some way analogous to sensation. In no other way is it possible to have a direct and characteristic revelation of the ultimate Reality. Any other method, such as that of intellectual apprehension, is confined to manifestations, which however true, and they are very true, may be infinitely remote from the inmost nature of that Reality. The ultimate unity must be known to us, if we are to have a real knowledge of it, as the unity of a whole which is exhaustively realised in its diversity, and not simply as a heuristic principle which is only realised in so far as it can interpret the diversity. This does not mean that God must be known to us as extensive magnitude coterminous with the boundaries of existence, but that what we know of Him must be expressive of Himself as He is for Himself and not a problematical conception. It is impossible to think that we are unprovided with a power of apperceiving what is beyond the grasp of

Imagination and Understanding. We do not need to appeal with Kant to an Intuitive Understanding outside of us. The Intuitive Understanding is within us; for, as was shown in the preceding chapter, the nature of the ultimate Ground of existence and the nature of the human mind are of the same character, namely, purposive reality without a purpose or indeterminate coherence. And it is not wonderful if this intuitive power, which is the motive of all Science and productive of its schemata, should also exist in us independent of the discursive Understanding which it institutes. This intuitive or empathic consciousness is alone capable of apperceiving God, precisely because it transcends the distinction between a hypothetical unity and its particular instances, between possibility and actuality, between Understanding and Imagination, between sensation and thought. This is that peculiar form of sensation which does not refer to any determinate object and whose content is indeterminate coherence. It is also the purest form of Science because it realises most perfectly the ideal conditions of Science. Even in Art, where the unity between whole and part is very close, there may be a discrepancy: for example, there are musicians who prefer reading the score to hearing the music. Even in an organic whole the unity is hypothetical or incompletely realised in the parts. But in Empathy it cannot be so, for the Imagination, the highest faculty of Sense, is not allowed to compete with thought but is produced at will by the intuitive power of thought itself. Someone can say: 'I believe in God, but I cannot express what I feel. It is not enough to say that God is Father, it is more than that; I simply feel that I live in Him and He in me, but I cannot form any conception or image of what it means to me.' That is enough. But it is not logically coherent !

Unde mihi lapidem, unde sagittas?

If it cannot be approved as logical coherence, it is because it is more than logical coherence. It is the apprehension of the whole not as it is hypothetically, but as it is exhaustively, realised in its diversity ; and still it is not that whole as it is imaged extensively, but as it is intensively revealed to us in the elemental feeling of our own identity. The ideational Imagination only enters into this experience as a negative factor, in so far as its futile effort to grasp the divine totality provokes the creative energy of our moral nature. This moral power of Imagination is not the private possession of Genius but is in the gift of our common humanity, and we have not realised it only because we have not cultivated it. In the consecrated effort to live the life that is in God, to appropriate the inmost essence of Truth as Spirit, our wills become perceptive. Heavenly things find expression in heavenly speech. It is in this progressive culture that the reconciliation of Nature and Freedom is realised. By long dwelling in fellowship with spiritual things, the eyes of our spiritual Understanding are enlightened; and while the Imagination of common apperception sacrifices its freedom, it acquires " an extension and a might greater than it sacrifices."—" But we all, with unveiled face reflecting as a mirror the glory of the Lord, are transformed into the same image from glory to glory, even as from the Lord the Spirit."